Left-Wing Extremism and Human Rights

Left-Wing Extremism and Human Rights

The Role of Civil Liberties Groups in Andhra Pradesh

K.V. Thomas

SAGE www.sagepublications.com
Los Angeles • London • New Delhi • Singapore • Washington DC

First published in 2014 by

SAGE Publications India Pvt Ltd
B1/I-1 Mohan Cooperative Industrial Area
Mathura Road, New Delhi 110 044, India
www.sagepub.in

SAGE Publications Inc
2455 Teller Road
Thousand Oaks, California 91320, USA

SAGE Publications Ltd
1 Oliver's Yard, 55 City Road
London EC1Y 1SP, United Kingdom

SAGE Publications Asia-Pacific Pte Ltd
3 Church Street
#10-04 Samsung Hub
Singapore 049483

Published by Vivek Mehra for SAGE Publications India Pvt Ltd, typeset in 10/12 Palatino Linotype by RECTO Graphics, Delhi and printed at Saurabh Printers Pvt Ltd, New Delhi.

Library of Congress Cataloging-in-Publication Data

Thomas, K. V.
  Left-wing extremism and human rights : the role of civil liberties groups in Andhra Pradesh / K. V. Thomas.
    pages cm
  Includes bibliographical references and index.
    1. Human rights—India—Andhra Pradesh. 2. Right and left (Political science)—India—Andhra Pradesh. I. Title.
  JC571.T456   323.0954′84—dc23   2014   2014002659

ISBN: 978-81-321-1158-0 (HB)

The SAGE Team: Shambhu Sahu, Archita Mandal, Nand Kumar Jha and
                Rajinder Kaur

Dedicated to victims of human rights violations world over

Thank you for choosing a SAGE product! If you have any comment, observation or feedback, I would like to personally hear from you. Please write to me at contactceo@sagepub.in

—Vivek Mehra, Managing Director and CEO,
SAGE Publications India Pvt Ltd, New Delhi

Bulk Sales

SAGE India offers special discounts for purchase of books in bulk. We also make available special imprints and excerpts from our books on demand.

For orders and enquiries, write to us at

Marketing Department
SAGE Publications India Pvt Ltd
B1/I-1, Mohan Cooperative Industrial Area
Mathura Road, Post Bag 7
New Delhi 110044, India
E-mail us at marketing@sagepub.in

Get to know more about SAGE, be invited to SAGE events, get on our mailing list. Write today to marketing@sagepub.in

This book is also available as an e-book.

————— ଏ)ଓଃ —————

Contents

Abbreviations

AHRC	Asian Human Rights Commission
AICCCR	All India Coordination Committee of Communist Revolutionaries
AICCR	All India Coordination Committee of Revolutionaries
AIFOFDR	All India Federation of Organizations for Democratic Rights
AIPRF	All India People's Resistance Forum
AJYCP	Assam Jatiyatabadi Yuba Chatra Parishad
AMS	Adivasi Mahila Sanghathana
ANF	Anti-Naxalite Force
ANLA	Adivasi National Liberation Army
AOB	Andhra–Orissa Border
APCCCR	Andhra Pradesh Coordination Committee of Communist Revolutionaries
APCLC	Andhra Pradesh Civil Liberties Committee
APDR	Association for the Protection of Democratic Rights
APRCP	Andhra Pradesh Revolutionary Communist Party
APSRTC	Andhra Pradesh State Road Transport Corporation
ARC	Administrative Reforms Commission
ASDC	Autonomous State's Demands Committee
ATR	Action Taken Report
AWARE	Action for Welfare and Awakening in Rural Environment
BSF	Border Security Force
BSP	Bahujan Samaj Party
CAF	Chhattisgarh Armed Force

CAG	Christian Action Groups
CAPART	Council for the Advancement of People's Action and Rural Technology
CARD	Creative Action for Rural Development
CBI	Central Bureau of Investigation
CC	Central Committee
CCC	Committee of Concerned Citizens
CCOMPOSA	Coordination Committee of Maoist Parties and Organisations in South Asia
CCR	Centre for Constitutional Rights
CEDAW	Convention on the Elimination of All Forms of Discrimination against Women
CEHRD	Centre for Environment, Human Rights and Development
CERD	Committee for the Elimination of Racial Discrimination
CHRI	Commonwealth Human Rights Initiative
CIA	Central Intelligence Agency
CISF	Central Industrial Security Force
CMC	Central Military Commission
COVA	Confederation of Voluntary Associations
CPC	Chinese Communist Party
CPDR	Committee for the Protection of Democratic Rights
CPI	Communist Party of India
CPM	Communist Party of India (Marxist)
Cr Pc	Criminal Procedure Code
CREDS	Chaitanya Rural Education and Development Society
CRESA	Centre for Reconstruction through Social Action
CRPF	Central Reserve Police Force
CRZ	Compact Revolutionary Zone
CSPSA	Chhattisgarh Special Public Security Act of 2006
CWS	Centre for World Solidarity
DARC	Dalit Action and Research Centre
DDS	Deccan Development Society
DGP	Director General of Police
DOPT	Department of Personnel and Training
DSS	Dalit Sangharsh Samiti

DVAF	Dalit Voluntary Associations Federation
ECOSOC	Economic and Social Council
EFA	Education for All
ESC	Economic, Social and Cultural
FFC	Formation of Fact Finding Committees
FIR	First Information Reports
FRA	Forests Rights Act
FRC	Forests Rights Committee
GONGO	Government Organized NGOs
HRI	Human Rights Initiative
IAP	Integrated Action Plan
IAS	Indian Administrative Service
ICCPR	International Covenant on Civil and Political Rights
ICESCR	International Covenant on Economic, Social and Cultural Rights
ICLU	Indian Civil Liberties Union
IEDs	Improvised Explosive Devices
IFAD	International Fund for Agricultural Development
IGOs	Inter-Governmental Organizations
ILO	International Labour Organization
INSAS	Indian Small Arms System
IPF	Indian People's Front
IPHRC	Indian Peoples Human Rights Commission
IT	Information Technology
ITBP	Indo-Tibetan Border Police
ITDA	Integrated Tribal Development Agency
ITDG	Intermediate Technology Development Group
ITDP	Integrated Tribal Development Projects
JFM	Joint Forest Management
KAMS	Krantikari Adivasi Mahila Sangathan
KLO	Kamtapur Liberation Organization
LAMPS	Large Area Multi-purpose Cooperative Societies
LIC	Low Intensity Conflicts
LRSA	Legal Resource and Social Action
LTTE	Liberation Tigers of Tamil Eelam
LWE	Left-Wing Extremism
MCC	Maoist Communist Centre

MLM	Marxist–Leninist Movement
MNREGP	Mahatma Gandhi National Rural Employment Guarantee Programme
MOCA	Maharashtra Control of Organised Crime Act, 1999
MOU	Memorandum of Understanding
MP	Minister of Parliament
MRG	Minority Rights Group
NAWO	National Alliance of Women's Organisations
NCDHR	National Campaign on Dalit Human Rights
NDA	National Democratic Alliance
NDHRC	National Dalit Human Rights Committee
NGOs	Non-Governmental Organizations
NHRC	National Human Rights Commission
NNEGA	National Network of Employment Guarantee Assurance
NSA	National Security Act
OCDR	Organisation for Civil and Democratic Rights
OHCHR	Office of the High Commissioner for Human Rights
OIC	Organization of Islamic Countries
OPDR	Organization for the Protection of Democratic Rights
OVRA	Organization for Vigilance and Repression of Anti-Fascism
PACS	Primary Agricultural Cooperative Societies
PCAPA	The People's Committee against Police Atrocities
PDF	People's Democratic Front
PDS	Public Distribution System
PESA	Panchayats (Extension to Scheduled Areas) Act
PFI	Popular Front of India
PIL	Public Interest Litigations
PLA	People's Liberation Army
PLGA	People's Liberation Guerrilla Army
POTA	Prevention of Terrorist Activities
PPSS	POSCO Pratirodhi Sangram Samiti
PSU	Public Sector Undertakings
PUCL	People's Union for Civil Liberties

PUDR	Peoples Union for Democratic Rights
PWG	People's War Group
R&D	Research and Development
RDT	Rayalaseema Development Trust
RIDES	Rural Integrated Development Educational Society
RIM	Revolutionary International Movement
RPF	Revolutionary People's Front
RWA	Revolutionary Writers Association
SC	Scheduled Caste
SDP	Substantive due process
SEZ	Special Economic Zones
SHG	Self Help Group
SHTG	Self Help Thrift Groups
SIDUR	Society for Integrated Development in Urban and Rural Areas
SIKASA	Singareni Karmika Samakhya
SIMI	Students Islamic Movement of India
SLP	Special Leave Petition
SMC	State Military Commission
SNIRD	Society for National Integration through Rural Development
SPO	Special Police Officer
ST	Scheduled Tribe
STL	Special Tribunal for Lebanon
TADA	Terrorist and Disruptive Activities (Prevention) Act
TCOC	Tactical Counter-Offensive Campaign
TDP	Telungu Dessom Party
TMC	Trinamool Congress
TRS	Telangana Rashtra Samithi
UCCRI	Unity Centre of Communist Revolutionaries of India
UDHR	Universal Declaration of Human Rights
ULFA	United Liberation Front of Assam
UNCHR	United Nations Commission on Human Rights
UNDHR	UN Declaration of Human Rights
UNHCHR	United Nations High Commissioner for Human Rights

UNW	UN Women
URMCA	United Reservation Movement Council of Assam
USSR	Union of Soviet Socialist Republics
UT	Union Territory
VANI	Voluntary Action Network of India
VHF	Very High Frequency
VIRASAM	Viplava Rachayithala Sangam
VRO	Village Reconstruction Organization
WPB	Workers Party of Belgium
WTO	World Trade Organization
YIP	Young India Project

Preface

When bombs explode and kill hundreds of civilians, terrorists terrorize the civil society and play death game with hostages, spine-chilling stories of encounter killings prick our conscience, refugees uprooted from their homeland live in inhuman conditions, people die in the streets and villages due to starvation, 'prisoners of conscience' languish in jails and detention camps and the atrocities against women and marginalized sections go unabated, we hear more and more about the protection and promotion of human rights. Even the most authoritarian regimes, known for their dismal record of human rights, proclaim their deep commitment to these rights. Such rhetoric ends even before the aching memories of bizarre incidents fade from our minds. This dichotomy between what nations and governments profess and practise in the case of human rights is, perhaps, the greatest tragedy confronting the 21st century.

This evokes a number of pertinent questions. What compels the states to practise this dichotomy? Whether it is domestic- and foreign-policy compulsions or their eagerness to present clean image at international plane? Are the states alone responsible for this tragedy? What role can the civil society and human rights, non-governmental organizations (NGOs) in particular, play in such situations? Should they fall in line with the approach of the states or truly uphold the spirit of international covenants and declarations on various aspects of human rights? To what extent NGOs and civil rights groups can take up these challenges?

The main effort of this research was to examine the role of civil liberties groups and NGOs in the protection and promotion of human rights that, for the study, have been interpreted in the broader terms, covering political, civil, economic, social and cultural rights of the people, as enunciated by Vienna Declaration and Programme of Action (1993) on human rights. From the historical and empirical sources, bulk of the data has been collected and incorporated in the study. The first and most conventional of the historical sources came from books, journals, newspapers, magazines, documents, monographs, annual reports of National Human Rights Commission (NHRC), NGOs and civil liberties groups and so on, whereas the empirical data were collected from samples, structured interviews, interactions with a wide spectrum of people and case studies of selected organizations.

Setting of the theme of research, the historical evolution of the international human rights, legal and institutional milieu, codification of humanitarian and human rights laws and India's Constitutional structure of rights and institutional mechanisms like NHRC and law-enforcement agencies in the protection of these rights has been brought out. Through the qualitative and quantitative methodologies, the research has been undertaken and the significance of the study in the present national and international polity has been amply highlighted.

As left-wing extremism (LWE) and counter-extremist operations have become the major sources of human rights violations in the country, the pan-Indian scenario of the movement bringing out its genesis, organizational structure, ideological moorings and the differential demographic and geographic spread has been elaborately dealt with. Certain cardinal findings such as the difference in responses of the tribals and the Dalits to Naxal movement, with mainstream political parties more successful in weaning the Dalits away from revolutionary ideologies, have been arrived at on the basis of detailed analysis of facts and figures. The natural resources that are driving rapacious land acquisition at the instance of multinationals backed by political power centres and displacement of the marginalized and underprivileged in the extremist-affected areas have opened new areas of conflict.

An empirical study of the movement in Andhra Pradesh, once the citadel of LWE, clearly manifests that it is an offshoot of various socio-economic and developmental issues, and thus the social-reform role of Maoist/Naxalite activism in the neocolonial set-up cannot be ignored. This analysis brings out yet another significant finding that marginalized sections, especially the tribals who were neglected and exploited for many decades through insensitive planning and developmental strategies, continue to be the main support base of LWE movement. Sandwiched between the extremists and security forces in action, they are the worst victims of the naked violations of civil and human rights in the contemporary Indian polity. These aspects were deeply probed into on a pan-Indian basis and the ground-level empirical study of the problem in the state of Andhra Pradesh proved that the trend can be well applied to other states as well. An action plan to deal with the LWE threat and the discontent and frustration of marginalized sections through institutional and voluntary mechanisms with the active participation of civil society is the need of the hour.

In this regard, the conceptual framework of civil liberties organizations and NGOs, the emergence and functions of human rights NGOs, major international human rights NGOs and the procedures available to even individuals to access international and national mechanisms were discussed in detail. The debate over state and non-state violence that impinges upon Amnesty International, Human Rights Watch and so on assumes considerable importance, especially in the light of the polemics among major civil liberties/human rights groups in India on this issue. A detailed profiling of civil liberties organizations/NGOs and the emerging trends such as 'networking of NGOs' and foreign-funding patterns with particular reference to Andhra Pradesh is incorporated in our analysis. Case studies of NGOs, one each from civil rights front, women, Dalit, tribal, rural poor, minorities and urban poor, inter alia, bringing out their aims and objectives, major areas of operation, notable achievements in the human rights field, major sources of finances and so on have proved that NGOs/civil rights groups have made significant contributions in the protection and promotion of human rights.

Through qualitative and quantitative analysis of data collected from relevant groups/categories, especially the police, the target sections like Dalits/tribals and experts, the contributions of the NGOs and civil liberties organizations in creating human rights awareness amongst marginalized and vulnerable communities, enabling them legal redress against patterns of violations and providing access to socio-economic entitlement have been empirically evaluated. The data analysis has vindicated the main hypothesis that the NGOs and civil liberties groups have made contributions in promoting human rights especially of weaker sections. The extent of their contribution on the basis of the analysis of data, case study of selected organizations and interaction with a wide spectrum of individuals was rated as 'moderate' to 'high' depending upon the areas/fronts in which NGOs are working for promotion of human rights and related issues.

Significantly, more impact could be made in the Dalit/tribal front, where the ongoing process of resurgence through 'social-engineering' could be accentuated by NGOs active in these fronts. New strategies like 'networking' of NGOs have created a positive impact in accelerating the socio-economic development, particularly of marginalized sections. However, the emergence of different players in the voluntary sector such as conventional NGOs espousing social/developmental issues, human rights NGOs vociferously taking up issues of human right violations, particularly by the state, government-organized NGOs (GONGOs) acting as mouthpieces of governments in international forums, pseudo-religious and revivalist outfits assuming voluntary role and civil-liberties groups trying to occupy their separate space by concentrating on more radical issues have considerably hampered the potential of NGO sector in vigorously pursuing action-oriented programmes for protecting and promoting human rights. Thus, a paradigm shift in the strategy of NGOs and civil liberties movement has become necessary to jointly focus their attention on issues of common concern such as protection of individual freedom and liberty.

Such an approach has become necessary for civil liberties groups and NGOs to play a major role in containing the growth of LWE or similar violent movements that have become the biggest challenge to the internal security of the nation. The prominent civil rights leaders, having accessibility to the top leadership of LWE groups, can operate as the best interlocutors or intermediaries in any political dialogue/negotiation between the state and extremists, as they had shown during crucial 'hostage negotiations' and ceasefire dialogue in Andhra Pradesh in the past. Similarly, conventional NGOs, having decisive sway over the marginalized sections in extremist-affected areas, through their campaigns and activities have the potential to wean away these sections from the influence of Left ultras. After all, the state should understand the reality that a socio-economic-political movement like LWE should be dealt with 'people-centric' action plan in which political negotiations play a crucial role along with specific developmental agenda for the target groups of the affected areas.

In any such developmental agenda, reputed community or NGOs, aptly described as the most representative characters of 'third way' (*The Third Way—The Renewal of Social Democracy* by Anthony Giddens [Cambridege: Polity Press, 1995]), can play a key role in socio-economic development. They can assist state in delivering social goods such as basic education, healthcare, sanitation, poverty alleviation, gender justice and so on, which are inextricably intertwined with the very broad concept of human rights.

The healthy interrelation between the state and voluntary sector has now developed as a global agenda in which the United Nations (UN) and other international bodies have a decisive role. The Nobel laureate, Dr. Amartya Sen, has given it international recognition through his concept 'neo-classic welfare economics', which he advocates for the socio-economic development and social justice of the various cross sections of the society. The success of the concept, according to him, depends much on the participation of voluntary organizations in the developmental process as state has limitations for the effective implementation of land reforms, elimination of the underutilization of agricultural labour and the generation of high domestic savings, which are the three vitals of the 'welfare economics' for any developing country. His 'idea of justice' apparently emanates from this welfare economics and suggests that a perfectly just society is an utopian concept and that a comparative approach that focuses on the actual realization of justice and the prevention of the manifestation of severe injustice is the need of 21st century.

The crucial question is how the 'remedial injustice' could be rectified, especially in countries like India where a mosaic of socio-economic and political factors coupled with the omissions and commissions of governance breed severe forms of injustice including naked violations of civil and human rights. Dr. Amartya Sen has rightly suggested that the better solution lies in properly addressing obvious forms of injustice as oppression of minority groups, subjugation of women and other weaker sections or extreme exploitation of workers. Essentially, what matters more is how the political executive and state superstructures would respond to these areas of severe injustice which we see all around in our day to day life.

1

Human Rights: Historical Background and Constitutional Framework

The concept of human rights is perhaps the most powerful new addition in the international agenda. But the concept of an individual having inalienable rights has its origin in the doctrine of natural law and justice. These rights are based on the belief that all human beings are born free with equal dignity, esteem and honour. Thus, 'human rights' are the rights that every human being is entitled to enjoy and have protected. The underlying idea of such rights—the fundamental principle that should be protected in the treatment of all men, women and children—existed in some form or the other in all civilizations and societies.

Over two thousand years before Christ, we find the rudimentary form of these rights in the instructions of Pharaohs[1] of ancient Egypt, in the sermons of Moses to Israelites, in the charter of Cyrus[2] the Great and in the code of Hammourabhi[3]—the kings of Persia and Babylon, respectively. The Oriental civilizations had rich legacy on human rights. The Indian epics and scriptures have many references to these rights. *Rig Veda*[4] talks about three civil rights pertaining to the body, dwelling place and life. *Atharva Veda*[5] says about right to equality of all—the very source of human rights. Mahabharatha speaks about civil liberties. In Ramayana, Lord Rama is depicted as an epitome of divine and natural justice transcending beyond family bonds and relations. *Bhagavadgita* is nothing but a compendium of right and rational sermons and instructions by Lord Krishna, proclaiming the virtues of right deeds and actions and the enforcement of true justice. Vasudhaiva Kutumbakam[6] is ample proof that long ago our great ancestors believed that the whole world is one family. Kautilya[7] of ancient India dealt with civil and legal rights along with economic rights.

The evolution and crystallization of human rights has been a very long process in which the contributions of philosophers and political thinkers were significant. Thomas Aquinas[8] (1225–1274) sowed the seeds of 'natural laws' and 'liberty of individuals'. The thinkers of the West strengthened philosophical foundations of the concept of human rights. Grotius[9] (1588–1645), the Dutch jurist through his classical work, *De Jure Belli ac Pacis*, originated the concept of *jus genitum* [law of nations] and laid down the basic principles of international law underlining the basic rights and privileges of aliens, prisoners of war and so on. Benedict Spinoza[10] (1632–1677) of Holland strongly defended the natural rights and the value of freedom of thought and expression essential for the proper development and dignity of individual, as well as the security and welfare of the state. The French philosophers like Montesquieu (1689–1775), Voltaire (1694–1778) and Rousseau (1712–1778)[11] gave new dimensions to the concept of human rights when they advanced the slogan that 'all men are born and remain free and equal in their rights'.

England was a playground of different schools of thought on natural rights—the fountainhead of human rights. Thomas Hobbes (1588–1679) and John Locke (1632–1704)[12] were the leading political thinkers who interpreted these rights on different lines. While Hobbes advocated the total surrender of the natural rights to the absolute governmental authority, Locke talked about the partial surrender of these rights for the assurance of social peace. Locke highlighted the inalienable right of man to uphold his right to life, liberty and property and the legal and moral obligation of any state to protect these rights. Thomas Paine (1737–1807),[13] through his work 'Rights of Man', also immortalized the basic rights of man such as 'right to life, liberty and property'. A utilitarian like John Stuart Mill (1806–1873)[14] emphasized the role of state to protect the rights of individuals particularly the women and other weaker sections. Samuel Pufendrof[15] (1632–1694) of Germany gave birth to the idea of civil society and the spirit of individual freedom. Immanuel Kant[16] (1724–1804) advocated that men are by nature free and equal and their natural rights should be protected by the state. Johann Fichte[17] (1762–1814), who followed the liberal and individualistic doctrines of Rousseau, sanctified the law of nature, rights of individuals and security of the people. Hegel, through 'historical materialism', and Karl Marx,[18] through 'dialectical materialism', broadened the scope of human rights, interlinking them with the moral and legal obligations of the state to promote and protect these rights.

Wars, revolutions, rebellions and liberation struggles contributed to the growth of human rights concept. In England, 'Magna Carta' of 1215 guaranteed to citizens freedom from imprisonment or dispossession from property or prosecution and exile 'unless by the lawful judgment of the peers or by the law of the land'. The revolution of 1640[19] and the Glorious Revolution[20] of 1688 led to the Habeas Corpus Acts and the Bill of Rights of 1689, which assured the freedom of speech, the right to bail and freedom from unusual punishment and right to trial and jury. The Industrial Revolution, Free Trade Union Movement and the concept of 'collective bargaining' affirmed the rights of workers against physical and economic exploitation.

The revolutions in America and France led to the genesis of important governmental policy declarations and documentation in which the human rights philosophy was crystallized. In USA, the Declaration of Independence (1776), the Resolutions of the Colonial Assemblies and Continental Congresses, the Articles of Confederation and the Virginia Bill of Rights (1771)[21] were the most significant ones upholding the dignity of individuals, irrespective of their socio-economic background. The French Revolution had also produced remarkable series of documents and constitutions, which formed the mainstream of the historical and legal foundations of the modern concept of human rights. The Declaration of the Rights of Men and Citizens (1789), which was the basic foundation of the French Constitution, was the most significant one. The Communist Manifesto of 1848 and the Russian Revolution paved the way for the genesis of the 'socialist concept of human rights', which emphasizes the primordial role of the state as protector of human rights with overriding emphasis on Marxism–Leninism and the concept of the 'dictatorship of the proletariat'[22] and socialist production relations. Above all, the Second World War, which witnessed devastating consequences of most heinous crimes, mass killings, genocide, gang rapes and unprecedented use of brutal force by the perpetrators of Fascism and Nazism led to strong determination among nations to create a world order in which the fundamental human rights are respected.

The genesis of UN and adoption of its charter were major landmarks on the evolution of human rights. The preamble of this charter underlines that 'the peoples of the United Nations determined to reaffirm faith in fundamental rights, in the dignity and worth of human person, in the equal rights of men and women and of nations large and small have resolved to combine efforts to accomplish these aims' (UN Charter, 1945). However, the most important provisions are probably those contained in Articles 55 and 56 of the charter. Article 55 provides that UN shall promote 'universal respect for and observance of human rights and fundamental freedom for all without distinction as to race, sex, language or religion', while in Article 56, 'all member nations pledge themselves to take joint and separate action in co-operation with the organization for the achievement of the purposes set forth in Article 55' (UN Charter, 1945).[23]

The most significant contribution of UN in the direction of promoting human rights was the adoption of UN Declaration of Human Rights (UNDHR)[24] on 10 December 1948. As underlined in its preamble, this declaration containing 30 articles 'reaffirmed the faith in the fundamental human rights; in the dignity and worth of the human person and in the equal rights of men and women and have determined to promote social progress and better standards of life in larger freedom'. In line with the preamble, the rights as enshrined in the declaration cover a wide spectrum of issues such right to life, right to property, right to education and work, social justice and the role of state in protecting these rights through the implementation of the rule of law and due process of law. While ensuring right to life, liberty and security (Article 2) of all human beings, the declaration specifically states that no one shall be subjected to torture, cruel, inhuman or degrading treatment or punishment (Article 5) or arbitrary arrest, detention or exile (Article 9). It underlines right to life with dignity, for which individuals should be ensured of equality before law and equal protection of law (Article 7), right to work/equal pay for equal work (Article 23), along with the freedom of thought, expression, religion, association and movement (Article 13 and 18). Equally important are the rights concerning individual's status as a citizen, such as the right to nationality and democratic rights (Article 21). In fact, as succinctly highlighted in the preamble, 'the recognition of the inherent dignity and of the equal and inalienable rights of all members of the human family is the foundation of freedom, justice and peace in the world'. Perhaps, the reservations by individual nations and the world community at large to recognize this reality is the greatest challenge confronting the world in the present millennium, jeopardizing peace and justice in many parts of the world.

Since its adoption, the declaration has been and continues to be a source of inspiration for national and international efforts to promote and protect human rights and fundamental freedoms. The declaration, translated into around 350 national and local languages, is the best known and most cited human rights document in the world. The former UN Secretary General Kofi Annan, had rightly commented: 'Humanity will not enjoy security without development; it will not enjoy development without security; and it will not enjoy either without human rights'.[25] The words of Kofi Annan are more relevant in the present-world scenario in which there are many challenges like terrorism, conflicts, poverty, political repression and discrimination that continue to undermine the respect for basic human rights.

The broad spectrum of human rights that one envisages in the present millennium is the outcome of a number of national and international issues that had cropped up in the world during the second half of 20th century. These included (*a*) the national liberation struggles and civil wars; (*b*) ethnic conflicts and organized moves of 'ethnic cleansing'; (*c*) global terrorism and counterterrorism operations; (*d*) disintegration of nation states; (*e*) displacement of persons; (*f*) economic disparities and lopsided development; (*g*) large-scale migration of people due to famines, poverty and internal disturbances; (*h*) refugees and stateless persons; (*i*) environmental issues and so on.

The UN had adopted a number of covenants and declarations in order to confront these challenges in the human rights field. The International Covenant on Civil and Political Rights (ICCPR) came into existence in 1966. In the same year, UN General Assembly adopted the International Covenant on Economic, Social and Cultural Rights (ICESCR) which focuses more on the socio-economic and cultural development of underprivileged communities. They include healthcare, education, food security, housing, right to employment with equal pay for equal work and so on. UN adopted similar covenants and declarations in order to safeguard the rights of specific groups such as children, women, displaced persons, undertrials, ethnic–religious minorities, shelterless and so on. Special mention should be made about the International Convention on the Elimination of all forms of Social Discrimination (1969),[26] Convention against Torture and Other Cruel Treatment and Punishment (1987)[27] and Convention on the Rights of Children (1990).[28]

Side by side good deal of thought had been given to the question of extending the scope of human rights to new areas such as right to development, right to the environment, right to share the common heritage of mankind, right to peace and so on. These rights were christened as 'new human rights' which according to their protractors should receive international recognition. Over the last one decade, a plethora of such issues had come up in the international scenario and the advanced, affluent and developing countries are in the midst of these problems which need a closer look of UN and international community. A time has come for a thorough review and amendment of various UN charters, covenants and declarations in order to effectively deal with new challenges to the human rights at national and international level.

The setting up of human rights committees,[29] under Article 28 of ICCPR, as a principal organ for implementation of the ICCPR with the power to monitor and review the enforcement of these rights was a major step in the direction of protecting and promoting human rights. The real test of effectiveness of an international system for the protection of human rights vests on the question whether it permits individuals who believe that their rights have been violated to seek a remedy from an international situation? With the inclusion of a separate Optional Protocol[30] in 1977, UN had improved the position of individuals who are the victims of human rights violations. The Optional Protocol provides that any state party to the covenant which ratifies the protocol, thereby recognizes the competence of human rights committee to receive and consider communications from individuals who claim to be victims of a violation by the state party of any of the rights set forth in the covenant. Similarly, the prominent NGOs that have no right to lay information before the human rights committee when they were considering the report of a government have been empowered (1993) to send their information to the committee which would distribute the same to all members as official documents. This has improved the status of human rights NGOs throughout the world.

The Resolution 1503 Procedure[31] (adopted by the Economic and Social Council in 1970), empowering UN Human Rights Commission[32] to examine and 'communicate together with the replies of governments if any' which appears to reveal a consistent pattern of gross human rights violations, and the setting up of a Sub-Commission on Prevention of Discrimination and Protection of Minorities were important breakthrough and a move away from the apparent neglect of human rights by UN on many crucial issues. Similarly, the Resolution 1235 Procedure,[33] which enabled the commission to give annual consideration to an item entitled, 'Questions on the violation of human rights and fundamental freedoms including the policies of Racial discrimination and segregation and of Apartheid in all countries particularly colonial and other dependent countries and territories', helped NGOs to play a crucial role in exposing human rights violations and corner those nations which were gross violators of these rights. However, the restrictions imposed by the nation states on the activities of individuals and NGOs strongly espousing the human rights issues at national and international level, through a plethora of draconian legislations, have, to a great extent, nullified UN initiatives in this direction.

The 1990s witnessed certain spectacular international developments in the direction of protecting human rights. During the beginning of 1990, there were no International Criminal Courts (ICCs) and no pending universal jurisdiction cases. However, the next two decades saw a sea change in the international criminal law with many steps taken at national and international courts to bring to justice those responsible for the worst crimes such as genocide, crime against humanity and war crimes committed anywhere in the world. In the same decade, many states rejected the idea that economic, social and cultural (ESC) rights could not be justiciable and accepted in principle that these rights can be enforced through courts. Two decades later, an increasing number of national courts and regional human rights bodies are now enforcing ESC rights.

The appointment of first Human Rights Commission[34] in 1994, with responsibilities such as protection and promotion of human rights, co-ordination of human rights activities within UN and outside and assistance to other UN organs by performing delegated tasks and so on, have broadened the scope of UN to intervene in specific areas of human rights violations. Simultaneously, a number of other bodies had also come into existence closely intertwined with the concept of the protection of these rights. The International Criminal Tribunal for Rwanda was set up to prosecute genocide, crimes against humanity and war crimes committed in Rwanda. In 1995, Additional Protocol to the European Social Charter was adopted enabling collective complaints on violation of ESC rights. South Africa adopted a new constitution in 1996, guaranteeing citizens' ESC rights as well as civil and political rights. Another landmark development was the adoption of Rome Statute in 1998[35] which led to the establishment of the first ICC. The arrest of Augusto Pinochet,[36] the former Chilean president by the United Kingdom in 1998 on charges of gross violation of human rights gave an impetus to many countries to use universal justice system against perpetrators of crime against humanity. In the beginning of the new millennium, the UN played a proactive role in motivating the member nations to adopt a more conducive approach in the enforcement of economic and social rights of people. UN Commission on human rights created a Special Rapporteur on adequate housing and right to livelihood in 2000 and another Special Rapporteur on the right to health in 2002.

Similarly, in a groundbreaking move, UN adopted Optional Protocol to ICESCR in 2009. This Optional Protocol is highly significant in that it corrects a lacuna vis-à-vis the covenant, namely the lack of complaint mechanism. The above Protocol enables individuals and groups from acceding state parties to petition the UN committee mandated to monitor the enforcement of the ICESCR against transgressions when domestic remedies have been exhausted. In addition, the committee is authorized to recommend interim measures to avert further deterioration of conditions and even to enquire into cases of gross and systematic violations. The effectiveness of Optional Protocols, accompanying human rights treaties may have been moderate in terms of the actual operation of the complaint procedures. They, nevertheless, establish a sound moral basis in the realm of argument that when human rights are regarded as universal, the accountability and transparency of the states should likewise transcend geographical boundaries. The case is more compelling in the age of globalization, wherein the challenges of food shortage, energy crisis and climate change are all global. These moves had, had some impact on nations as manifest by the decision of the Apex Court of India recognizing the right to food as a fundamental right.[37]

The ICC was opened in The Hague in 2002, marking a new era on international criminal jurisprudence. ICC had been pursuing investigations into war crimes, genocide and crimes against humanity allegedly committed in Northern Uganda, the Democratic Republic of Congo, and Central African Republic and in Darfur, western Sudan. It was for the first time in 2009 that ICC issued an arrest warrant against a sitting head of state, Omar al-Bashir of Sudan,[38] on serious charges of human rights violations in that country. This indictment had evoked sharp division in the international community when the G-77 group of developing countries, the African Union, the Arab League and the Organization of Islamic Countries (OIC), along with China, strongly opposed the prosecution move. Special tribunals were constituted for Lebanon, Cambodia and so on for the trial of offenders. It is significant that as of middle 2010, 111 countries have signed up to ICC, which is a clear indication that the campaign on international justice has moved down. However, the effective functioning of the court depends much on the approach of countries, especially the political support as rightly observed by Richard Goldstone,[39] former chief prosecutor in the Yugoslav and Rwandan tribunals, 'International Courts like other international bodies require the co-operation of States to make them function efficiently ... If political will is absent, they will flaunder'. A number of international and internationalized courts have been created and countries have ensured that national courts can, and increasingly do, prosecute gross human rights violations committed anywhere in the world. But there is a long way to go to end the present impunity.

While appreciating the contributions of UN in the field of human rights since the adoption of UNDHR, one can easily find that the international body has done some work in the field of standard setting and promotion through Universal Declaration and two covenants (ICCPR and ICESCR) and numerous conventions dealing with specific topics and a variety of soft-law instruments and declarations. But in the case of actual protection of human rights and implementation measures, UN's record is less impressive. The main bottleneck was that many of the member countries failed to ratify the UN covenants and declarations under one pretext or other, whereas UN had no effective structural mechanism or instrument to persuade or prompt the nations to ratify them. Similarly, the trial and investigation of war crimes by ICC or the special tribunals in Lebanon or Cambodia[40] could not make much headway due to the lack of effective institutional mechanisms or differences in international community. Kofi Annan, former UN secretary general highlighted this aspect as:

> The humanitarian challenge is heightened by the fact that the international community does not respond in a consistent way to the humanitarian exigencies. In the foreseeable future the international community should remain prepared to engage politically—if necessary militarily—to contain, manage and ultimately resolve conflicts that had gone out of hand. This will require better functioning collective security system than exists at the moment. It will require, above all a greater willingness to intervene to prevent gross violations of human rights.[41]

The *UN Millennium Report*[42] has also highlighted the inherent issues in respect of 'humanitarian intervention'. While humanitarian exigencies have been used by many countries as a cover to interfere in the internal affairs of sovereign states, they worked as catalysts to deliberately encourage secessionist movements, thereby provoking governments to commit gross violation of human rights, which in many cases led to external intervention. Moreover, 'there is little consistency in the practice of intervention owing to its inherent difficulties and costs as well as perceived national interests.'

In fact, such issues could not be conveniently buried under the carpet, especially in the backdrop of the recent international developments and the polemics on 'humanitarian militarism'.[43] For example, though Sadam Hussain's attack on Kuwait was generally condemned by the international community, there were sharp reactions from the Arab world against US attack on Iraq and the liquidation of Sadam Hussain. Similarly, neither UN nor the international community could do much to stop the naked violation of human rights in Libya for many decades under the iron hands of Colonel Muammar Gaddafi. The intervention of North Atlantic Treaty Organization (NATO) forces in Libya in the wake of national uprisings in the country was also a bone of contention. The reality is that rather than humanitarian or human rights considerations, power equations and economic interests influence the major powers to interfere in the affairs of sovereign states while UN remains a silent spectator. Thus, there is growing reaction among many nations against the violation of sovereignty in the name of humanitarian issues.

Apart from the principles of sovereignty and non-interference, there are certain practical difficulties to effectively engage in humanitarian intervention. First and foremost is that if the people cannot make their state institutions deliver human rights, how can UN, a representative organ of the international system of states get this done? Secondly, gross violation of human rights never occurs overnight. The conditions that lead to such violations should be identified on time and eliminated by the comity of nations. Third, very often the root cause of a human rights tragedy in a particular state would be deep-rooted in its history and legacy, as in the case of erstwhile Yugoslavia or Rwanda. Thus, proper intervention at emotional level can very well defuse the situation. Fourthly, the contemporary state system does not recognize any international mechanism adequately empowered and capable to intervene in the affairs of a state without its consent, however badly that state runs internally. Ironically, geopolitical compulsions force many nations to keep silence or support the worst violators of human rights. Such situations can be tackled through proactive role of civil society or action groups. Action should be taken to encourage home-grown human rights institutions in each state and strengthen them by mobilizing adequate resources through international co-operation. Similarly, international responses to emergency humanitarian situations should be based on consensus and in conformity with the principles of impartiality, fair play, non-eclecticism and uniformity of application of standards. In short, the international community should take the lead to avoid power politics in the area of human rights. In fact, the UN Security Council can play a pivotal role in this regard. But the crucial question is whether the Council can think and act above power politics.

Political Regimes and Human Rights Violations

History is full of tragic episodes of brutal violation of human rights by individual rulers or political regimes that resulted in the genocide of millions. Ideologies or 'isms' seldom had any decisive role in such naked violation of human rights. Ironically, the regimes established on the pillars of democracy, socialism, communism, theocracy, monarchy, military junta or dictatorship of proletariat contributed to the bizarre scenario of violence and killings by these regimes and opposing groups. Thus one of the main hallmarks of the 20th century was 'democide', that is, organized genocide or mass murder by a regime or ruler to perpetrate their interests and to safeguard their seats of power.

R.J. Rummel[44] chronicled the history of major democides through a series of his works on the subject, covering almost all the continents. Though his findings, especially the figures pertaining to the murders, in these democides are debatable, it is established beyond doubt that the phenomenon of death by government/rulers was astronomical in nature during the 20th century and all forms of governments were involved in such dastardly acts. One thing was clear that even democratically elected governments in many countries failed to protect and promote human rights in their true spirit. According to Rummel, the total democide murders of 20th century were 169,202,000 and pre-20th century democide murders were to the tune of 133,147,000. He accounted the highest number of such murders in 'Soviet Gulag' (61,911,000) followed by the Communist Chinese Ant Hill murder (35,236,000); the Nazi genocide (20,946,000) and the depraved nationalist regime murder (10,214,000). The other democides chronicled by him included: Japan's savage military (5,964,000), Khmer Rouge hell state (20,35,000), Turkey's genocidal purges (1,883,000), the Vietnamese War (1,670,000), Poland's ethnic cleansing (1,585,000); the Pakistani cut throat (1,503,000), Tito's slaughter (1,072,000), Orwellian North Korea (1,663,000); barbarous Mexico (1,417,000) and feudal Russia (1,066,000).

Just like Rummel, 'The Case Studies of Jewish Holocaust'[45] projected horrendous pictures and statistics of mass execution of European Jews by Nazi regime. The abiding hatred of Jews as 'untermenschen' (subhumans) was the main ideology and political program of Nazism, the movement that seized power in Germany in1933. Adolf Hitler, who took over the regime in 1934, set about using his police and paramilitary forces to murder political opponents, especially Jews and Bolsheviks (Communists). The Jewish dead numbered more than 5 million: about 3 million in killing centres and other camps, 1.4 million in shooting operations and more than 600,000 in ghettos. Traditional estimates are closer to 6 million (Hilberg).[46] It is estimated that the Nazis succeeded in killing 60 per cent of all the Jews in Europe. In addition to the Jews murdered in Poland (3 million) and the Union of Soviet Socialist Republics (USSR) (1 million), the worst-hit communities were in Hungary (550,000 Jews killed), Romania (275,000), Lithuania (150,000), Germany (135,000–140,000), and the Netherlands (100,000).[47]

The Communist dictators like Joseph Stalin and Mao Zedong probably killed more people than Adolf Hitler. But 'in ferocity, hate, sadism and horror, the Nazi genocide of the Jews of Europe has no peer'.[48] The element of sadism has attracted considerable recent notice:

> The Germans debased and inflicted pain upon Jews with a regularity calculated not just to cripple their bodies but also to plunge them into a state of perpetual terror. The ideal guiding the Germans' treatment of the [Jews] was that it ought to be a world of unremitting suffering which would end in their deaths. A Jew's life ought to be a worldly hell, always in torment, always in physical pain, with no comfort available.[49]

Thus, Noam Chomsky has rightly commented the mass execution of Jews as 'the most fantastic outburst of collective insanity in human history'.[50]

The establishment of Communist regimes in many countries witnessed mass executions mainly on class/ideological lines. Over 10 million people perished in the USSR during the 'state purge' by Joseph Stalin during 1937–1938.[51] The great terror in the country during this phase also led to the mass arrest of around 8 million, execution of around one million, death in camps of around

2 million and incarceration of over 1 lakh. The Stalinism also created major ripples in Europe and Communist satellite countries like Romania, Bulgaria, Hungary, Poland, Yugoslavia, East Germany, Cuba, Czech Republic and so on, where human rights were trampled down for many decades by the unpopular rulers/governments installed by the Soviet Union. The outside world was almost totally dark about the actual situation of these satellite countries till the disintegration of the Soviet Union, as a fall out of the 'glasnost and perestroika'[52] vigorously pursued by Soviet Premier Mikhail Gorbachev. One disgusting feature of these regimes was the total negation of personal freedom or liberty to the people in contrast to the absolute powers enjoyed by the state and its superstructures like police, bureaucracy and so on.

The dissidents and progressive intellectuals like Aleksandr Isayevich Solzhenitsyn[53] had immortalized such trends in the former Soviet Union and her satellite countries. The popular works of Solzhenitsyn had dramatized the all-pervasive powers of state and bureaucracy as: 'anything you saw was yours; any apartment you looked at was yours; any beautiful woman was yours; any enemy was struck from your path; the earth beneath your feet was yours and the heaven above you was yours'.[54] It is a sad truth that many ambitious career-oriented individuals clamp up the ladder and experience the taste of absolute power by collaborating with such regimes in the naked violation of human rights.

The disintegration of Soviet Union and her satellite East European countries opened a floodgate of major human rights issues during the last decade of 20th century. The entire Balkan belt was in great turmoil. Bosnia-Herzegovina turned into a bloody battlefield where the Serb strategy of gender-selective mass execution of non-combatant civilian Serb population had inflicted the severe strain to the minority Muslim population. 'As of December 1994, between 200000 to 400000 people died since June 1991, as a result of the conflicts between Serbs and non-Serbs; over 2.7 million people had been left as refugees and 20000–50000 Muslim women were raped by Serb-soldiers'.[55] Though Serb soldiers were mainly responsible for the mass execution of non-Serbs, Slobodan Milosevic, Yugoslavian premier and his wife Mirjana Markova played the leading role in perpetrating the mass murder of non-Serb population in Balkans. They are now facing the trial before the Special Tribunal constituted to try the culprits of Balkan genocide.

The world witnessed a number of such dictators, the epitomes of cruelty and brutality, who were instrumental for the cold-blooded killing of innocent men and women to retain their seats of power. Some among them like Louis XIV (Louis the Great, 1638–1715) of France, who was the longest reigning monarch in European history, attributed monarchy as divine gift and ruled the masses with iron hand. His absolute monarchial rule in France denying basic rights of people led to the French Revolution. But the revolution did not immediately change the fate of French people. Robespierre,[56] who emerged to power with the active support of radical Jacobeans glorified terror 'as nothing other than justice, prompt and inflexible', suspended civil liberties, forgot the promise of the Declaration of the Rights of Men and was instrumental for the elimination of over 30,000 people in France in early 1790s. In the neighbouring Italy, Benito Mussolini (1883–1945) emerged as the first fascist ruler of the Europe in 20th century and liberally used his secret police, Organization for Vigilance and Repression of Anti-Fascism (OVRA), to mercilessly eliminate his opponents.

Irrespective of continents or the system of governments, 20th century was full of such rulers/dictators who are still remembered by the world for their brutalities against civil population in the name of reforms or development. Though the Communists hail Mao Zedong as the architect of Peoples Republic of China, the Cultural Revolution alone had resulted in the killing/death of over 30 million people. The annexation of Tibet in 1949 led to a series of human rights violations against the Buddhist minorities, while the tragic memories of Tianamen Square massacre still remain afresh in our minds. Meanwhile, Chiang Kai-Shek of Taiwan let loose a reign of terror in his country resulting in the killing of thousands in his conflicts with mainland China. Fidel Castro of Cuba (1959–1999), Tito of erstwhile Yugoslavia (1945–1987), Kim Il Sung of North Korea (1948–1994), Ho Chi Min of Vietnam (1953–1956) and Slobodan Milosevic of Yugoslavia (1992–1999) were other prominent Communist rulers who adopted all repressive measures of torture and execution of opponents/civilians to retain their hegemony. But Cambodia/Kampuchea witnessed the worst form of genocide and killing under the command of Khmer Rouge (Cambodian Communist Party) headed by Pol Pot and his gang during 1975–1979. Around 2 million Cambodians, including noted intellectuals, affluent urbanites and various ethnic minorities had perished due to the combined result of political execution, starvation and forced labour. The strong human rights proponents implicated former Soviet Premier Leonid Brezhnev for the execution of thousands of civilians in Afghanistan (1979–1982). Almost on the same vein, they blame former US presidents, Lyndon Johnson and Richard Nixon, for the killing of civilians in Vietnam (1963–1974) and Cambodia.

A more distressing scenario prevailed in the Islamic world. Colonel Gaddafi of Libya ruled the country with iron hand till his unceremonious exit and execution by rebels in 2010. Similarly, Saddam Hussein of Iraq ruthlessly eliminated his opponents during 1980–1990 and Kurdistan rebels (1987–1988).The 'Khomeini brand of conservative Islam' in Iran, in their attempt to wipe out last remnants of Shah regime, adopted all oppressive measures in the country (1979–1989).The Islamic Republic of Pakistan never attached any sacrosanct for human rights within the country or outside. Yahya Khan (former president of Pakistan) was blamed for the large-scale massacre of people in the erstwhile East Pakistan during Bangladesh liberation struggle in 1970–1971. Sukarno of Indonesia, through his anti-Communist purge, liquidated thousands of his opponents, while his successor Suharto is blamed for East Timor crisis. Hassan Turabi (Sudan, 1989–1999), Hafez Al-Assad (Syria, 1980–2000), Al Zarqawi (Iraq, 2004–2006) and so on were the other Islamic rulers who adopted ruthless measures against their own people. Meanwhile, Osama Bin Laden of Al Qaeda was responsible for worldwide terrorist activities, in which thousands of innocent people sacrificed their lives. Mullah Omar of Taliban adopted similar strategies and killings in Afghanistan since 1986.

Global Human Rights Scenario: A Matter of Serious Concern

Richard Reoch's[57] (editorial co-ordinator of independent newspaper: *Terra Via*) report on the human rights scenario in the world on the eve of World Human Rights Conference (Vienna, 1993) was thought-provoking. According to him, around 120 million people were killed in 20th century both in peace time and armed conflicts as a result of government intervention, including tens of thousands sentenced to death or who disappeared in over 60 countries in the last decade. The toll of economic injustice and deprivation was equally horrendous. Fourteen million children die every year before they reach the age of five. Slavery is banned in international law, yet about 200 million people were held in conditions amounting to slavery, including some 200 million children as victims of child labour. Torture and ill-treatment of persons in jails, police stations or detention camps have been reported from over 100 countries. Despite guarantee of freedom of expression and association, 'prisoners of conscience' — people jailed solely for non-violent exercise of human rights — are held in more than 60 countries. Estimated political refugees run to 14–17 million and the informally displaced people range 12–24 million.

On the economic, social and cultural front, the figures are profoundly disturbing. Worldwide, nearly 140,000 under five die from the combined effects of hunger and disease every three days. Over 100 million people were affected by famines in the opening year of this decade. More than a quarter of world's population does not get enough food and nearly 1 billion go hungry. Over 1 billion people still lack access to health services. One hundred and thirty million people lack access to primary education. Nearly 1 billion adults are illiterate of which 600 million are women.

The overall global human rights scenario continues to remain serious with new shades of violations and abuses, especially against the poor and marginalized sections. A recent report of Amnesty International has clearly indicated these trends. One major finding is that many nations are not serious on the protection of human rights, nor sincere in their approach in effectively dealing with human rights violations. For example, though International Criminal Court had come into existence almost one decade ago, 81 countries have not signed unto the ICC. Incidentally, this includes seven countries[58] of G-20 set-up, considered to be a group of advanced nations committed to human rights. This is quite contrary to the declared motto of G-20 that 'governments should ensure that no one is above law and that everyone has access to justice for all human rights violations'. Similarly, violators of human rights enjoyed immunity in at least 61 countries, whereas people were tortured or otherwise ill-treated in at least 111 countries; their freedom of expression was restricted in at least 96 countries and 'prisoners of conscience' were held over 48 countries. Above all, unfair trial and illegal practises to defeat due process of law were rampant in 48 countries.

Majority of nations, irrespective of their political system or economic advancement, adopt double standards in respect of what they profess and practise in the case of human rights. Sir Stephen Sedley rightly observed in 'Human Rights—A 21st century Agenda' that 'human rights are a commodity like any other capable of being traded for political or economic advantage and the rhetoric little, more the conduct of politics by other means'.[59] Many a time a complex of factors—strategic, economic, trade, political and diplomatic—condition the approach to human rights. The super powers are not an exception to this trend. For example, during the second half of 20th century, both USA and USSR potentially used their veto power in the UN to defend their allies like Israel, Cuba, Afghanistan, Pakistan, Egypt, Philippines, North Korea and so on, on many graver issues of human rights violations. Similarly, USA has imposed major 'sanctions' against around 90 nations, covering more than half of the world population, overriding the provisions that relate to human rights under Articles 1, 55 and 56 of the UN Convention on ESC rights. Their impact was most distressing and devastating in countries like Iraq, where more than 575,000 children perished in 1990s due to starvation and acute shortage of life-saving medicines.

The US policy towards Libya was the latest example of its double standard towards human/civil rights issues. Colonel Muammar Gaddafi, the strong man of Libya who never bothered about the civil/human rights of his countrymen, was the arch enemy of US when he was vigorously pursuing anti-US line among the Arab countries. But the oil-rich Libya and Gaddafi came closer to US when he diluted his anti-American line. Naturally, US conveniently ignored the sufferings and naked violation of human rights of large majority of Libiyans under his oppressive regime till Libiyans revolted against Gaddafi in 2011. Taking cue of the revolt, US strategically switched over their loyalties towards the new movement. Ultimately, Gaddafi was butchered on the streets of Tripoli under the nose of the joint NATO forces headed by US.

US adopted extreme steps when US citizens were subjected to human rights violations by terrorists or other organized groups. On the other hand, they were less concerned about the fate of nations or people under the constant threat of transborder terrorism or Low Intensity Conflicts (LIC). Thus, when a bomb exploded in a night club in West Berlin (5 April 1986) in which an American citizen was killed, US administration concluded it as the handiwork of Colonel Gaddafi's (Libya) men and soon started the bomb attack in Tripoli and Benghazi, killing the innocent civilians. In Mogadishu, a UN soldier was killed and five were wounded (9 September 1993). The US helicopter gunship went into action and over hundred Somalis, including children, were killed as a result of 'strafing'. In the same year, USA resorted to extensive bombing in Baghdad which resulted in the killing of eight Iraqis and injury to many civilians. US warplanes made repeated attacks in Basara state (Iraq). In the Northern Iraq, US dropped 'cluster bombs' which caused extensive damage to civil establishments. When US diplomatic establishments in Nairobi and Darussalam were struck by Islamic terrorists in September 1998, US resorted to massive missile attack in Sudan and Afghanistan which caused major causalities to civilians and civil establishments.

On the other hand, strategic and economic considerations continue to dominate US perception on human rights violations by terror groups in many countries of Asia and Africa, including India. A typical example of the recent past was the US approach towards Pakistan in respect of Mumbai terror attack in which many Indian civilians lost their lives.

The 11-September World Trade Centre (WTC) attack and the subsequent counterterrorism operations worldwide with US at the helm of affairs led to a plethora of human rights issues. Ironically, any brand of terrorism is itself an extreme denial of the most basic human right, namely life, and it creates an environment in which the people cannot live in freedom from fear and enjoy their other rights. This universal truth has been conveniently forgotten by many countries like USA while dealing with human rights or related issues in other countries.

Another distressing aspect was the eagerness of governments to enact special draconian legislations that strip away many civil liberties and personal freedoms on the pretext of countering such threats. Any number of examples can be cited from different countries, irrespective of their form of government or judicial set-up. In the Indian context, legislations like Terrorist and Disruptive Activities (Prevention) Act (TADA), Prevention of Terrorist Activities (POTA), Armed Forces Special Powers Act, Disturbed Areas Act and any number of state legislations such as Maharashtra Control of Organised Crime Act (MOCA), 1999, Chhattisgarh Special Public Security Act of 2006 (CSPSA), Madhya Pradesh Special Areas Security Act, 2006, and so on should be interpreted as such moves. These legislations contain provisions such as reversing the burden of proof, that is, those accused of terrorist or connected activities or who sympathise or even are guilty by association on the basis of accusations by anonymous channels are presumed to be guilty until they can prove their innocence of unspecified charge. The heart of the matter is that governments use such activities as an alibi to stifle dissent and criticism and imprison or threaten those who do not fall in line with their agenda. Through such exercises, the state becomes more authoritarian in its character and human and civil rights suffer.

Obviously, such strategy was found more predominant in 'soft states' of Asian and African countries where human rights were found to be the biggest casualty. The arrest and detention of Patrick Barigbalo Naagbanton,[60] a well-known human rights activist of Nigeria, against the military regime, for his organized efforts to improve the working conditions of working class and protection of environment and river waters was a typical example in this regard. Same was the case with Dr. Binayak Sen, an equally well-known activist, vice president of the People's Union for Civil Liberties (PUCL) and also a paediatrician who was detained in Raipur Jail, Chhattisgarh for over two years on charges of abetting Maoist activity, sedition and waging war against state under various sections of CSPSA.[61] The reality was that Dr. Sen raised his voice against *Salwa Judum* (state-sponsored force to counter Maoists in the state) and disappearance and fake encounters in the state. There were other well-known cases of victimization of human rights activists in other states as well. They included Ms. Shamin Modi, a leading activist of Shramik Adivasi Sanghatana and functionary of Samajwadi Jana Parshad, Madhya Pradesh; Abhay Sahu, president of POSCO Pratirodhi Sangram Samiti (PPSS) of Orissa and so on. Ms. Modi along with her husband, Anurag Modi, was in the forefront of various campaigns in

Harda district of Madhya Pradesh, focusing on issues like minimum wages for workers/tribals, ownership of forest land, bonded labour, illegal mining in forest areas, atrocities and large-scale corruption by political leaders. On the other hand, Abhay Sahu (PPSS) was spearheading a movement against the establishment of 12 million tonne mega steel plant by POSCO, displacing tribals and indigenous population in Orissa.

US anti-terror operations had wider ramifications in the area of human rights. The US priorities shifted from upholding of human/civil rights to victory in the global war against terrorism, for which they adopted distasteful practise. The civilized world closely watched images of caged and shackled detenus at the US naval base at Guantanamo Bay in dismay and anguish. The tragic images of torture at the Abu Gharib prison in Iraq and the Gulfstream jets that were used to transport unfortunate detenus to the secret prisons at Bagram Airbase, Afghanistan, and around the world had seared into the public consciousness. The disclosures of Justice Department on the 'enhanced interrogation techniques', violating the basic canons of law enforcement in any civilized society and laws, used against the detained terror suspects and secret Central Intelligence Agency (CIA) prisons have exposed the dark face of US counterterrorism operations, especially from human/civil rights angle. Ironically, Bush administration had legally sanctified such abuses and naked violations of human and civil rights with the help of the Justice Department. Unfortunately, many other democracies joined the US in the war against global terrorism and shifted the balance of law and administrative practises towards state/nation's security. For example, in Australia and Great Britain the post 9/11 hysteria was harvested by the governments to introduce tough immigration and detention laws against illegal migrants in defence of the policy of strengthening nation's security.

However, in the midst of dark clouds hovering over the horizon of human and civil rights in the present millennium, there are occasional silver lines of hope. They appeared in the form of political and judicial processes as well as the lobbying of domestic and international civil society. The counterterrorism operations of US have undergone significant transformation with the elevation of Barack Obama to White House. Though US policy formulations on global terrorism or international relations cannot be changed at a stroke, Obama administration has adopted certain significant human rights friendly measures.

The first and foremost one was the Obama's declaration to close down Guantanamo detention and torture centre after interpreting the entire episode as 'sad chapter in American history'.[62] It is true that Obama took this brave decision in the light of supreme court's criticism of Bush administration for the treatment of the detainees and the resignation of prosecutors from the military tribunals, which tried the detainees on the grounds of biased trial procedures. The second development was the release of a lengthy secret report by Judicial Department highlighting CIA's interrogation techniques such as staging mock executions, intimidation with hand gun and power drill, threat of sexually assaulting members of detainee's family, 'water dousing' (laying a detainee on a plastic sheet and pouring water over him for 15–20 minutes), blowing cigarette or cigar smoke into prisoners' faces and so on.

The above report prompted US Justice department to order an investigation by a veteran federal prosecutor. Ironically, the senate/house intelligence committees have fully defended the harsh interrogation techniques, describing them as the main tools in the current US counterterrorism operations and expressed genuine doubts that the Justice Department enquiry would jeopardize these operations. However, Obama administration was less convinced of these arguments and seriously went ahead with a number of serious steps to make CIA more accountable to the civil society in USA and to refurbish its image at international level. It is yet to be seen as how far these measures would succeed, considering the fact that intelligence agencies whether in USA or in other countries, under one pretext or other, try to remain unaccountable to the political executive or to the 'due process of law'.

Meanwhile, Australian government and judiciary that handled Dr. Mohammed Haneef episode (charged by the Autralian police with abetting the Glasgow terror attack and deported to India) demonstrated their commitment to human rights values, even in the thick of counterterrorism operations, by openly condemning the extra judicial detention of Dr. Haneef, who was unconditionally released and exonerated from all charges. The Australian community, including legal fraternity, civil liberties groups and other sections of the society, strongly responded to the prima facie abuse of executive power by the government. Dr. Haneef episode and the approach of Australian community have sent a clear message to the entire world that we should not privilege security and order to such an extent as to destroy our most cherished values of liberty and justice in the search of unattainable cent per cent absolute security. Thus, Benjamin Franklin, one of the fathers of American independence, was perfectly correct when he commented: 'those who would sacrifice essential liberty to temporary safety deserve neither liberty nor safety'.[63]

A different scenario exists in India where decades-long insurgency activities in the North East and Jammu and Kashmir (J&K), and LWE in different states have considerably influenced mass psyche and approach of various institutions. The new shades of extremism, militancy and violence have created the so called 'terror-phobia' among large segments of the population. This, to a great extent, gives 'public sanction' for various institutions to adopt apparently illegal methods to contain the menace of extremism and terrorism. Naturally, the biggest casualty of this trend is the human/civil rights. Thus, in many instances, the counterinsurgency and counterterrorism operations by police and security agencies violate the 'due process of law' and open a floodgate of human/civil right issues. Sad reports of encounter killings, custodial deaths, mass rape, disappearances and mass graves pour in from such areas. A number of apparently convincing official arguments such as brutality of terror groups, heavy casualties to security personnel and civilians, foreign links, destruction of public and private properties and so on would come up to justify such actions. Organized 'cover-up' operations are stage-managed to shield the perpetrators of such dastardly crimes. Another equally disturbing trend is the tendency of the security/law-enforcing agencies to fabricate false criminal cases and ruin innocent persons in body, mind and reputation. The infamous 'ISRO espionage case', terror-related cases in Malegaon and Mecca Masjid (Hyderabad) and so on are a few examples in this regard.[64]

Another equally disturbing trend is the reservations or limitations of various institutions to uphold the 'due process of law' or constitutional safeguards, especially in terror/extremist-related cases. Ironically, the political and electoral compulsions force the mainstream parties to play hide-and-seek game in such sensitive matters. Even on serious issues of extremist violence or naked human rights violations, they tactfully play the 'vote-bank' politics and do everything to keep their flocks together. A typical example was the post-Godhara riots in Gujarat in 2002, perhaps, the biggest human carnage in the history of independent India. While the ruling establishment tried to play down the carnage, highlighting the theme of development and pride of the state, other mainstream parties were eager to use the issue to make a political capital. Most significantly, it was at the instance of civil liberties groups/independent NGOs and activists like Teesta Setelvad, Mukul Sharma and Mrinalani Sarabhai[65] that gruesome killings and atrocities at Gulberg Society, Naroda Patiya and Best Bakery[66] were taken up and legally fought within the state and outside. The tragic part of the entire episode was that there were attempts to influence various institutions to toe the line of the state establishment in such macabre incidents of killings, rape and other violations.

While lauding the role of judiciary in upholding the constitutional safeguards on personal liberty and civil/human rights, one should not forget the reality that the hype on terrorism and extremism, which has been amplified through pervasive media, at times influences the judiciary as well. This will lead to unhealthy trends like sanctioning liberal powers to investigation agencies in contravention of the legal procedures and practises, incarceration of thousands of innocent youth in jails as undertrials for years on flimsy charges, which amount to serious violations of human rights. Thus, sacrosanct institutions like judiciary also come under the critical radar of activists and progressive intellectuals in the context of their role in protecting civil/human rights of citizens. In the words of former Chief Justice K.G. Balakrishnan of supreme court:

> Instead of offering a considered response to the growth of terrorism, country may resort to questionable methods such as permitting indefinite detention of terror suspects, the use of coercive interrogation techniques and the denial of the right to fair trial. Outside the criminal justice system, the fear generated by terror attacks may also be linked to increasing governmental surveillance over citizens and unfair restriction on immigration.[67]

He also cautioned the citizens on the organized moves from certain sections to make changes in our criminal and evidence law—such as provision for longer periods of preventive detention and confessions made before police officials to be made admissible in court. The former chief justice has rightly observed that: 'While the ultimate choice in this regard lies with the legislature, we must be careful not to trample upon constitutional principles such as 'substantive due process'.[68] This guarantee was read into the concept of 'personal liberty' under Article 21 of the Constitution of India by our supreme court. Incidentally, Chief Justice Balakrishnan has also acknowledged the fact that the judiciary of USA and UK has played moderating role in checking the excesses that have crept into the response against terrorism.

Viewed in this backdrop, the civil society or their representative independent organizations in India have a crucial role to play in checking the increasing incidence of human/civil rights violations as a fall out of the organized efforts by the state to contain terrorism. Significantly, activists and human rights NGOs backed by progressive intellectuals were in the limelight in various states, particularly Gujarat, Chhattisgarh, the Punjab, Andhra Pradesh and J&K in carrying out campaigns and legal battles against the naked violation of human/civil rights of citizens by the state and it superstructures. Ironically, such NGOs and their functionaries attracted the wrath of the state and its agencies. The civil/human rights activists were branded as staunch supporters of terrorists/extremists, subjected to death threat or torture, prosecuted through the use of judicial system and silenced through introduction of security laws. In the recent past, smear campaign and defamatory tactics have been used to delegitimize the works of these activists, with the media often colluding in the dissemination of slanderous accusations and attacks on their personal integrity and political independence. Internationally renowned social activists/intellectuals like Ms. Medha Patkar, Ms. Arundhati Roy and so on were targets of such attack; the sole reason being that they failed to endorse the official line of the government or its agencies on sensitive issues like development and displacement, environmental protection, empowerment of tribals and other marginalized sections or the state-sponsored violence against left-wing extremists in the name of counter-extremist/insurgency operations.

Such persecution and resistance against genuine human rights defenders are in contravention of the provisions and safeguards endorsed by the international community, notably the UN. The UN

Declaration on Human Rights Defenders of 1998 sets out the prime responsibility of the states to take all necessary steps to ensure the protection of all those who exercise their rights to defend human rights. Among the other things, the Declaration affirms the rights to defend human rights, to the freedom of association, to document human rights abuses, to seek resources for human rights work, to criticize the functioning of government bodies and agencies and to access to international protection bodies. Moreover, general guidelines have been issued to human rights bodies in different countries to adopt a proactive approach in protecting the interests of such defenders.

Differences in the economic, social and political philosophies of the nations also create impediments in the protection of human rights. For example, authoritarian regimes seldom accord any importance to the concept of these rights on the pretext that too much freedom to individuals would breed chaos and instability, adversely affecting development. Such perceptions turn them as worst violators of human/civil rights. Many Islamic regimes adopt a similar line, linking up these rights with religion, customs and practises. For example, Iran and Saudi Arabia argue that human rights should be recognized as different in different religious contexts. With the spread of Taliban and emergence of highly puritanical and fundamentalist outfits in many Islamic countries, many governments are under great pressure to denounce these rights. A few governments in South-east Asia have begun to argue that the very idea of human rights conflicts with very specific characteristics of regional customs and culture.

The liberal democracies in Western countries have been described as strong protagonists of human rights. But they have different perceptions on these rights. For example, USA, UK, Canada and so on place more weight on individual rights and have effective institutional mechanisms to protect these rights, especially those relating to privacy. On the other hand, many other countries in the Europe, influenced by the remnants of Nazism and similar ideologies, attribute that state is the source of all rights. The protagonists of the 'socialist concept of human rights', comprising of countries which follow Marxian philosophy, interpret citizens' rights as state's rights. The oriental societies, especially in developing countries of Asia, attach more importance on 'community or groups' and their rights.

Such wide divergence in the perception and practise of human rights has made the universal application of these rights a myth. Instead, the emerging trend in the present century is the genesis and spread of regional human rights' forums and organizations influenced by local and indigenous factors. This, to a great extent, has adversely affected the efforts of UN and other international bodies to take human rights beyond countries and continents as laid down in the UN Charter of Human Rights.

Regionalism and Asian Concept on Human Rights

A major trend in the field of human rights is the formation of regional-level conventions. The European Convention on Human Rights (1953), American Convention on Human Rights (1975), African Charter on Human and Peoples Rights (1986) and Arab Charter on Human Rights (1994) were the major regional systems that came into existence. This was followed by the formation of such regional systems in Asia and Pacific. Asian Human Rights Commission (AHRC), which came into existence in late 1990s, while endorsing the universality and indivisibility of human rights, emphasized the concretization of these rights in Asian countries.

It has been widely debated on the relevance of regionalism of human rights. The main question is whether the regional conventions would facilitate the implementation of human rights more effectively or weaken the UN efforts to protect and promote human rights at global level. One generally accepted conclusion is that the regional bodies which operate in consistence with the norms and principles set out in the UN Declaration can accelerate the enforcement of these rights among the member countries. After all, the local voice and reaction of human and civil rights activists on serious human rights issues would be better appreciated by the respective states that are sensitive to the concept of human rights than the mere rhetoric and peaceful sermons of UN or other international bodies

The dichotomy exhibited by the advanced 'Northern governments' in the concept and practise of human rights sharpened the differences between the West and Asian countries mainly on the question of important areas of human rights. The affluent North have come to use the term human rights in the very narrow sense, referring only to the civil and political rights, thereby denying or neglecting the social and economic rights of the people in less developed southern nations. The argument of southern nations is that 'the right to subsistence is the most important of all human rights without which the other rights are out of question'.[69] These polemics have now intertwined with the concept of development.

The practise of Western countries attaching 'strings' (conditionalities) relating to human rights safeguards such as protection of political or civil rights and holding of regular elections and so on for developmental assistance to the developing countries in the Asia and Africa has been strongly resisted by the poor nations of these continents. For example, Indonesia took a strong stand that most of the Asian countries happen to be at low level of development and hence should be accorded priority in fulfilling their most basic rights such as eradication of poverty, elimination of illiteracy, improvement of health and creation of employment opportunities without any conditionality. Malaysia had taken a sterner line when its former President Mahathir Mohammed questioned the relevance of UDHR and held that 'political rights were outdated and unsuited to developing countries'. Singapore went a step ahead and advised former Philippines President Ramos in 1994 to sacrifice a degree of democracy for the sake of political stability and economic growth. However, Ramos outrightly rejected the advice, which is a clear indication that even South Asian countries have different perception on the concept of human rights and development.

Needless to mention that Asian concept of human rights has been influenced by a number of factors. The prominent factors include: reservation of Asian leaders to relinquish sovereignty by allowing foreign interference; fragile political institutions, coupled with the combination of ethnic diversity and economic vulnerability; and general apprehension of the leaders that strict adherence to human rights norms may lead to economic decline and moral decay. Moreover, many of the Asian countries have complex societies that attach more importance to 'community rights' which are intertwined with customs and traditions. The legacy of colonialism and historic freedom/liberation struggles in majority of these countries has influenced their political set-up, which, in many respects, interprets human rights as 'alien'. Further, the sad saga of the disintegration of many of the newly independent sovereign republics and the political turmoil and instability made many of these states adopt a negative approach towards human and civil rights. Added to this were the genesis and spread of 'sub-nationalist tendencies' in some of these countries that became insensitive to these rights. All these trends clearly reflected in the Asian concept of human rights vis-à-vis the approach of political regimes in these countries towards human rights.

Vienna Declaration (1993)—A Major Landmark in the Growth and Consolidation of Human Rights

The challenges and issues confronting the human rights move-ment such as different perception of nations on human rights, the concept of 'new human rights' and so on were the major agenda of the World Human Rights Conference held in Vienna in 1993. Vienna Declaration and Program of Action in 1993[70] settled a number of issues on the intergovernmental agenda. The univer-sality of human rights was reaffirmed and the entire spectrum of human rights was endorsed without division. The Declaration had unequivocally upheld that 'all human rights are universal, indivisible, independent and inter-related'. The human rights were reaffirmed as that consisting both civil and political rights, the broader range of ESC rights and the right to development. Thus, the Declaration which emphasized the need for develop-ment stated: 'Democracy, development and respect for human rights and fundamental freedoms are independent and mutually reinforcing. The international community should support the strengthening and promotion of democracy, development and respect for human rights in the entire world'.[71] It also reiterated the significant role that the NGOs can play in the protection and promotion of human rights.

Legal framework of human rights—Humanitarian Law and Human Rights Law

The genesis of international humanitarian law is closely inter-twined with the history of wars from time immemorial. Even the primitive societies had traditionally grappled with a set of ethical or moral guidelines that should be followed by the conflicting groups or warriors in war or armed combat. History tells us that Alexander the Great during his historic battle race through Himalayas/Indus valley meticulously followed these codes while dealing with a defeated and demoralized King Porus. The settled principle of international humanitarian law is that the methods of warfare employed must, at all times, conform to the bonds of legality.

The first major attempt to modernize or codify these laws of war was made at the International Peace Conference convened in Hague in 1899. What was more significant of the 1899 Hague Convention was the adoption of a preambular paragraph known as 'Martens Clause', highlighting the legal protection that combatants and civilians were entitled to in a conflict could not be circumscribed by what countries were willing to accept, either collectively or individually, at any moment of time. Until a more complete code of the laws of war are issued, the clause highlighted:

> the High Contracting Parties think it right to declare that in cases not included in the Regulations adopted by them, population and belligerents remain under the protection and umpire of the principles of International law, as they result from the usuages established between civilized nations, from the laws of humanity and the requirements of the public conscience.[72]

However, neither the principles of international law nor the public conscience have remained static, but were subjected to major changes depending upon the actual conduct of war and the outrages thereof. For example, the use of poisonous gas and chemicals during First World War and the maltreatment of grounded soldiers, sailors and prisoners by Nazi Germany and Imperial Japan during the Second World War greatly influenced the changes in international humanitarian law. Perhaps, the single most factor which greatly contributed to a fundamental reappraisal of humanitarian law and its codification was the cataclysm of Second World War which caused the death of around 50 million people, who included around 26 million combatants and over 24 million civilians, of which one and a half million were civilians killed in air raids. The result was four Geneva Conventions of 1949 which relate to:

1. The amelioration of the condition of the sick and wounded in the field
2. The amelioration of the condition of the wounded, sick and shipwrecked members of armed forces at sea
3. The treatment of prisoners of war
4. The protection of civil population at time of war

In 1977, two protocols to Geneva Convention of 1949 were concluded representing a significant further step in the development of humanitarian law. The first protocol relates to the protection of the victims of international armed conflicts and expands the protection provided by the Fourth Geneva Convention, especially in regards to the use of weapons of mass destruction and protection of civilian population. The second protocol pertains to the protection of the victims of non-international armed conflicts. It builds upon an article found in four Geneva Conventions—Common Article 3—prohibiting violence against civilians in conflicts 'not of an international character' and expands the explicit prohibitions to include forcible displacement (Article 17) as well as acts of threats of violence, the primary purpose of which is to spread terror among civilian population (Article 13).

The second protocol of 1977 was basically intended to extend protection of human rights to areas of civil war, national liberation struggles and insurgency movements, in which the civil population is sandwiched between the combatants and the security forces countering them. Article 3 sets out rules which apply 'armed conflicts not of an international character occurring in the territory of one of the High Contracting Parties'. In such cases 'persons taking no part in the hostilities including members of armed forces who have laid down their arms and those placed "hors de combat" by sickness, wounds or any other means are in all circumstances to be treated humanely without any distinction founded on race, sex, color, religion or faith or wealth or any other similar criteria'.[73]

Nevertheless, there has been considerable difficulty in ensuring the effective application of these provisions. In many cases, various situations of civil conflicts have never been accepted as internal conflicts by the governments in power, which treat them as local insurrections or 'proxy wars' and adopt inhuman and barbaric means to suppress them. The application of humanitarian law becomes extremely difficult in situations of civil strife, especially when insurgents receive assistance from sympathetic foreign powers.

LIC or 'cross-border terrorism' has become a major international issue which needs to be tackled by international community by adopting sound principles upholding human rights concept. The fight against 'global terrorism' has become the prime concern of all nations, especially after 11-September attack on World Trade Center (WTC) towers. The UN had also risen to the occasion and the Security Council adopted Resolution no. 1373[74] on 28 September 2001, which made it obligatory for the states to take a number of specific measures and to co-operate in the fight against terrorism. However, the Security Council in January 2003 adopted Resolution no. 1456, to which is attached a declaration highlighting as to how this challenging task should be undertaken by the states. That declaration inter alia asserts: 'States must ensure that any measures taken to combat terrorism comply with all other obligations under international law and should adopt such measures in accordance with international, in particular international human rights, Refugee and humanitarian law'.[75] The above UN resolution cum declaration was adopted in the light of gross human rights violations in many countries targeting minorities and ethnic groups in the name of fighting terrorism.

The hiatus between international humanitarian law and human rights law is of considerable significance when we discuss various ways and means to protect human rights. Mr. Jean Pictet has written, 'Humanitarian law comprises two branches—the law of war and the law of human rights.'[76] But the extension of human rights to different areas—political, social, economic and cultural—has led to a different interpretation that 'humanitarian law is one branch of the law of human rights and human rights provide the basis and underlying rationale for humanitarian law'. In the other words, human rights law is the genus whereas humanitarian law is the species. The major human rights treaties which form the core of the human rights law are so fundamental that they must be respected at all times, even in periods of armed conflicts. This, of course, is one of the foundations of humanitarian law. A number of rights which the humanitarian law seek to guarantee to the victims of armed conflicts are also included in human rights treaties as rights which should be guaranteed to everyone.

From the Universal Declaration of 1948—the first international text to list the human rights—the modern human rights law has developed into an elaborate network of treaties and covenants. At universal level, the most significant treaties are the two United Nations Covenants of 1966. At regional level, pride of place must be granted to the European Convention of 1950, the first in terms of effectiveness. The aforementioned Convention by virtue of its feasibility and value of regional adjustment has greatly influenced the subsequent American Convention of 1969 and the African Charter of 1981. Similarly, other conventions, protocols and agreements dealing with more specific aspects of human rights broadened the scope of human rights law. For example, 1966 Convention on the Elimination of All Forms of Racial Discrimination[77] and 1979 Convention on the Elimination of All Forms of Discrimination against Women (CEDAW)[78] have made important contribution in developing human rights law against discrimination. In the field of economic and social rights, the treaties and recommendations from International Labour Organization (ILO) have generated an effective code of international labour law. These covenants and protocols and subsequent additions to humanitarian law demonstrate that treaties that form the basis of modern law are constantly being modified and added to. However, the real test of legal progress is not the number of new agreements but the extent to which human rights are ratified. Even if no human rights treaties are to be concluded, human rights law develops if those already agreed were being more widely accepted by the nations. If the growing network of treaty obligations is one measure for the growth of human rights law, creation of proper means for their implementation is more significant. Now, there are a number of international bodies such as human rights committees, UN commissions, European and Inter-American courts of human rights and so on, which have the competence to supervise the performance of the treaties and obligations. But the deficiencies such as optional implementation procedures, reluctance of the states to accept and ratify optional protocols and so on defeat the effective application of human rights law. Encouraging the states to accept the competence of human rights committees or optional provisions of regional conventions is therefore necessary to strengthen human rights law.

Constitutional-Legal Framework of Human Rights in India

The philosophical foundations of the concept of human rights were laid down at varying degrees in the constitution of almost all nations, especially those run by parliamentary system. For example, belief in natural law as the basis of certain rights and duties finds expression in the Constitution of Ireland (1937) which recognizes the family as a moral institution possessing inalienable rights and antecedents superior to all positive law. The British, French and American Constitutions inherited the basic canons of the Magna Carta of 1215, Declaration of the French National Assembly of the Rights of Men and Citizens and the Virginia Bill of Rights, respectively. They had sanctified the concept of human rights.

The adoption of Constitution of India in 1950 was a major land-mark in the history of the development of human rights in India. The preamble, fundamental rights and the directive principles of the state policy, along with a number of amendments, cover a wide spectrum of human rights issues and guarantee them for the people of India. While the fundamental rights stress on the protection of existing rights, the directive principles provide the dynamic movement towards the goal of providing these rights to all by the state and the amendments to the Constitution give an impetus for the implementation of these rights in line with the rapid socio-economic and cultural changes. The preamble of the Constitution declares that the people of India have solemnly resolved to constitute India a sovereign, socialist, and secular democratic republic and to secure to all its citizens:

Justice	Social, economic and political
Liberty	Of thought, expression, belief, and faith and worship
Equality	Of status and opportunity and to promote among them all
Fraternity	Assuring the dignity of the individual

The fundamental rights as enumerated in Part-II of the Constitution which can be described as 'Indian Magna Carta' of human rights are:

Right to Equality

Article 14   Equality before law
Article 15   Prohibition of discrimination on ground of religion, race, caste, sex or place of birth
Article 16   Equality of opportunity in matters of public employment
Article 17   Abolition of untouchability
Article 18   Abolition of titles

Right to Freedom

Article 19   Protection of certain rights on freedom of expression
Article 20   Protection in respect of conviction of offences
Article 21   Protection to life and personal liberty
Article 22   Protection against detention in certain cases

Right against Exploitation

Article 23   Prohibition in traffic in human beings and forced labour
Article 24   Prohibition of employment of children in factories

Right to Freedom of Religion

Article 25   Freedom of conscience and free pursuit of profession, practice and propaganda of religion
Article 26   Freedom to manage religious affairs
Article 27   Freedom as to payment of taxes for promotion of any particular religion
Article 28   Freedom as to attendance at religious instruction or religious worship in certain educational institutions

Cultural and Educational Rights

Article 29   Protection of interests of minorities
Article 30   Right to minorities to establish and administer educational institutions

Right to Constitutional Remedies

Article 32   Right to constitutional remedies

The directive principles and various social legislations uphold an array of human rights pertaining to the rights of workers, children, women, Dalits, Adivasis, and minorities. Despite such constitutional safeguards, numerous social legislations and democratically elected government committed to the cause of protection of human rights, these rights have been violated in various fronts, especially in the case of marginalized sections. From human rights perspective, the mundane provisions in the Constitution can be well equated with a plethora of UN covenants, protocols and declarations on human rights which on many occasions are not ratified, nor implemented by the member countries. It is pertinent to note that the framers of the Constitution, who were a galaxy of men with great vision and sagacity, sincerely desired that the provisions in the Constitution be implemented for the larger interests of all sections of people. But their hopes were belittled due to overriding political, caste, communal, social and economic factors. Thus, social justice, egalitarianism, equality and equal opportunity, human rights and so on remain a myth for the larger segments of Indian masses. In such a scenario, especially in cases of blatant violation of fundamental rights, natural justice and human rights, the judiciary steps in, especially at the instance of Public Interest Litigations (PIL) by NGOs or social activists. The judicial pronouncements by progressive judges of supreme court of India and high courts have considerably contributed to the development of human rights and humanitarian law in India. Thus, Justice (retired) V.R. Krishna Iyer of supreme court has rightly observed, 'Human Rights jurisprudence in India has constitutional status now'.[79]

The above observation emanates from the fact that many human rights—though guaranteed by Universal Declaration and various covenants, yet not specifically enshrined as enforceable rights in Indian Constitution—have been given such status by the Indian Judiciary through the instrumentality of placing reliance upon the declarations, while interpreting the provisions of the Constitution and laws of the land. Unlike the other branches of the Indian law where statutory provisions outstrip 'judge-made law', in the matter of human rights we owe more to the courts than legislations. The apex court has explained this position (AIR1980SC470PP-473-74) as:

> the remedy for the breaches of international law perse or 'proprio vigore' has not the force or authority of civil law, till under its inspirational impact, actual legislation is undertaken' Declaration of human rights merely sets a common standard of achievement for all people and nations, but cannot set a binding set of rules. Member states may seek through appropriate agencies to initiate action, when these basic rights are violated, but individual citizens cannot complain about their breach in the municipal courts, even if the country concerned has adopted the Covenants and ratified the Protocol. The individual cannot come to the Courts but may complain to the Human Rights Committees or bodies which in turn set in order procedures. In short, the basic human rights as enshrined in the International Covenants may at best inform judicial institutions and inspire legislative action within member States.[80]

Apart from such deep reverence, remedial action at the instance of an aggrieved individual is beyond the area of judicial authority. The apex court, in a number of leading cases, such as 'Premshanker case (AIR1980SC1535 P.1537); Sunil Batra (AIR1980SC1578PP1600-1603); regional director, ESI Corporation versus Francis De Costa (AIR1993 Supp (4)SAC100) and so on, had taken due note of international covenants and instruments on human rights, while dealing with the issues of human rights violations. However, legal luminaries are of the view that municipal courts should be given more teeth for dealing human rights issues. The human rights courts, as envisaged in Article 30 of the Protection of Human Rights Act, 1993, would become more effective only when municipal laws are having such provisions.

Protection of Human Rights Act, 1993 and National Human Rights Commission

The first major legislation enacted in India for protecting human rights was The Protection of Human Rights Act, 1993, which came into force on 28 September, 1993. The Act that provided for the Constitution of a NHRC under Article 3, State Human Rights

Commissions (Article 21) and Human Rights Courts (Article 30) was meant 'for better promotion of human rights and for matters connected therewith or incidental thereto'.[81]

The NHRC which came into existence during 1993 could play moderate role in strengthening the concept of human rights in Indian society. It dealt with a myriad of issues ranging from 'encounter killings' and 'custodial deaths', disappearances, from child labour to bonded labour, violence and atrocities against women, Dalits and minorities, from refugees to migrants, from complaints about the way in which special legislations like TADA took its toll, to submissions questioning the constitutional validity of other acts like Armed Forces Special Powers Act, Disturbed Areas Act and so on. Apart from enquiry/investigation into various complaints and recommending remedial measures such as compensation to the victims or their kith and kin for human rights violations, the Commission had also taken up other issues like jail reforms/revision of Indian Prisons Act, insulation of the investigation functions of police from political and other extraneous pressures as per the recommendations of Police Reforms Commission, abolition of child labour by enacting suitable legislations for free and compulsory education to all children until the age of 14 as enshrined in Article 45 of the Constitution and so on. The Commission, with the help of NGOs, drafted a new Prison's Act and conducted extensive research on child labour with the particular reference to the patterns of exploitation in which violence, money, caste, community and social weakness had played their part. The promotion of human rights literacy/awareness among various sections of the society was another major area of activity of the Commission. As part of this agenda, training modules for police personnel on human rights have been compiled and circulated to all states' police establishments in the country, The Commission also entered into certain areas beyond the purview of its statute and entertained the complaints of people, resulting from death or disability due to public health and environmental hazards.

NHRC's stringent recommendations to contain 'fake encounters' and 'custodial deaths' evoked criticism from section of police and security personnel on the plea that such actions would adversely affect operational efficiency and morale of the forces, dealing with extraordinary situations such as terrorism, insurgency, radical extremism and so on. The Commission or any agency committed to the cause of the protection of human rights should not be disturbed by such criticisms so long as the Constitution of India upholds the fundamental rights to life guaranteed under Article 21, which the apex court ruled as 'right to life with dignity' (Bandhu Mukthi Morcha versus Union of India, 3SC, 161, 183 & 84). Thus, the Commission had rightly highlighted in its third annual report as:

> ... the Commission worked on the premise that the human rights whether civil, political, economic, social or cultural are in the words of 1993 Vienna Declaration & Program of Action, are universal, indivisible, interdependent and inter-related and it was necessary for the Commission to remain keenly aware of this, when deciding whether to take cognizance of particular complaint or issues. This was all the more necessary in a country where the seeds of unrest or grievance arising from the human right violations often resulted from a complex mix of reasons that were historical, social, economic, and cultural and in which particular groups, not least for caste or community, economic deprivation or gender continued to be especially vulnerable.[82]

Though India has a vibrant democracy, independent judiciary, a Constitution upholding the sanctity of human rights and sensitive media, the country's overall human rights scenario is far from satisfactory. Human rights violations continue unabated in various fields in spite of the fact that India is a signatory to the UN charter, covenants and protocols and other international instruments on human rights. The annual reports of the NHRC demonstrated the distressing trend of gross violation of human rights in the country. A 10-year study of these reports (1993–2003) showed that the number of complaints received by NHRC, which was 496 in 1993–1994 (October 1993 to March 1994) has increased to 6,987 in 1994–1995; 10,195 in 1995–1996; 20,514 in 1996–1997, 36,791 in 1997–1998; 40,724 in 1998–1999; 50,634 in 1999–2000; 71,555 in 2000–2001; 69,083 in 2001–2002 and 68,779 in 2002–2003.[83] Thus, during the last one decade since the inception of NHRC in 1993, the Commission had received a total of 375,758 complaints of which 365,995 were taken up and 338,111 were disposed of. Total 169,459 complaints (50.16 per cent) were dismissed; 77,400 (22.89 per cent) were disposed of with specific directions and 91,252

(26.95 per cent) were concluded after receiving reports on the notices issued by the Commission. Only in 559 cases interim relief was recommended to the victims or to their relatives, while 295 cases involving government/service personnel were referred for initiating departmental proceedings.

These complaints manifested an array of human rights violations such as 'fake encounters', custodial deaths, custodial rapes and other police brutalities, dowry deaths, indignity to women, excesses against civilians by personnel of armed/paramilitary forces, illegal detention, 'disappearances', false implications, terrorist/Naxalite violations, atrocities against Adivasis/Dalits/ minorities and other marginalized sections, caste–communal conflicts, discrimination in employment, bonded child labour, trafficking in human beings and so on.

An analysis of these complaints and the action taken by NHRC revealed certain clear trends. Demographically, the marginalized and underprivileged sections were the worst victims of human rights violations. In majority of the instances, they failed to get due justice from various institutions of the state. From geographical point of view, two Hindi-speaking states, viz. Uttar Pradesh and Bihar accounted for the largest number of these violations. These states not only topped in the number of complaints, but they also accounted for an average of over 50 per cent of the total complaints annually registered with the Commission. The above statistics is reflective of the socio-economic-political fabric of these states where upper caste and landed gentry backed by the political set-up had all pervasive powers. Added to this were degenerated and decayed customs and traditions prescribed and practised on rigid caste lines creating social barriers and conflicts. This has also led to unhealthy trends like oppression and exploitation of Dalits and backward sections, which sharpened the conflicts and clashes with the active involvement of 'private armies' constituted on caste lines. The criminalization of politics and politicization of crimes have resulted in the crime graph taking a steep upward curve. The situation was further compounded leading to a plethora of human rights issues when an unholy nexus of politicians, law enforcement personnel, criminals and the underworld have emerged with impunity. The genesis and steady spread of left-wing radical groups in parts of undivided Bihar (now Bihar and Jharkhand) and their depredations against the so-called 'class enemies', especially the landed gentry, added new dimensions to the law and order and human rights scenario.

Ironically, almost all the states of the country had human rights complaints, which according to the NHRC reports were the reflection of growing human rights awareness among various cross sections. But, the reality is that only a marginal percentage of affected sections approach NHRC with complaints as the majority of the rural, poor and marginalized sections silently suffer their agonies and humiliation and are afraid to knock at the doors of bodies like NHRC.

The role of NHRC in dealing with human rights issues is yet another bone of contention. It may be mentioned that UN played a key role in promoting and strengthening NHRCs all over the world. The UN had envisaged a wider role for these bodies in the field of human rights issues. Their tasks, inter alia, included (a) issuing annual reports in individual countries, (b) holding public sitting on large scale and organized human rights violations, and (c) advising governments and nongovernmental agencies on questions of human rights. They are also assigned other supplementary tasks such as (a) submitting recommendations, proposals and reports on any matter relating to human rights to the government, parliament or any other competent body, (b) promote conformity of national laws to international standards, (c) receive and act upon individual complaints of human rights violations, (d) encourage ratification and implementation of international human rights standards and contribute to the reporting procedure under international instruments, and (d) promote awareness of human rights through information and education and carry out research and co-operation with UN, regional and national institutes of other countries and NGOs. The Paris Principles[84] emphasized functional autonomy and independence of NHRCs to effectively play their role. These principles highlighted comprehensive provisions to equip NHRCs in this regard. Some of the major guidelines as enunciated were (a) need for founding constitutional and legislative statutes, (b) ensuring as broad a mandate as possible, (c) independent appointment procedures with terms of office specified by law, (d) a pluralistic and representative composition, (e) regular and effective functioning, (f) independence from the executive branch, and (g) adequate funding. Ironically, many of the tasks as indicated by UN and guidelines contained in

Paris Principles could not be complied with by NHRCs in different countries. Thus, the formation and functioning of NHRCs in many countries had come under sharp criticism.

Some of the serious criticisms against NHRCs, including that of India are as follows: (*a*) lack of enforcement powers—the commission lack enforcement powers in respect of the recommendations/directions that they give to the government or other bodies. The main complaint by the alert public, human/civil rights activists and a number of NGOs is that an institution or body that is unable to enforce its own decisions lacks credibility and is nothing more than 'window dressing'. In the case of NHRC, India, such instances had occurred in a number of cases of serious human rights violations in which the Commission *suo motu* or on the basis of complaints had initiated proceedings and made recommendations to the central or state governments to extend relief to the victims or to take stern measures against the naked violation of human rights, but could not enforce them. Two unique examples are the Commission's recommendations pertaining to the 'Gujarat pogrom' in February 2002 and the activities of *Salwa Judum* (self-defence group) set-up by Chhattisgarh state government to tackle left-wing extremist (Naxalite) menace.

The state of Gujarat had witnessed unprecedented human rights violations in February–March 2002. Considering the seriousness of the violations, the Commission took *suo motu* cognizance of the situation in March 2002, initiated proceedings during the same month, arranged the visit of a high-level team including the chairman to the state from 19–22 March 2002, held subsequent proceedings on 1 April 2002 and 31 May 2002 and made a set of recommendations to the state government for the restoration of normalcy, rehabilitation and settlement of uprooted victims and sterner measures to bring all culprits to book by upholding the administration of criminal justice system. A Special Rapporteur in Gujarat had done commendable work by undertaking extensive tours to the riot-affected areas, relief camps and collected first-hand inputs regarding the ground level post-riot scenario in Gujarat. The Commission, on the basis of the reports submitted by the Rapporteur made further recommendations to the state government. Unfortunately, the state government adopted a negative approach in respect of these recommendations and made all efforts to scuttle the findings and recommendations of the Commission, negating the very concept of natural justice and canons of criminal justice system. Another discernible trend was that the bureaucracy and police, acting on behalf of the government, also collaborated with the perpetrators of heinous and barbaric crimes and were deeply involved in 'cover-up operations', apparently ignoring or neglecting the recommendations of the Commission. Though the Commission directed chief secretary and Director General of Police (DGP) of Gujarat to submit Action Taken Report (ATR) on the recommendations of the Commission, they were dilly-dallying on the entire issue without clarifying the points raised by the Commission. The concern and dilemma of the Commission on the apathetic attitude of Gujarat government was clear from the letter of Justice J.S. Verma, the then chairman of the Commission, addressed to the then Prime Minister Shri A.B. Vajpayee:

> ...with great respect, that if our country falls short in rendering justice, promptly and effectively to the victims, dependents and other persons or groups connected with the victims, a serious travesty of law will occur with potentially grave consequences not only to those immediately affected but also to the reputation of our country and its institutions of governance including National Human Rights Commission.[85]

The letter also specifically referred about the negative approach of the state government on such matters as:

> Regrettably to date, in spite of the recommendations made by the Commission, not enough has been done to assure the victims, the country and the world at large that the instruments of the State are preceding with adequate integrity and diligence to remedy the wrongs that had occurred.

Justice Verma, before concluding this letter to the highest political executive in the country, had also indicated the need of strengthening institutions like NHRC in protecting human rights:

> Contemporary human rights jurisprudence requires that the victims must have ready access to the legal system; that prompt and effective steps are taken to ensure that effective disciplinary, administrative, civil and criminal action is taken against those

guilty of omissions and commissions resulting in the violation of human rights, the reparation provided individually or collectively to those who have suffered; that the reparations proportionate to the gravity of violations and damage that occurred and that includes restitution, compensation, rehabilitation and satisfaction and guarantees of non-repetition.[86]

Justice (Dr. A.S. Anand) who was the successor of Justice Verma vigorously pursued the Gujarat episode, despite the negative and dilatory tactics of the state government in implementing the recommendations of the Commission or instituting effective investigations in respect of major cases such as Godhra, Chamanpura (Gulbarga society), Naroda Patiya, Best Bakery and Sadarpura, for which the Commission had earlier recommended probe by Central Bureau of Investigation (CBI) in view of large-scale violation of human rights on the lines of 'ethnic cleansing'. On the contrary, the approach of the state administration was to scuttle all investigations by misusing state instruments, intimidating and terrorizing witnesses and framing weak and fabricated charge sheets, as was manifest in Best Bakery case in which all the accused were acquitted by the trial court. There were also organized efforts from the part of the state government to silence the human and civil rights activists who raised their voice against such serious abuses and aberrations in criminal justice system on the behest of the state. The NHRC could not remain as a silent spectator of such naked violation of human and civil rights in the state, as highlighted in its report:

> Deeply concerned about the damage to the credibility of the criminal justice system and negation of human rights violations, the NHRC on the basis of the reports submitted by its Special team to Vadodara filed a Special Leave Petition (SLP) in the Supreme Court of India under Article 136 of the Constitution with a request to SC to set aside the impugned judgment of the Best Bakery case by the Trial Court.[87]

Similar issues had also come up in Chhattisgarh state which witnessed serious human rights violations in the wake of large-scale violence by left-wing Maoist groups in the form ambushes, bomb blasts and so on, targeting security personnel and counter-operations by security forces killing innocent civilian population, raping and molesting tribal women and incarcerating human and civil rights activists by fabricating false charges against them. The arrest and detention for over two years of Dr. Binayak Sen, a medical doctor engaged in philanthropic services among tribals and weaker sections and the national vice president of Peoples' Union for Civil Liberties (PUCL), had evoked worldwide condemnation by various human and civil rights groups, Over the years, it had also become a testing ground of state-sponsored vigilantism nicknamed as *Salwa Judum*, an armed self-defence group set up by the state to fight against left-wing Maoist groups having no dearth of sophisticated weapons. Irony was that in many places *Salwa Judum*, instead of confronting Left radicals, turned against villagers and tribals, opening yet another saga of large-scale violations of human rights. A specially commissioned report by NHRC has catalogued scores of gross human rights violations and made recommendations to the state government for taking sterner measures against the perpetrators of such violations particularly *Salwa Judum*. Having failed to get these recommendations implemented by the state, the NHRC submitted a sealed report to the supreme court requesting the intervention of the court. The supreme court, in September 2008, while directing the state government to implement some of the recommendations of the Commission appreciated the role of NHRC as:[88]

> The Commission has done a meticulous work. It has given a series of recommendations. It is very painful to read the report. It says there is arson and looting, people are armed and they [Salwa Judum] are committing serious offences. It says people who are subjected to serious problem are still afraid of coming out.

The court virtually denounced the state vigilantism as:

> When somebody is given arms, he claims to be a pseudo police. Once he is given arms, he will commit an offence though he has no right to do any such act. Some remedial measures have been suggested in the report and State may consider implementing them. Whatever is urgently required to be done, do it.[89]

But the irony was that far from heeding the directions of the apex court in true spirit, the Chhattisgarh government fully justified *Salwa Judum* with a dangerous promise that 'Chhattisgarh model' will be used for counter-Maoist operations elsewhere in the country. For anybody who believes in the rule of law and the existing criminal justice system in the country, *Salwa Judum*, the main feature of this model, is a dangerous concept which should be abandoned so that tens of thousands of people whose homes and livelihoods have been destroyed by the cycle of vigilante and Maoist violence are given a chance to return home and live in peace.

Another serious lapse of the Commission is functional duplication and lack of functional autonomy. The critics of NHRC allege that the Commission by virtue of its charter and duties tries to perform the role of judiciary or may be in many respects a complaint-redressal body of the government. They also highlight that NHRC becomes irrelevant if other safeguards for rights and freedoms such as constitution, various Acts and judiciary exist and effectively function. But the reality is that NHRC do not replace or undermine the role of any of the government agencies or institutions like judiciary, parliamentary committees and so on, but only compliment them. Another equally important factor is that functional aberrations do occur in the functioning of all these agencies in any system of government. On the other hand, the Commission generally lacks independence in their functioning as there are several restrictions imposed by the statute or the government itself in discharging their responsibilities. This is all the more glaring in the case of human rights violations, involving government departments or personnel. In many instances, the Commission has limitations to sternly act against government functionaries, especially police and paramilitary personnel responsible for gross human rights violations by misusing their 'sovereign' or official powers. Unique examples are the fate of probe on large number of complaints of fake encounters, custodial deaths, third-degree methods and so on. Such limitations of the Commission could be overcome through functional autonomy, which, to a greater extent, will check direct or indirect governmental interference on its functioning.

There are other organizational and structural factors which adversely affect the functioning of the Commission. One major bottleneck is the absolute powers of the governments to select the members of NHRC and State Human Rights Commissions. Majority of these hand-picked members, more loyal to the governments or their functionaries, show reservations to make recommendations against the governments or their functionaries even in gross issues of human rights violations. Thus, many civil rights groups describe these commissions as a puppet in the hands of governments who manipulate it to fulfil their political objectives. Such propaganda erodes the credibility and public image of human rights commissions. Another equally important factor impacting the role and functioning of the Commission is lack of adequate resources—professionally competent manpower, logistics, specific locations or grass-roots level offices and, above all, sensitivity towards human rights issues. This also leads to another bottleneck of Commission's lack of access to numerous victims of human rights violations, majority of them are poor and marginalized rural sections. This problem of accessibility is ironical as access to justice to victims of human rights violations was one of the main objectives of human rights commissions, as it was conceptually felt that these institutions may play a significant role that may not be performed by the government or the judiciary in entertaining complaints of human rights violations directly from the victims themselves.

On a closer appraisal, human rights commissions have been criticized for their ineffectiveness in fulfilling their foundational objectives. They have the inherent dangers of becoming players in the hands of the states, if they are not in consonance with certain standards. They suffer from different limitations that hinder their independent functioning. It is in this background that the internal reforms of these commissions through their recommendations to the governments assume considerable significance. These reforms should include more enforcement powers, functional autonomy, grass-roots level spread ensuring accessibility and more resources and so on. It is appreciable to note that NHRC has already made a number of such recommendations which need to be implemented on priority so that it can play a more constructive role in protecting and promoting human rights in India.

Significantly, some of these aspects have figured prominently in the report of UN Accreditation Panel in Geneva, 2011[90] which considered UN special status for NHRC. The letter from the UN High Commissioner for human rights laid down a number of stringent conditions to be fulfilled by NHRC for considering its case for special status. One main lacuna, pointed out by the panel, was the lack of pluralism in the composition of NHRC, as the body is dominated by judiciary. It is observed that majority of members from judiciary restrict diversity and plurality and adversely affects its functional efficiency. The panel felt that the principle of diversity has to be achieved by inducting 'deemed members' from minorities, women and schedule caste (SC)/scheduled tribe (ST). NHRC's justification that the body has to perform quasi-judicial role was unacceptable to the panel which observed that 'it was one among the ten functions'.

Another aspect was on the present pattern of selection of secretary general and director of investigations, who, according to the panel, lacked proper investigation skills. They suggested that the present scheme of deputation should be shelved and merit-based selection process to these posts should be initiated with suitable amendments in the Act. The third point was on the question of engagement of human rights defenders. The panel questioned NHRC's claim to have complied with Paris Principles' requirement of engaging with civil society and human rights defenders. It felt that the expert group constituted by NHRC has not been functioning effectively as means of engagement/co-operation with civil society. The panel also found that the present mechanisms are inadequate to effectively handle the large number of complaints received by the NHRC. During the visit of the UN Rapporteur to India in January 2011, one main grievance of human rights defenders was that the complaints received by the NHRC were handed over for investigation to police who are the major violators of rights. Thus, in majority of the complaints, there were no effective, unbiased and timely investigations. Finally, the panel was highly critical of the inordinate delay in publishing the annual reports. The delay was mainly due to the stipulation that the report should not be made public till the government is ready with the ATR. Surprisingly, the latest annual report was of 2007–2008.

There is no surprise on the comments/observations of the panel. The greatest irony is that a body like NHRC, which has a crucial role to play in the protection and promotion of human rights, is governed typically on political and bureaucratic lines without any accountability to people or to the victims of human rights violations. The best example in this regard is the controversy/allegations of corruption centring around the selection and appointment of the present incumbent (2011) to the post of chairman. The body has the dearth of manpower, infrastructure and resources. Deputation and other ad hoc arrangements of personnel in vital areas like investigation or research have eroded the efficiency, professionalism and credibility of this body.

Major Areas/Categorization of Human Rights Violations

Sumanta Banerjee[91] a civil rights activist had categorized the major areas of human rights violations in India as (*a*) state repression on various mass struggles and violation of human rights of ordinary citizens, (*b*) coercion resorted to by certain revolutionary groups notably left-wing extremists, engaged in struggles against the Indian State which has led to violation of fundamental rights of innocent citizens, (*c*) Religious-communal parties/organizations and xenophobic forces which have wrecked nation-wide havoc by unleashing riots that destroyed the lives and properties of common people, (*d*) Indian State's coercive measures like arrest, detention under draconian laws or punitive actions against the perpetrators of various struggles.[92]

The above categorization mainly from civil liberties point of view has not touched the areas of socio-economic, cultural rights of people, particularly the marginalized and underprivileged sections. A compilation made by Legal Resource and Social Action (LRSA) in Tamil Nadu,[93] to a great extent, covered those areas and categorized the violation of human rights in the broad spectrum of political, civil, social, economic and cultural rights as:

1. Violation by Law enforcement Agencies/Paramilitary forces.
2. Laws that create conditions for violation of human rights such as National Security Act (NSA), POTA, TADA and so on.
3. Special legislations such as Armed Forces Special Powers Act, Disturbed Areas Act and wide powers extended to security and law-enforcement agencies under the various provisions of these Acts, which are extensively misused.
4. Insurgency areas where threat to life and property is faced by civil population from armed opposition groups on one side and security forces from other.

5. Undertrials who constitute more than 10 per cent of prison inmates; majority of them are from marginalized or poor sections that often are unable to reach the corridors of justice.
6. Women are the worst victims of human rights violations, especially during communal/ethnic conflicts, counter-insurgency operations and so on. Indian women are worst victims of custodial rape, dowry deaths, domestic violence, discrimination and deprivation in normal and crisis situations. Vienna Declaration of 1993 had categorically highlighted violence against women as major human rights issue in many countries.
7. Dalits and tribals: Large-scale atrocities against these sections are common in many parts of the country besides day to day blatant human rights violations against them in the form of untouchability, harassment, bonded labour, social ostracism, displacement in the name of development, oppressive forest and natural resources laws, denial of minimum wages, lack of developmental opportunities and political space for participation.
8. Communal violence and lack of security for minority communities and ethnic groups, especially due to organized moves of fascist/semi-fascist forces organized on political and religious lines.
9. Issues such as child/bonded labour affecting children and deprived sections.
10. Lack of access to national and state human rights commissions, courts and other government agencies, especially for rural and underprivileged sections. In many cases, ordinary affected civilians with genuine issues are prevented from deposing before such bodies due to intervention of government functionaries/political parties, security forces and vested interests.

Law-Enforcement Agencies and Human Rights Violations

The above categorization of human rights violations and the ground-level statistics of these violations indicate that law-enforcement agencies, though conceptually considered as the protectors

of human rights in a democratic society, sometimes turn as violators of these rights. In fact, an analysis of the complaints received
by NHRC during the first one decade since its inception in 1993
revealed that majority of these complaints centred around the
omissions and commissions of police and other security agencies.
The custodial deaths, perhaps the most barbaric and inhuman
acts which could never be expected from any civilized law-
enforcement agency showed an alarming increase of almost cent
per cent during the period 1995–1997 (444 in 1996–1997 and 888 in
1997–1998).[94] Despite modernization of state police forces, application of scientific and technical means for investigations, and
organized efforts to make the police humane by ensuring better
living and working conditions, there is no major positive change
in respect of custodial offences. According to NHRC, 2,318 cases
of death in police custody and 716 fake encounters have been registered with it since 1993. The reality is that such numbers are
only indicative. It is an open secret that custodial deaths are routinely registered as suicides and encounters are frequently staged
to murder of those under detention. There were also other violations such as 'fake encounter killings', 'custodial rape/molesta-
tion', illegal detention, forced disappearances, use of third-degree
methods, falsification of evidence and non-registration of First
Information Reports (FIR) of poor and less-privileged sections of
society. Human rights violations during day to day policing, on
many occasions, evoked controversies which gave leverage to the
detractors of police to malign police image through orchestrated
propaganda and campaign.

The human rights violations by law-enforcement agencies are
due to a confluence of factors such as the legacy of the police of
total subservience to the authority in power and influential sections, outdated legislations like the Indian Police Act of 1861,
political interference in all areas of police functioning, improper
police training, lack of application of science and technology
in police work, lack of resources and poor working conditions of
personnel at cutting-edge level, public pressure and 'media trial'
in sensational cases and so on. Moreover, the increasing tendency
of senior echelons of police to remain in the good books of political executive for ensuring plum postings and privileges at the cost
of free and fair policing leads to steady increase in illegalities and
human rights violations.

It is an established fact that human rights violations will continue to persist as long as the police organization maintain their present status quo. Definitely, things will improve if the police change their present style of functioning. The NHRC has rightly observed, 'an efficient honest police force is the principal bulwark of the nation against violation of human rights'[95] Ironically, the history of various attempts at police reforms and the fate of the respective commissions clearly showed an inbred resistance among all governments to embark on real reforms in line with the democratic aspirations of the masses.

The first National Police Commission (NPC) (1977–1981) of the independent India submitted eight comprehensive reports to the government, covering all aspects of the police organization and works including a draft Police Act to replace the archaic Police Act of 1861. No worthwhile action was taken on this report for the next decade and half. However, in 1997, Inderjit Gupta, former union home minister in the United Front Government, took up the issue with the state governments and suggested that the important recommendations of the Commission such as formation of State Security Commission and so on be implemented urgently to bring about required changes in the functioning and behaviour pattern of police. But nothing happened in the states. Thereafter, the Rebeiro Committee of 1998 and Padmanabaih Panel of 2000 made a number of recommendations to implement radical reforms on the organizational structure, recruitment, command and control, functioning and accountability of the force. Meanwhile, Prakash Singh, a retired DGP, had moved the apex court and made a plea that the police reforms, in line with the recommendations of NPC and other panels, be expedited.

However, the inertia continues without any major reforms or changes in the police set-up. On the contrary, negative signals on implementation of police reforms, especially in transforming the police to be more people/human rights friendly had come from senior political leaders like L.K. Advani, former deputy prime minister cum home minister in National Democratic Alliance (NDA) government. Advani, being in the capacity of the home minister, asserted in one of the seminars organized by human rights organizations in Delhi during October 2002 that:

Government had the political will to bring police reforms but in a different perspective from that of human rights activists ... for you it is important from the point of view of human rights, for me it is important from the point of view of governance.[96]

The type of governance, as envisaged by many political leaders, is of 'Chhattisgarh model' which totally negates civil and human rights, but promotes state vigilantism in the form of *Salwa Judum* or other state-sponsored forces in the name of fighting terrorism or extremism, endangering the rule of law and basic canons of a free civilized society. The final truth is that no political party or government headed by them desires to deny itself the power to use or misuse police for political manipulations. Perhaps, what Leo Tolstoy wrote of the hypocrisy and sympathies of Russian landed gentry to the serfs appear apt in the case of our modern political leaders in respect of their approach to police: 'I sit on a moving back, chocking him and making him carry me, yet assure myself and others that I am very sorry for him and wish to ease his lot by all possible means except by getting off his back'.[97]

However, we should not be carried away by the propaganda that political interference is the source of all evils in police. After all, we cannot simply wish away the control of political executive over police in democracy. There are genuine apprehensions among all sections of people, notably progressive intellectuals as to how far the proposed reforms even if implemented would help to refurbish the public image of police, their competence and professionalism, unless there is radical transition on the attitude and approach of police leaders who govern the police. Such apprehensions are not unfounded if we make a thorough objective analysis on the exact role played by police in a number of recent sensational cases like Best Bakery, Sohrabuddin—Kasumbi,[98] Jessica Lal,[99] Priyadarshini Mattoo,[100] Nitish Katara,[101] Nithari[102] and so on. Some pertinent questions come up to our mind. Whether the political interference was the sole causative factor for serious lapses which derailed the entire investigation and evoked widespread criticism and commotion among various cross sections of the society? Can the police be exonerated from the lapses in the investigation of these cases? How many of the police leaders attempted to resist apparently illegal orders or directions from political masters? The cardinal truth is that a symbiotic relationship exists between political masters and majority of senior police leaders at the cost of impartial and unbiased policing. Gujarat scenario was an eloquent testimony to this truth which at varying degrees is applicable to other states as well.

The police organization cannot be freed from this unholy nexus by a set of reforms initiated at the instance of police leaders and political executive. Any future strategy on police reforms should be focused on the qualitative improvement on the behaviour pattern, temperament and professionalism of personnel at cutting-edge level. Only such reforms can ensure better functioning of the police at law and order, investigation and other vital areas of policing. Unfortunately, such demands never emanate from higher echelons of police who are more concerned about autonomy or unlimited powers for police, better pay scales and perks, parity with officers of Indian Administrative Service (IAS), more modernization grants and increase in police–population ratio and, last but not the least, cosy posts and lucrative post-retirement assignments. Thus, there is an urgent need of bodies like Administrative Reforms Commission (ARC), NHRC, Department of Personnel and Training (DOPT), independent NGOs and so on to come out with a blue print of police reforms that would reform the police in line with the aspirations of common people, especially minorities, Dalits, tribals and marginalized sections.

Meanwhile, the police leadership should initiate internal reforms involving all sections in the force. Serious corrective mechanisms should be taken in order to make law-enforcement agencies human rights friendly. Some of these measures should include: (a) Improvement in police professionalism for which sound recruitment, training and human resource development policies should be formulated in tune with the future challenges in the law-enforcement field; (b) minimization of political interference in policing, especially in investigation field, for which police leaders should uncompromisingly endorse rule of law and due process of law; (c) creation of human rights awareness in police, especially at constabulary level with the inclusion of subjects/topics like human rights, legal and constitutional provisions and international covenants and protocols in training modules/in-service courses; (d) replacement of outdated legislations like Police Act of 1861, Indian Prisons' Act and so on with new legislations containing provisions to make police and prison officials more human rights friendly; and (e) better resources, manpower and scientific technological devices in order to equip the police, make them professionally competent and liberate them from 'third-degree culture'.

A code of conduct for police should be framed and meticulously followed by personnel to avoid human rights violations. This code invariably should include:

1. Personnel should show full allegiance to the constitution and uphold the rights.
2. Personnel should not question the propriety/necessity of any law enacted. They should enforce the law firmly and impartially without fear or favour, malice or vindictiveness.
3. Personnel should respect the limitations of their powers and functions. They should not usurp or seek to usurp the functions of judiciary or sit in judgement on cases to avenge the individuals.
4. In securing the observance of law or maintaining of order, the police, as far as practicable, should use the methods of persuasion, advice and warning. When application of force becomes inevitable, only the irreducible minimum force required in the circumstances should be used.
5. The prime duty of police is not to prevent crime and maintain order, but police should recognize that test of their efficiency lies in the absence of problems of both crime and order and not the visible evidence of harsh police action in dealing with such problems.
6. They should recognize that they are the members of the society with the only difference that, in the interest of the society and on its behalf, they are employed to give full-time attention to the duties which are normally incumbent upon every citizen to perform.
7. They should realize that efficient performance of their duties will be dependent on the extent of ready co-operation that they receive from the public. This will depend on their ability to secure public approval of their conduct and actions and to earn and retain public respect and confidence.
8. They should always keep the welfare of the people in mind and be sympathetic and considerate towards them. They

should always be ready to offer individual service and friendship and render necessary assistance to all without any regard to their wealth or social standing.

9. They should always place duty before self, remain calm in the face of danger, scorn or ridicule and should be ready to sacrifice their lives in protecting those of others.

10. They should always be courteous and well mannered, be dependable and impartial and should possess dignity and courage and should cultivate character and trust of people.

11. Integrity of the highest order is the basis of the prestige of police. Recognizing this, police should keep their private lives scrupulously clean, develop self-restraint and should be truthful and honest indeed in both personal and official life, so that people treat them as exemplary citizens.

12. They should recognize that their full utility to the country and society is best assured only by maintaining high standards of discipline, faithful performance of duties in accordance with law and implicit obedience to the instructions of the commanding rank.

13. As members of a secular democratic state, the police should strive continuously to rise above personal prejudices and promote harmony and common brotherhood among all the people of India, transcending religious, linguistic, regional and sectional diversities. They should further denounce any practises derogatory to the dignity of women, and the less-fortunate sections in the society.

2

Human Rights Scenario in Andhra Pradesh: A Ground-level Study

With the end of 'cold war', the subject of human rights is perhaps the most powerful new addition to the international agenda. The growth of global terrorism and the organized moves of the comity of nations to contain the threat have posed new issues relating to political and civil rights of individuals. On the other hand, globalization and liberalization have created new frontiers of social and economic rights closely intertwined with the survival and dignity of human beings, especially in developing countries. However, the double standard maintained by nations in respect of what they profess and practice in the case of human rights and the efforts of the 'affluent' Northern governments to use the concept as a potential weapon in pursuance of their global economic, strategic and military interests have created distressing human rights scenario in many countries. There is 'discernable lack of commitment on the part of many governments either to protect the human rights or to act their protection at international level'.[1]

The NGOs and civil liberties groups assume 'a significant role to exert pressure upon national governments and inter-governmental organizations (IGOs) for the horizontal enforcement of these rights'.[2] Encouraged by UN and other international human rights bodies, NGOs, notably human rights NGOs, adopt a number of mechanisms for the protection and promotion of these rights. These include: (a) fact-finding missions or information gathering and documentation on human rights issues; (b) open denunciation of human rights violations at international and national level; (c) lobbying in governmental and intergovernmental arenas; and (d) international solidarity and humanitarian relief. With all limitations and criticisms, the Amnesty International is a living example to the above trend. Added to these are myriad of projects/programmes, campaigns and action-oriented ventures undertaken by a large number of NGOs in the socio-economic and cultural fields targeting the poor and marginalized sections who are the worst victims of human rights violations in almost all countries, including India.

This brings us to the Indian scenario in which poverty, unemployment, undernourishment, illiteracy, lack of drinking water/ health facilities, deprivation and inequalities, exploitation and discrimination and denial of basic freedom have created serious strain and stress in our social, economic and political fabric. Despite globalization and liberalization and decisive economic growth and development, the gulf between the rich and poor has substantially increased and overwhelming majority of people is deprived of the basic requirements to lead a life with dignity. Think of a nation with hundreds of millions denied of basic minimums of life: 70–100 million children outside the schools; 30 million people without shelter and another 40 million unemployed; more than half of its 1,000 million people illiterate or semi-literate; and lopsided development leading to more and more areas of unrest and draconian legislations and insensitive state agencies playing havoc with the life and dignity of citizens. It is almost a Herculean task for any democratic government to resolve all these vexed issues in the present century. Over six decades of our experiments in independent India in the form of economic planning and development, rural-upliftment schemes, poverty-alleviation and employment-generation programmes, social justice and welfare demonstrate this cardinal truth.

The 'penalties of discrimination and deprivation will catch with all of us'[3] The Nobel laureate Amartya Sen's words are prophetic. In fact, these penalties have already caught us in many fields. LWE, different shades of terrorism, Insurgency, political violence, communal conflicts, ethnic and regional struggles and so on have seriously infested the nation. Many parts of the country in the Northeast, J&K, Andhra Pradesh, Chhattisgarh,

Jharkhand, Orissa, Uttar Pradesh, Rajasthan and so on have witnessed such conflicts and violence. New battlefields have been opened in these states where the depredations and violence by struggling groups/extremists/militants and counter-operations by state agencies have led to large-scale violations of civil/human rights of people, especially women, Dalits, tribals, children and rural poor. Basically, the root cause of many of these struggles/conflicts are socio-economic issues. Dogged battles are being waged in many areas by marginalized sections for land, water, forest resources and for their mere existence.

Of the various struggles and movements, LWE is the most serious challenge to internal security and democratic institutions. More than one-third of total districts in the country are, in one way or other, affected by this challenge causing serious impact to our economy, development, peace and security. Perhaps, the Left radicalism and interrelated conflicts account for the largest number of human/civil rights issues in the country. Ironically, the marginalized sections like tribals, Dalits, rural poor and women, who otherwise are the victims of ill-conceived policies, misgovernance and lopsided development, are worst affected sections of the LWE imbroglio in the country. A thorough analysis of the movement, including the interplay of various socio-economic factors contributing to its genesis, spread and consolidation along with its current organizational/structural profile, is necessary to better appreciate its impact in the polity and system including human rights scenario. Such an approach is much needed when we search for serious solutions to solve or contain Left extremism in the country.

The state of Andhra Pradesh was specially focused for this research project as the state in many respects was a seething claudron of all the above-mentioned issues. Political extremism perpetrated by LWE groups has affected the entire Telangana and adjoining districts, in which the people, particularly the tribal and rural poor, were sandwiched between the extremists and forces fighting against extremism. Large segments of the tribals were a deprived lot, immersed in issues such as the alienation of their land, lack of development and neo-cultural invasion. Equally distressing was the condition of large majority of Dalits who were subjected to exploitation and maltreatment by the landed gentry.

Caste discrimination and social atrocities like untouchability prevailed in many parts of the state.

The conditions of rural poor were equally distressing. Unsettled land issues on settlement of title deeds, lack of irrigation facilities, erratic power supply, the 'debt trap' laid by moneylenders and absence of effective marketing mechanism added to their miseries. The tragedy of large-scale suicide of cotton growers in many districts during 1997–1998 was the culmination of these factors. A study by P. Sainath, leading journalist and expert on rural issues, revealed that a total of 23,279 cases of suicide of farmers were registered during the period 1997–2008 of which 13,465 cases were reported during 2003–2008.[4] This was only the tip of the iceberg of the problem as a large number of suicides or deaths due to extreme poverty of farmers seldom found place in such official statistics. Side by side, the remnants of feudalist tendencies still existed in rural areas in the form of bonded/child labour, untouchability, exploitation of women and so on. The above social and economic milieu of the state has led to the genesis of civil liberties movements and NGOs that, during the last two decade, have been actively involved in intricate and complex issues like human rights, 'state violence' and the protection and promotion of the rights of poor and weaker sections. The study has unfolded these issues and reached conclusion/findings on the exact role that NGOs and civil liberties movements can play in the protection of human rights in a civil society, inflicted with stress and strains arising out of conflicts and struggles

Objectives and Hypotheses

The main objectives of the study were: (*a*) to examine the role of state and its agencies in the protection and promotion of civil/human rights, especially in the wake of the mounting threat by LWE groups and encroaches/excesses on the rights and privileges of marginalized sections like Dalits, tribals, women, rural poor and so on; (*b*) to assess the extent of success attained by NGOs/civil liberties groups in the promotion of human rights through their various campaigns/activities and programmes; (*c*) to study the projects and programmes of selected NGOs/civil liberties groups with a view to assessing their impact in the human rights field; and (*d*) to arrive at conclusions on the future role that NGOs/ civil liberties groups can play in the promotion of human rights. In line with the above objectives, the following hypotheses were formulated to undertake the project:

1. Despite constitutional and legal safeguards to promote and protect human rights of all sections, the state and its agencies could not fully protect these rights, especially of the marginalized sections. The violence and depredations of left-wing radicals and the counter-strategies by the state to contain them have added the dilemma of the state in the protection of these rights.
2. The NGOs/civil liberties groups, through their campaign and activities, had promoted the concept of human rights among various cross-sections of the society.
3. The activities of NGOs had accelerated the process of socio-economic changes in many sectors with corresponding fillip to the growth of human rights concept.

Research Design

Various research tools were used to undertake the project. From the initial pilot study, it was found that the subject of research was not a very familiar one for common people who are unable to cater precise data or critical evaluation of the role of NGOs or civil liberties groups in promoting human rights. Thus, data from knowledgeable people was collected. For that purpose, the 'decisional' and 'reputational'[5] approach often used in community-research studies, with some modifications was adopted. One hundred persons comprising functionaries of civil rights groups/ NGOs (40), legal experts (15), bureaucrats (15), academicians (12), media personnel (10) and police personnel (08) were contacted for eliciting their views on the subject of research. Besides, experts (75) on human/civil rights movement and interrelated issues from Andhra Pradesh and other states were interviewed and their feedback was incorporated in the analysis.

The police being the main instrumentality of the state play a crucial role in the protection as well as abuse of human rights. While a professionally competent and unbiased police can very well safeguard these rights, a corrupt and partisan police set-up playing second fiddle to the whims and fancies of the state are a threat to civil and human rights, especially of marginalized sections. Taking cue of this reality, the views of different ranks of police personnel (sample strength of police personnel contacted: 100) of the rank of constables to superintendent of police from Andhra Pradesh have been ascertained in respect of NGOs/civil rights movement and complexities associated with policing in LWE-affected areas of Telangana.

Just like police, civil society has a decisive role in the protection and promotion of human rights in a democratic setup. A society insensitive or indifferent towards the concept and practice of human rights either consciously or due to lack of awareness of rights can seldom play this role. Interaction has been made with general public (200) belonging to different class, caste/community and religion, from all the 23 districts of Andhra Pradesh and their awareness about the human/civil rights groups, basic policing aspects vis-à-vis rights and privileges of public, NGOs and their contributions in the protection and promotion of human rights of different sections of the society has been ascertained.

Data-gathering Instruments

The conventional data-gathering instruments for empirical research viz. questionnaire/opinionnaire and interview schedule were used on the basis of the knowledge gathered from the study of literature and insights from the pilot study. These included: (a) Questionnaire on 'the role of NGOs in promoting human rights' (prepared on a five-point-scale Likert model); (b) two open-ended questions—one pertaining to the suggestions for improving the effectiveness of NGOs in the human rights field and the other on the suggestions for better understanding between NGOs and police in order to protect and promote these rights; (c) questionnaire for eliciting views of police personnel on NGOs/contributions to human rights; (d) an open-ended question eliciting suggestions from the samples to improve the relations between the police and NGOs; (*d*) questionnaire for the general public on the contributions of NGOs in promoting human rights (prepared on a three-point-scale Likert model); (*e*) an open-ended question seeking suggestions to improve the human rights scenario in the country; (*f*) observation schedule for NGOs/civil liberties groups with a self-assessment opinionnaire (prepared on a Likert model, five-point scale.

Procedural Steps

The research data were collected from historical sources and by qualitative and quantitative empirical research methodologies. The study of literature comprising books, documents, journals, pamphlets, annual reports of NGOs and work reports and other publications helped to collect useful data on conceptual and legal framework of human rights/NGOs, the genesis, growth and current profile of LWE groups and the statistical profile of NGOs and civil liberties organizations in Andhra Pradesh. The personal interaction/interview with different category of samples provided deeper and more detailed information on the subject of study. The case study of civil liberties organizations/NGOs — one each from civil liberties front (Andhra Pradesh Civil Liberties Committee [APCLC]), women (ASMITA) tribal (LAYA), Dalit (Society for Integrated Development in Urban and Rural Areas [SIDUR]), rural poor (Action for Welfare and Awakening in Rural Environment [AWARE]) and minorities (Confederation of Voluntary Associations [COVA]) helped to collect specific data on the main hypotheses of the research.

For example, APCLC despite its pro-LWE proclivities tried to uphold the civil and constitutional rights of extremists in the wake of a large number of extra judicial actions by the police and security agencies. It was formed in 1973, mainly as a pro-Left civil rights movement by pro-Left intellectuals like lawyers, academicians, journalists and women activists. APCLC has organizational set-up in all the 23 districts of Andhra Pradesh, but is more active in Telangana. The outfit undertakes a wide spectrum of campaign and activities like (*a*) fact-finding mission on encounter killings, police excesses/atrocities, particularly against LWE, Dalits and so on; (*b*) Dalit issues such as untouchability, atrocities by caste Hindus; (*c*) violence against women such as rape, molestation, dowry deaths and other atrocities; (*d*) child and bonded labour; (*e*) suppression of workers' rights like denial of minimum wages; (*f*) discrimination in development, particularly the economic backwardness of Telangana; (*g*) environmental issues like pollution from cement factories, mining projects; (*h*) petitioning the administration on issues of civil/human rights and environment; (*i*) publication of literature; (*j*) conduct of public meeting and other peaceful mass activities; (*k*) filing cases in courts on civil/human rights issues and presenting evidence before enquiry commissions or other bodies such as NHRC. All these activities have considerable sway in influencing the state and its various agencies in the protection of civil and human rights of people especially vulnerable sections in a democratic set-up.

The legal battles fought by APCLC in the apex court, Andhra Pradesh High Court and NHRC for the protection of civil, democratic and human rights in 1980s and 1990s when anti-Naxalite operations were at their peak were significant. A number of significant directions/recommendations were passed by these bodies in the light of these battles. As a consequence to the acceptance of the recommendations by Andhra Pradesh government, NHRC, on 29 March 1997, issued a letter to all chief ministers of the states to follow the guidelines in respect of the investigation of 'encounter deaths' (full text available on NHRC website). Through this landmark direction, a clear message had been given to the law-enforcing agencies in the country that they should uphold the 'due process of law' while dealing with emergency situations like extremism or militancy. APCLC also maintained rapport with a number of civil/human rights bodies such as Committee for the Protection of Democratic Rights (CPDR), Bombay, Peoples Union for Democratic Rights (PUDR), Delhi, Organisation for Civil and Democratic Rights (OCDR), Tamil Nadu, Indian Peoples Human Rights Commission (IPHRC), Bombay, and so on and took up issues of human rights violations, especially of marginalized sections.

By espousing the civil and human rights issues of different sections, APCLC could make major contribution in protecting and promoting these rights. Its wide range of activities closely fit in the mode of a typical 'human rights NGO'. However, its uncompromising stand on civil liberties and human rights and practical approach in pursuance of its aims and objectives, rather than the mere rhetoric and propaganda on such issues, have attracted the wrath of the establishment ever since its formation. Added to this was their bold and open stand sympathetic to many issues projected by LWE groups and other radical/militant sections. APCLC's reservations to denounce 'violence perpetrated by revolutionary groups' in contrast to the organized violence by the state and its superstructures gave an opportunity to its detractors to brand the organization as pro-Maoist.

The case study of AWARE, Hyderabad, unfolded an entirely different story. It manifests the ground-level reality that sincere and committed NGOs can make substantial contributions in improving the lot of rural poor by ensuring their basic human and civil rights. AWARE a 'giant NGO' with its activities spread over to 6,000 villages in the states of Andhra Pradesh, Orissa, Maharashtra, Uttar Pradesh, Kerala, Karnataka and Tamil Nadu could prove this reality. AWARE's 'development model' mainly focuses on the creation of awareness among the downtrodden sections like Dalits, tribals, women and rural poor at the instance of AWARE volunteers. Then they would be elevated to a phase of social and economic advancement through apex organizations of their own and cluster of activities in different sectors like agriculture, health, literacy and marketing, supported by AWARE for a period of 8 to10 years and finally preparing them to carry out the process of development by themselves. This model has much relevance in the Indian context of rural development.

An analysis of the impact/achievements of its projects for a period of 25 years revealed that over 10 lakhs population out of a total of around 25 lakhs people in their operational area could be covered of which more than 50 per cent were women belonging to marginalized sections. A mosaic of developmental and welfare activities such as employment generation, improved irrigation for agriculture, rehabilitation of bonded labour, distribution of land to landless, increased agricultural production, better marketing facilities for farmers, and cultivation of trees and literacy among rural poor could be undertaken in these areas. These achievements among the target groups' notably marginalized sections speak of the success and viability of the model. The major target groups, who have been benefitted through AWARE's programmes are tribals (Lambadas, Koyas, Nayakpodus, Yonadis, Yerukalas, Chenchus and Panas), Harijans, fishermen and other weaker sections of rural areas. Moreover, at the instance of the outfits/societies such as Lambada Service Society, Girijan Seva Samity and Harijan Seva Sangh were floated and they worked as second-line organizations of these groups. AWARE's mega-project for the development of the tribal belt of Dandakaranya which covers five districts of Andhra Pradesh, five of Orissa and one of Madhya Pradesh needs special mention. The above region with 21 sects of tribals, numbering about 8 lakhs, was the hot bed of LWE where the tribals were sandwiched between the extremists and security forces. The scheme was meant to promote every tribal as an entrepreneur in production and marketing of over 60 forest products without any heavy machinery or manpower involvement that would disturb environment. Intermediate Technology Development Group (ITDG) of United Kingdom[6] and 'NISSET' (leading NGO of Denmark; commonly known in that name) of Netherlands, were also associated with the project, which is estimated at ₹21 crores and spread over five years.

AWARE had a number of legal struggles on human rights issues. The full-time lawyers of AWARE work for human rights education, out-of-court settlements by mediation and land retrieval from the big landlords who are in illegal possession of poor peoples' land, especially tribal land. Around 150,000 families were provided with free legal service; 44,000 acres were taken from the landlords by legal means and redistributed to landless tribal families. Its Centre for Human Rights Education and Development provided training for lawyers, social investigators and barefoot legal workers on human rights and related issues. Formation of Women Brigade (Chaitanya Sakthi), particularly of tribal villages was a serious move for the empowerment of women. The trained members of 'Chaitanya Sakthi' motivated other women to fight for their rights, equalities and economic independence. About 6,000 women, who were trained under this scheme, work voluntarily for achieving gender justice by forming Mahila Mandalis and so on. They launch campaign against bonded labour, illiteracy, alcoholism and fight for land rights. Similarly, specific schemes for poverty alleviation, health care, environmental education, ecology and development have been launched for marginalized sections. These programmes have created major changes among the tribals/Harijans and rural poor, who live with more dignity, equality and social justice.

Just like the rural poor, the exploitation of women in the family and outside is very common. When their constitutionally and legally sanctioned rights are deprived under one pretext or the other, a big question arises in respect of their basic human or civil rights. Thus, there is no exaggeration that the overwhelming majority of rural women still lives in the four walls of the kitchen in the most depressed conditions, devoid of real human dignity and status. The existing legislations and various enforcement mechanisms have inherent weakness or limitations to safeguard the interests of women, especially of rural and marginalized sections. It was in this backdrop that political and apolitcal women organizations were floated in different states.

ASMITA was one such outfit which was formed in Secunderabad by prominent women activists of Andhra Pradesh like Kalpana Kannabiran (daughter of late K.G. Kannabiran, noted civil rights activist), P. Lalithakumari alias 'Volga' (leading feminist writer in Telugu) and Vasantha Kannabiran (wife of K.G. Kannabiran). It basically works for the empowerment of women and its declared objectives are to provide (*a*) a space for women to come together, (*b*) a context for creative writing, dialogue, analysis and reflection, (*c*) a space for feminist action on critical issues, (*d*) necessary resources to empower women from underprivileged groups, and (*e*) context for building solidarity networks with other movements for civil and democratic rights. Its campaigns are mainly focused on issues such as (*a*) violence against women, (*b*) child marriage, (*c*) health, (*d*) education and (*e*) human rights.

As a major NGO in the women's front, partner of National Alliance of Women's Organisations (NAWO) and nodal agency for the follow-up of Beijing Declaration (on women rights), ASMITA could create moderate influence among large chunk of women population in Andhra Pradesh. Apart from women empowerment programmes, such as adoption of urban slums, gender training on women issues, its campaigns for creation of awareness among rural women on their rights and privileges and weakness and strength are more important from human rights angle. The translation of human rights documents to Telugu and their dissemination among rural people, encouragement given to human rights activists and feminist writers to bring out literature on the conceptual and creative aspects of women issues and mobilization of women on socially important issues like anti-liquor/anti-communalism campaigns have contributed to the promotion of human rights concepts among women. The interlinkages of the organization with women movements within the country and outside could also facilitate ASMITA to project human rights and interrelated issues with much clarity and precision.

Another equally exploited section is Dalits. Despite economic planning and a plethora of schemes and programmes for the development of Dalits, they still leave a spectre of poverty, starvation deaths and unemployment. The steady exodus of rural people to urban areas in search of job has created a disturbing trend of sprawling slums, devoid of basic amenities for life. While tenancy, bonded labour, caste discrimination and exploitation by the landed gentry virtually deny the basic human rights for sizeable section of Dalits, the bulk of the slum dwellers are deprived of hygiene or health facilities and are the victims of antisocial activities such as prostitution, drug peddling, child labour and so on. The very concept of human and civil rights is a mirage for the majority of these unfortunate citizens. This case study of SIDUR was intended to assess the extent of their impact among these target groups. SIDUR, one of the prominent NGOs in rural/Dalit front, was started in Hyderabad (Andhra Pradesh) in 1990.

The declared aim of the society is to work for the equality of human beings, irrespective of caste, creed, religion and sex. Its foremost aim is to strive for an egalitarian society that is just, free and equal to everyone. An analysis of the main objectives and activities of the organization such as rehabilitation of street children, slum dwellers and women empowerment revealed that many of its programmes are meant to promote basic human rights, especially of the marginalized sections. The activities of SIDUR are spread over all the 23 districts of Andhra Pradesh through around 150 NGOs, which are supported by the organization. These NGOs are members of Dalit Voluntary Action Forum (DVAF), which work for the empowerment of Dalits through literacy/adult education campaigns, awareness programmes and legal education.

Tribal population of India are the worst victims of human rights violations. Sandwiched between extremist/militant elements and state security agencies in majority of their traditional habitats, they are subjected to social, economic and cultural exploitation from time immemorial. The steady displacement of tribals from their homeland due to the establishment of a number of mega-developmental projects including the Special Economic Zones (SEZ) has aggravated the 'tribal dilemma'. Though the state has initiated a number of ambitious schemes for the integrated development of these sections, overwhelming majority of tribals in the country still remain as the most backward and exploited lot. A number of NGOs and action groups have stepped into this sector with the declared aim of all-round development of tribal community and bringing them to national mainstream. A case study of such an NGO predominantly working among the tribal population of Andhra Pradesh–Orissa–Maharashtra belt was undertaken in order to evaluate their contributions to the upliftment of tribals with particular reference to human rights field.

'LAYA' was formed in Visakhapatnam, Andhra Pradesh in 1989 with the declared aim to end exploitation of tribals and to attain their all-round progress. In-line with the above aim, the body has identified its goals: (*a*) increase the access and control over local resources and ensure its better utilization by the tribal community, (*b*) developing and facilitating the tribal activists with the capacities to intervene in the problem situation in the context of a macro-development perspective, (*c*) empowerment of tribal women as co-partners of sustainable socio-economic development (*d*) promotion of people's organization at grassroots level, (*e*) promotion of sustainable development activities in the region and (*f*) research, documentation and dissemination of information on life systems, tribal culture and identity and development experiments in relation to tribals.

Its functional strategy included (*a*) networking with groups working among tribals to promote local communities network/platform; (*b*) documentation of all major aspects that touch the lives of tribals, with special emphasis on the basic issues relating to land, water and forests; (*c*) training at grassroots level that will aid in the process of promoting a people's platform and/or effective micro-level intervention; (*d*) promotion of micro-level interventions for demonstrating effective and equitable institutional mechanisms that tackle the basic issues affecting tribals; and (*e*) empowerment of women.

Over the years, LAYA has extended its activities to more and more areas. Its interventions are now mainly in the fields of: (*a*) land alienation and human rights; (*b*) natural resource management, especially for the upliftment and welfare of tribals; (*c*) application of science and technology for welfare and development; (*d*) developing herbal-based health-care system; (*e*) micro-credit for marginalized sections; (*f*) Microenterprises; (*g*) empowerment of youth; (*h*) women empowerment; (*i*) networking and (*j*) campaigns. The organizations could make significant impact in the civil society/target groups through their interventions/activities.

As an active 'NGO' in the field of tribals, 'LAYA' could make major contributions in promoting the rights and interests of tribals, one of the most exploited lot in the country. Issues such as tribal-land alienation by non-tribals, depletion of forest resources which adversely affect the socio-economic balance/living conditions of tribals, displacement of tribals due to the construction of big dams and the indifferent or ineffective functioning of government agencies in tribal belts/scheduled areas could be well projected by LAYA through its legal struggles, extensive research and documentation and mobilization of affected sections. Such campaigns/programmes could be given more impetus and momentum through networking with like-minded groups and NGOs. The availability of adequate funds and a set of experienced persons helped the organization to go ahead with its campaigns/projects/programmes /documentation and researches in the tribal field, in spite of veiled threats from LWE groups. Visibly, there is a wind of change among the target population which is a positive trend on the increasing human rights awareness of tribals.

Communal riots and conflicts which result in cold-blooded killings and organized atrocities against women and other weaker sections account for substantial number of human rights violations. Our old cities, having mixed population, had had the past history of such major communal holocausts which on many occasions could not be effectively handled or contained by the state or its agencies. The latest example was the Gujarat carnage of 2002. This case study was intended to assess the exact role that a well-organized NGO can play in such a scenario of communal strife and conflicts posing serious threat to human rights.

Hyderabad is one such city that frequently witnessed communal conflicts. Independent organizations and NGOs were floated

in the city whenever the city witnessed such unfortunate tragedies. The Deccan Development Society (DDS) was one such body
which gave inspiration for the formation of COVA in 1994. COVA
has identified its main tasks as: (*a*) creation of awareness among
the general public and target groups on the social, economic and
other issues which create poverty, illiteracy, unemployment, disempowerment and communal disharmony; (*b*) encourage networking of organizations, groups and individuals, endeavouring
for communal harmony and empowerment; (*c*) formation of
women/youth groups in communally sensitive areas; (*d*) training to women, youth and men for employment, self-employment,
vocational and income-generation activities, (*e*) promotion of
microenterprise, co-operatives for women; (*f*) creation of awareness among all sections on environment concerns, regarding sanitation, safe drinking water, health care, ecological regeneration,
civic amenities and so on; (*g*) formulation of solutions to the social
and development problems of old city and sensitizing the plan-
ners and administrators on such issues. In pursuance of its goals
of communal harmony and empowerment through the active
participation of local groups and organizations, COVA identifies
groups and organizations active in different localities and forms
groups, especially in communally sensitive and economically
backward areas.

Ground-level assessment also indicates that COVA could make
its presence felt in the old city of Hyderabad which is unique in
respect of the socio-economic and religious milieu. Orthodoxy,
obscurantism and illiteracy are the main facets of the overwhelming population, which suffer from lack of development and infrastructure such as drinking water and sanitation facilities. Women
are the worst victims of such socio-economic and educational
backwardness. Added to this is the fear of communal conflicts
and riots. In such an atmosphere of tension and frustration, only
NGOs can win over the faith of the people. In fact, COVA plays
this role comparatively well. Its innovative schemes such as
spreading the message of communal harmony through students/
teachers in the schools, empowerment of women by constituting groups of volunteers in slums and imparting training to the
slum dwellers on income- generating trades and vocations and
working out a marketing network to sell out the products by local

entrepreneurs could considerably change the social and economic milieu of this area. Coupled with these changes, they could also effectively fight against the exploitation of women like the kidnapping of girls for flesh trade and the infamous 'temporary marriage' of poor girls by the alien visitors. All these activities could marginally promote the concept of human rights. Similarly, the interview with experts/prominent personalities helped to add more flesh and blood to the required empirical data. The qualitative and quantitative data analysis enabled to get conclusive findings in line with the objectives of the study.

An attempt has been made to define and explain the key words that constituted the main theme of the research.

Human Rights

The definition and interpretation of human rights vary from nation to nation. The US, in their policy document in 1978, defined human rights as 'Freedom from arbitrary arrest and imprisonment, torture, unfair trial, cruel and unusual punishment and invasion of privacy. It also involved Right to food, shelter, health care and education, freedom of thought, speech, assembly religion, press, movement and participation in government'.[7]

In India, the Protection of Human Rights Act, 1993[8] defined human rights as: 'the rights relating to liberty, equality and dignity of the individual guaranteed by Indian Constitution and embodied in the fundamental Rights and International Covenants and enforceable by Courts in India'. Two covenants of 1966, namely The International Covenant on Civil and Political Rights and The International Covenant on Economic, Social and Cultural Rights are significant in this regard.

The expression personal liberty in Article 21 of the constitution is of the widest amplitude and covers a variety of rights which go to constitute the personal liberty of man. Some of those rights have been raised to the status of distinct fundamental rights as enshrined under Article 19.

From human rights angle, Article 21 extends to the concept of life with dignity. According to (retired) Justice Bhagwati[9] of the supreme court:

... the right to live with human dignity as enshrined in Article 21 derives its life breadth from Directive Principles of State policy and particularly clause (e) and (f) of Article 39 and Articles 41 and 42 and at least therefore include protection of the health and strength of workers, men and women and of the tender age of children against abuse, opportunities and facilities for children to develop in a healthy manner and in conditions of freedom and dignity, educational facilities, just as humane conditions of work and maternity relief.

These are the basic requirements which must exist in order to enable a person to live with human dignity and neither the central government nor the state governments has the right to take any action which will deprive a person of the enjoyment of these basic essentials. Thus, in India, the concept of human rights in their broader plane, has been guaranteed by the Constitution and legal provisions.

However, different perspectives exist among individual nations in respect of human rights. The western concept of human rights has evolved over a long period of time responding to specific configurations of power and economic relationships. On the other hand, Asian countries are focusing on what is being recognized as the indivisibility of human rights. The Asian countries generally argue that economic underdevelopment renders most of the political and civil rights emphasized by the west irrelevant in Asia. Moreover, Asian countries are highly diversified and the unity of governments is more apparent than real. It is utmost fragile. Thus, uniform codes have to be minimal and spaces must be created for the full recognition and participation of the diverse communities

Non-governmental Organizations (NGOs)

Currently, there are two approaches to define NGOs—one broad and the other narrow. As per broad definition, 'every organization in society which is not part of government and which operates in civil society is NGO'. Thus, organizations like political groups, labour and trade unions, religious bodies and institutions, sports clubs, arts and cultural societies, trade and commerce bodies, professional associations and so on come under the broader definition of NGO. The problem with the broad definition is that it embraces a huge number and a variety of diverse organizations.

For research purpose, the narrow definition on NGO was applied. According to this definition:

> NGOs are those organizations which are not serving the self interests of members, but are concerned in one way or another with the disadvantage and/or the disadvantaged or with the concerns and issues which are detrimental to the well being, circumstances or prospects of people or society as a whole.[10]

Terms such as 'voluntary organization', 'private voluntary organization' or American terms 'non-profit organization', 'not for profit organization' and so on have also been used for NGOs. At international level, the concept of 'human rights NGOs' had been developed in late 1970s when a set of NGOs or IGO, through their case studies of human rights issues, could confront the abusive governments which tried to play down such issues. 'A human rights NGO is one established specially to do human rights work', Amnesty International, Human Rights Initiative (HRI),[11] American Institute for Human Rights,[12] PUCL, India and so on are described as such NGOs.

Civil Liberties

> Civil Liberty is said to consist of physical freedom from injury or threat to life, health and movement of body, intellectual freedom for the expression of thought and belief and the practical freedom for the play of will and the exercise of choice in the general field of contractual action and relations with other persons.[13]

Professor Earnest Barker[14] identified three key elements in civil liberty, viz. personal reputation, freedom especially of movement and personal property and the free use, enjoyment and disposal of all acquisitions (Principles of Social and Political Theory).

Third-degree Methods

'The illegal use of force or threat by police in extracting confession from the suspect/accused during investigation or compelling him/her to disclose facts bear on investigations.'[15]

The Constitution of India (Article 21 & 20(3)), Criminal Procedure Code (Cr Pc, Section 163), IPC (Section 330, 348, 376(2)), Indian Evidence Act (Section 27), Indian Police Act (Section 29), and various international instruments such as Universal Declaration of Human Rights, ICCPR, Declaration on the Protection of All Persons from being Subjected to Torture and Other Cruel, Inhuman and Degrading Treatment or Punishment, UN Declaration on all Forms of Racial Discrimination, International Convention on the Elimination of All Forms of Racial Discrimination,[16] International Convention on the Suppression and Punishment of the Crime of Apartheid,[17] Convention on the Prevention and Punishment of the Crime of Genocide,[18] Standard Minimum Rules for the Treatment of Prisoners and Vienna Convention on Consular Relation,[19] prohibit in uncertain terms the use of 'third degree' or 'custodial violence' by law enforcement personnel.

Custodial Death

Neither procedural nor substantive Acts give any definition of 'custodial death'. However, custodial death generally includes the death of a person in police custody and is considered to be the most acute form of custodial violence. The Final Report of the Royal Commission into Aboriginal Deaths in Police Custody in their recommendations (No. 41) enunciated the definition in custodial death as:

1. Death occurring in prison, custody of police or detention as juvenile
2. Whose death is caused or contributed to by traumatic injuries sustained or due to lack of proper care on custody or detention
3. Who dies or is fatally injured in the process of police or prison officers attempting to detain that person
4. Who dies or is fatally injured in the process of prison escaping or attempting to escape from prison or police custody or juvenile detention. David Bayle,[20] an author of many titles on policing has interpreted that the definition should include:

i) All cases where a person dies of whatever cause while in police custody, whether or not the custody is lawful and regardless of the actual location of death

ii) It should also include cases where the deceased was out of custody at the time of death where the death may have resulted from injuries sustained during the period of custody

iii) Where a person dies having escaped from police custody

The international community and international bodies have comprehensively outlawed against custodial violence. Article 5 of UNDHR stipulates that no one should be subjected to torture or cruel or inhuman treatment or punishment under detention. Similarly, Article 7 of ICCPR also upholds the same spirit.

Encounter Killings

'The extra legal killings or the obnoxious practice of killing persons belonging to political groups, sympathizers or others by branding them as extremists, terrorists or mafia men by police or security forces under the guise of confrontation or encounter.'[21] In UN parlance, such practices are described as 'extra judicial executions'. The UN and the international community, in the beginning of 1980s, drafted 'The Principle on the Effective Prevention and Investigation of Extra-legal and Arbitrary and Summary Executions' which was endorsed by UN General Assembly in December 1989. To supplement the principles, the Minnesota Lawyers International Human Rights Committee[22] prepared a manual in 1991 for thorough, prompt and impartial investigations in all suspected cases of extra legal, arbitrary and summary executions. However, these principles have not been adopted so far by many countries including India. In the Indian scenario, the issues of custodial violence and encounter killings have prominently figured in the context of various operations by state agencies against LWE and different shades of terrorism, militancy and insurgency. This has also become one of the main areas of campaign by human rights NGOs and civil liberties organizations.

3

Left-Wing Extremism: Pan-Indian Scenario

The LWE, popularly known as Naxalbari movement, which had its genesis at Naxalbari village (West Bengal) during May 1967, has now become a major threat to country's internal security. Though Andhra Pradesh was the citadel of this movement for many decades, LWE has now spread over to 200 odd districts, mainly in 14 states. The movement, notably Communist Party of India (CPI) (Maoists), is quite active in states like Chhattisgarh, Jharkhand, Orissa, Bihar and Maharashtra, whereas some activists and sympathizer groups can be found in West Bengal, Assam, Uttar Pradesh, Uttaranchal, Madhya Pradesh, Tamil Nadu, Kerala and Karnataka. The strategy of the left-wing extremists is to wage 'protracted people's war' against the state as part of its concept of 'new democratic revolution'[1] and the establishment of peoples' government. The revolutionary struggles by LWE groups and counter- extremist operations by the state have opened a saga of human/civil rights violations in the country. Thus, the pan-Indian scenario of the movement is closely studied with particular focus on the state of Andhra Pradesh in order to arrive at conclusions as to how the Naxalite movement had developed as a major source of threat to human rights in the country.

Of the various left-wing extremist groups in the country, CPI(Maoists) formed after the unity of People's War Group (PWG) and Maoist Communist Centre (MCC) in September 2004 has now become the vanguard of the LWE movement in the country with well-established organizational set-up and mass base in different states. The ideological base of CPI(Maoists) is deeply rooted in the initial Maoist stream enunciated by its ideologues like Charu Mazumdar and Kanu Sanyal in 1960s that led to the Naxalbari uprising in West Bengal in May 1967. The left intellectuals and neo-communists rightly described the movement as 'spring thunder over India'[2] considering its rhetoric and the strong ripples created by it in Indian polity. Just like these pioneer leaders, Maoists also characterize the Indian society as 'neocolonial and semi-feudal', one in which the influences of imperialism, feudalism, casteism, communalism, liberalization and Brahminical hegemony are predominant. According to them, the exploitation of Dalits, tribals, women and the other underprivileged sections, state-sponsored oppression of weaker sections and the steady exodus of foreign capital and technology into the country relegating the domestic economy and entrepreneurship to background are clear manifestations of the above trends. Added to these are the ever-deepening economic and political crisis in the country as part of the overall crisis in the international arena and the bourgeoning corruption and other malpractices eroding the faith of masses on democracy and constitutionally established institutions including judiciary.

The *Maoist leadership ideologically pursues a two-staged armed revolutionary struggle* to demolish the state power as part of its strategy of establishing a proletarian regime. The Party documents and disclosures by senior leaders clearly indicate that the task of first stage of this struggle is to change the semi-colonial, semi-feudal society into an independent new democratic society through the resolution of the two fundamental contradictions of the present Indian society, that is, the contradiction of the Indian people with imperialism and the contradiction of the broad masses with feudalism. Again, in its continuity, the task of second stage is to establish the socialist system and continue the revolution for advancing towards communism on the world scale.

Imperialism, the comprador bureaucrat capitalism and feudalism which block the political, economic and cultural development of the country and the people have been identified by the leadership as the main targets of this revolution. Thus, the whole focus of Maoists is to overthrow the semi-colonial, semi-feudal rule of the big landlord-comprador bourgeoisie classes, and imperialism that backs them, through armed struggle and thereby to establish the people's democratic state under the leadership of proletariat (the new democratic state). This new democratic state will comprise the proletariat, peasantry, petty bourgeoisie and the national bourgeoisie classes. The state will guarantee real democracy for the vast majority of the people while exercising dictatorship over the tiny minority of the exploiters. The minimum programme of the party is to establish socialism by accomplishing the new democratic revolution. The ultimate programme is to establish communism on a world scale.

The Maoists, in pursuance of their revolutionary struggles, have identified certain potential weapons which they intend to build up systematically over a period of time. These weapons are (*a*) a strong revolutionary party based on Marxism–Leninism–Maoism as its guiding ideological basis in all matters. A party that is well disciplined and build through revolutionary style and methods. This party which upholds democratic centralism would be closely integrated with the masses and should stand firmly on the class and mass lines and armed struggle. (*b*) A strong and well disciplined people's army under the leadership of the party. Primarily people's army will be built through the armed agrarian revolution mainly with the help of the landless poor peasants, agricultural labourers and the working class and (*c*) a united front of all revolutionary classes under the leadership of the proletariat based on worker–peasant alliance and on the general programme of people's democratic revolution. This united front will be built in the course of advancing the armed struggle for the seizure of political power.

The party organization is constituted according to geographical divisions and spheres of production. The highest decision-making body of the party is the Polit Bureau comprising 13/14 members (six of whom were either killed or arrested between 2007 and 2010). Among them, Kobad Ghandy is the senior-most member. Other arrested Polit Bureau members included Pramod Mishra, Ashutoseh Tudu and Amitabh Bagchi. Cherukuri Rajkumar, alias Azad, the spokesperson for the party, who was gunned down in Andhra Pradesh was another Polit Bureau member. Similarly, Mallojula Koteswara Rao, alias Kishenji, one of the senior Polit Bureau members who was instrumental for many dreaded operations against security forces in Andhra Pradesh, West Bengal and Orissa was killed in an encounter in November 2011. Present indications are that only six of the 13-member Maoist Polit Bureau still remain active—Mupalla Laxman Rao, alias Ganapathy; Prashanta Bose, alias Kishanda; Nambala Keshav Rao, alias Vasavraj; Vivek, Pratap and Misir Besra.

The Central Committee (CC) of the party, which takes command from the Polit Bureau and passes the information to its members, comprises of 32 members. This Committee is elected by the Party Congress. It represents the whole party and can take crucial decisions with full authority on behalf of the party. The CC elects the general secretary and the Polit Bureau depending on the requirements of the movement and will take all important political, organizational and military decisions in accordance with the party line. Muppala Lekshmana Rao, alias Ganapathy, who took over the leadership of erstwhile PWG from the legendary leader Kondapalli Seetharamaiah, is the present general secretary of the Maoists.

Below the CC, there will be special area/special zonal committee/state committee; regional committee; zonal committee/district committee/divisional committee; sub-zonal/sub-divisional committee; area committee and local-level committees such as village/*basti*/factory/college. The primary unit of the party is cell which consists of three to five members of a village or two or three villages combined, or in a factory or educational institution or a locality or two or three localities combined. Party is constituted with two types of members—professionals and part-timers.

The Maoists have constituted *People's Liberation Guerrilla Army (PLGA), the well-knit armed wing* which undertakes various actions/operations of the outfit. The PLGA is controlled by the Central Military Commission (CMC) which gives military, political and ideological directions to PLGA, besides ensuring supply of weaponry, ammunition, communication and intelligence to the dalam members for their operations. It comprises three components, namely main force, secondary force and base force. The highly trained and equipped main-force guerrillas, who are under the command of the state/special committees, are normally deployed for major operations. The secondary force have the special and local guerrilla squads whereas the base force includes people's militia with village or area defence squads or the ordinary men and women who are given rudimentary military training.

For co-ordinating their operations and training, each state has State Military Commission (SMC) which is assisted by sub-zonal military commands headed by state committee members/commanders. The details of the commanders of the armed dalams at various levels and their operational tasks are a highly guarded secret which is known to only limited number of leaders at highest level. These commanders operate in various pseudonyms and normally do not surface during routine organizational programmes. While the trained guerrillas use sophisticated weapons like AK-series rifles, Indian Small Arms System (INSAS), carbines and rockets, the local militia uses indigenously available weapons such as bows and arrows, axes, swords, knives, iron rods and so on. The trained cadres of people's militia participated in sensitive operations by CPI(Maoists) such as Jehanabad jail break in November 2005 and co-ordinated attack of police establishments in Koraput, Orissa during February 2004.

The organizational structure of CPI(Maoists), as revealed from the documents of the outfit and disclosures made by senior leaders, is roughly delineated below:

Polit Bureau/Central Committee
Central Military Commission (CMC)
Four Regional Bureaus (RB)
(Northern RB/South-west RB/Eastern RB/Central RB)
Zonal/Special Zonal Committees
State Military Commission
People's Militia

Geographically, the states of the Punjab, Haryana, Delhi and Rajasthan come under Northern RB, while Maharashtra, Karnataka, Tamil Nadu and Kerala are under South-west RB, Andhra Pradesh and Dantakaranya (Chhattisgarh including Bastar region) in Central RB and Assam, West Bengal, Bihar, Orissa and Jharkhand in Eastern RB.

Apart from central and SMCs, the Maoists have started constituting regional military commissions for proper supervision and co-ordination of PLGA and people's militia, especially during major operations.

Since 2007, Maoists have started establishing research and Development (R&D) units in urban centres like Bhopal and

Rourkela with the main aim to develop advanced weapons and explosives. They suffered a major setback when its Bhopal unit was busted in January 2007 and senior leaders of Central Technical Committee were arrested by police.

A closer look on various *historical, geographic, demographic and socio-economic factors* that contributed to the genesis and spread of LWE in the country is of considerable relevance for better appreciation of the current dimensions of the movement in Indian polity. This analysis also helps us to understand the basic human/civil rights issues closely intertwined with the movement.

Historically, even before India's independence, a section of nationalist leaders argued that communism and socialism were better suited for the emancipation of the large majority of the Indian masses who were the poorest of the poor, marginalized and exploited from time immemorial. Initially, these leaders were associated with Congress Socialist Party and socialist movement. However, they were sidelined in the halo of Mahatma Gandhi, who spearheaded the freedom struggle mainly on non-violent path. The formation of CPI in 1925 gave an impetus to those leaders who advocated a socialist–communist path for country's development and emancipation of the poor. The party formed a militant kisan movement which strongly espoused the cause of the peasants and landless agriculturists. Though the communist party was banned during British regime, they clandestinely built up the movement with the help of peasants and workers, occasionally resorted to sporadic violence and sacrificed comrades during confrontation with the British and native police. The Meerut-conspiracy case of 1929[3] and the Chittagong-armoury raid of 1933[4] were some of the leading 'armed actions' of the early communists in India. In fact, these violent struggles along with the martyrdom of patriots like Bhagat Singh, Chandrashekhar Azad and others sow the seeds of revolutionary movement in Indian polity.

Special mention is to be made about two movements. First one was the 'Tebhaga movement'[5] led by Kisan Sabha of CPI to increase the cropshare of peasants from half to two by third, thereby reducing the share of landlords to one by third. Charu Mazumdar, who was considered to be the father of left-wing extremist movement, was actively associated with this movement. The second one was the consistent campaign against the brutal repression of peasants by feudal landlords during the regime of Nizam in the princely state of Hyderabad. The movement was later transformed into a full-fledged armed struggle, Telangana Uprising, led by Andhra Pradesh unit of the Communist party. Thousands of acres of land was redistributed to landless poor peasants in People's Courts. Guilty landlords were tried and punished. People's Self-defence Corps defended the villages from attacks of army and police. Nehru sent the army in and Sardar Patel, the iron man of India, adopted the ruthless oppressive measures (known as 'SP' measures) to crush the uprising. Perhaps independent India for the first time witnessed the massive violation of human/civil rights perpetrated by state superstructures. Ultimately, the capitulationism of the CPI to electoral politics led to the surrender of the armed struggle.

The *ideological differences in CPI* and their shift in strategy and tactics considerably contributed to the genesis of left-wing extremist movement. The more radical sections in the party were sceptical of party policies and programmes, especially the compromises with the bourgeoisie/Indian ruling class as part of parliamentary ambitions in contravention of true Marxist–Leninist concept of class revolution. The formation of first Communist government in Kerala after the historical victory of the Communists in 1957 Assembly elections and the subsequent dismissal of the state government by the centre in 1959 after the prolonged anti-communist liberation struggle by the major communities in the state sharpened the internal contradictions in the party. Emboldened by the political developments, the radicals intensified their criticism, highlighting the futility of parliamentary path to pursue the true Communist class revolution in a country like India. They could effectively project the axis of 'comprador-big-bourgeois landlord', which, they alleged, had virtually defeated brave moves of the first Communist government in Kerala, especially in the fields of land reforms and education. The radicals sent a clear message to party comrades in different states that the bourgeois-landlord classes could be defeated only through 'protracted peoples war and armed national liberation struggles'[6] for which the Communists should shun the parliamentary path and switch over to armed struggle. The developments in the international Communist world also greatly influenced them. The major issue was the Sino-Soviet conflict and Indo-China war of 1962. A large section of the 'pro-China' group backed Chinese version on border dispute and branded India as 'aggressor'. This group also agreed with Chinese Communist Party (CPC) in their interpretation that Soviet Union was following 'revisionism' and 'Soviet imperialism and socialism', especially in their relations with East European countries.

These differences in Indian Communist party ultimately led to the split in the movement in 1964, leading to the formation of pro-Soviet CPI and pro-Chinese Communist Party of India (Marxist) (CPI[M]). In fact, the split in Communist party gave a fillip to Left radicals, especially in view of the pro-Chinese gestures of Marxists and their 1964 policies and programmes, upholding 'people's democratic revolution'. However, the wide dichotomy in the ideology and their actual practice by CPI(M) had soon belittled the expectations of the radicals in the party, especially when the leadership took initiative for floating united fronts in their strongholds like West Bengal, Kerala and Tripura with the sole aim to win the elections and capture power. The late 1960s witnessed such alliance politics in almost all CPI(M)-stronghold states. Ironically, the decision of party leadership to work out such opportunist alliance even with those parties which are ideologically opposed to them opened a floodgate of internal contradictions that had precipitated into major organizational crisis. In West Bengal, leaders like Charu Mazumdar and Kanu Sanyal openly revolted against the party leadership. Greatly inspired by Chairman Mao of China, they felt that the situation in India was ripe for armed revolution. Thus, in May 1967, a strong Marxist–Leninist Movement (MLM) led by these leaders was built up among peasants and workers of Naxalbari in the Darjeeling district of West Bengal. The movement soon spread like a wild fire to other states attracting intellectuals and youth, besides workers, peasants and marginalized sections.

Three distinct phases can be traced in respect of the geographical spread of the movement. Initially, during 1960s and 70s, the movement had its centre in West Bengal with its pockets of influence in Andhra, Bihar, Kerala and so on. The ideological halo of the movement and presence of charismatic leaders attracted sections of intellectuals, artists, literary men and students and youth during this phase. Thus, renowned Alma centres like St. Stephens College, Delhi, Presidency College, Calcutta, Osmania University, Hyderabad, Jawaharlal Nehru University, Delhi, and Regional

Engineering Colleges (present National Institute Technology [NITs]) in Warangal, Kharagpur, Calicut and so on became hot spots of left-wing extremist activities. Another notable trend was the active association of art and cultural movements with Naxalites. Leading lights of literary world of Telugu like Sri Sri R.V. Shastri, Khtuba Rao, K.V. Ramana Reddy, Cherabanda Raju Varavara Rao and C. Vijaylakshmi with others joined hands to form Viplava Rachayithala Sangam (VIRASAM) or Revolutionary Writers Association (RWA). Artistes from Hyderabad, inspired by Srikakulam struggle and the songs of Subharao Panigrahi, formed a group—Art Lovers (Jana Natya Mandali)—comprising of the famous film producer Narasinha Rao and the legendary Gaddar. In view of such developments, the movement was led largely by urban-based intellectuals during this phase. But the brutal repressive strategy adopted by the state apparatus, especially during the period of National Emergency, to crush the movement resulted in a geographical shift in its spread from the late 1970s.

This marked the second phase of the movement since the beginning of early 1980s when the LWE leaders and cadres who were under considerable pressure from state and central forces shifted their sphere of activities to inaccessible and difficult forest and tribal areas, especially of Andhra Pradesh, undivided Madhya Pradesh and Bihar, Orissa and Maharashtra. In fact, the movement, during this period, could augment their support base mainly due to the active support of indigenous tribal and backward population. The LWE groups strengthened their clandestine 'guerilla apparatus' in their stronghold states with the support of these sections. Despite the split within LWE movement and occasional fratricidal conflicts, the PWG and MCC made spectacular growth during this phase, especially in states like Andhra Pradesh and Bihar which had witnessed large-scale LWE violence. The two-pronged strategy of stepped-up operations and dialogue adopted by the state governments to tackle LWE menace in many respects helped the ultras to maintain their stranglehold in their stronghold areas which continued to be the forest and tribal belt.

However, in late 1990s, the police and other forces could get an upper hand against LWE. This was mainly through sustained 'anti-extremist action plan' such as increased combing operations, development of a vast 'informer network' and, of course, seriously addressing the problems of affected sections. Many top leaders including CC members and underground squad commanders notably of PWG and MCC were liquidated, giving a severe blow to their movement. This had forced LWE to bring about some changes in their tactics and strategy which marked the third phase of the movement in late 1990s. One significant development was the formation PLGA and the shifting of all squads and party organizations from the plains to forest areas. This phase also marked the beginning of more co-ordinated efforts to give practical shape to the concept of Red Corridor comprising the contiguous tribal areas stretching from India's border with Nepal in the north and slicing through Bihar, Uttar Pradesh, Madhya Pradesh, Jharkhand, Orissa, Chhattisgarh, Andhra Pradesh, Maharashtra, Karnataka and Kerala in the down south.

Meanwhile, systematic efforts were made by LWE, notably CPI(Maoists), to strengthen their clandestine apparatus by extending such 'modules' to urban and semi-urban areas. Formation of R&D units in urban centres like Bhopal, Rourkela, Jabalpur and so on under Central Technical Committee with a view to develop modern arms and explosives and open hideouts for senior leaders in urban areas and so on were certain moves in this direction. Simultaneously, Maoists also started urban-based organizational campaigns on issues like economic reforms, liberalization, exploitation of rich natural and mineral resources by multinationals and the displacement of tribals and indigenous people from their homelands. In Nandigram, West Bengal, a fact-finding committee has established that the Maoists were responsible for inciting the violence in places like Nandigram and Singur where major Indian corporate houses like TATA have ventured to start auto industries on the invitation of CPI(M)-led government in the state. A report submitted by the then West Bengal chief minister, Buddhadeb Bhattacharya, to Prime Minister Manmohan Singh on the Nandigram violence has blamed the left-wing extremists for the flare up. The report highlighted:

> It may be noted that left-wing extremists (LWE) have stepped up their propaganda pertaining to the espousal of the causes of farmers by raising the issue of displacement of farmers from their own land for industrial and infrastructural projects. Frontal organizations of LWE activists named the Gana Pratirodh Manch carried out propaganda against the acquisition of land in Singur and have

also generally opposed land acquisition for large projects throughout the state. [7]

The above developments, coupled with Maoists shifting their
focus on urban intrusion and recruiting 'elite' class, suggest that
the Naxal leaders have decided to adopt an approach that will
bring them out of the rural deep forest to the urban areas. Like
everything, this movement too is adapting and changing its working with time.

Thus, by the end of 2010, over 200 out of 625 districts in the
country were directly or indirectly affected by the activities of
LWE groups, accounting for about 40 per cent of India's total
geographical area. According to Union Home Ministry, around
60 districts are seriously affected mainly in the self-styled Red
Corridor belt. A state-wise profile of most seriously affected districts is present in Table 3.1.

Table 3.1:
State-wise List of Districts Worst Affected by Maoist Activities

Chhattisgarh	Jharkhand	Orissa	Maharashtra
(a) Jagdalpur	(a) Palamau	(a) Malkangiri	(a) Gadchiroli
(b) Bastar	(b) Garhwa	(b) Koraput	(b) Bhandara
(c) Kankar	(c) Latchar	(c) Gajapati	(c) Chandrapur
(d) Dantewada	(d) Gumla	(d) Rayagada	(d) Gondia
(e) Rajnandagaon	(e) Koderma	(e) Nowrangpur	
(f) Surguja	(f) Chatra	(f) Mayurbhanj	
(g) Jashpur	(g) Hazaribagh		
(h) Khawarde			
Bihar	Madhya Pradesh	West Bengal	UP
(a) Jehanabad	(a) Balaghat	(a) Midnapore	(a) Sonebhadra
(b) Buxar	(b) Dindori	(b) Bankura	
(c) Bhojpur	(c) Mandela	(c) Purulia	
(d) Rohtas			
(e) Gaya			
(f) Banka			
(g) Aurangabad			
(h) Bhabhua			
(i) Patna			

Source: Ministry of Home Affairs, Districts covered under Security Related Expenditure
(SRE) with list of 'Focus districts' most seriously affected by LWE activities, August, 2011.

The LWE activities have notably come down in Andhra Pradesh which was once the citadel of the movement. The Telangana districts (Khammam, Warangal, Nizamabad, Karimnagar, Adilabad, Nalgonda, Medak, Mehaboob Nagar, Rayalaseema, Anantapur and Kurnool) and Coastal Andhra districts, namely East Godavari, Srikakulam, Visakapatnam, Vizianagaram and Guntur were infested by this movement, which suffered serious reverses due to the anti-Naxal operations by 'Greyhounds'.[8] However, the ongoing agitation for separate Telangana state and increasing influence of CPI(Maoists) in Andhra–Orissa Border (AOB) gave an impetus to the Maoists to revive the movement in the Telangana region, especially Khammam, Warangal and Karimnagar districts. Besides Telangana issue, [9] they also try to exploit the sentiments of the people on Polavaram dam issue. As part of this strategy, the Maoists from Dandakaranya and AOB took a strategic decision during mid-2010 to work in the direction of re-establishing control over north Telangana by actively involving in local issues.

On the other hand, over three-decades-long CPI(M) rule in West Bengal coupled with the mounting anti-CPI(M) feelings among the rural peasants and workers due to major deviations of the party from 1964 policy and programmes led to the resurgence of left-wing extremist ideology among sizeable section of people in the state. Nandigram–Singur–Lalgarh developments were open manifestation of this trend. Maoist leader Kishenji claimed in an interview that the mass Naxalite movement in Lalgarh in 2009 was aimed at creating a 'liberated zone' against 'oppression of the Left by the establishment and its police'. He stated that this had given the Naxalites a major base in West Bengal for the first time since the Naxalite uprising in the mid-1970s and that 'we will have an armed movement going in Calcutta by 2011'. The Maoists and their supporters demonstrated their cult of violence through the dastardly act of the derailment of Janeswari Express in Midnapore district during May 2010 leading to the death of 148 people.

The disillusion among sizeable chunk of Marxists coupled with the political opportunism by mainstream and regional parties in the state also worked to the advantage of LWE to broaden their support base. It is an irony that mainstream and regional parties very often enter into tacit understanding with extremists and insurgents for making narrow electoral success and later try to wriggle out of embarrassing situations arising out of such unholy nexus. This has happened in West Bengal on the eve of last Assembly polls in 2011. The single-point agenda of these parties was to unseat CPI(M)-led Left Front from power. A number of anti-CPI(M) bodies came up in the political scenario of the state, which were directly or indirectly backed by the supporters of these parties. For example, Police Santrash Birodhi Janasadharanar Committee (People's Committee Against Police Atrocities [PCAPA]) which spearheaded the Lalgarh movement[10] with a lot of bloodshed and violence had large number of supporters of Trinamool Congress (TMC). Chhatradhar Mahato, one of the key figures of the movement, had close linkages with TMC.

The strategy of Maoists in West Bengal is to fully exploit these political trends to the benefit of the movement. Already some strong signals have come up from west and east Midnapore, Purulia and Bankura district after the arrest of five Maoists, including the secretary of the Nandigram Zonal Committee in June 2010. Inputs indicate that Maoists are engaged in an ambitious task of building the party in South 24 Parganas, especially the Sundarbans. Another significant strategy was the move of Maoists to build a safe corridor from coastal West Bengal to Chhattisgarh through Gopiballavpur and Nayagram in west Midnapore, bordering east Midnapore and Orissa. Meanwhile, there was a spurt in LWE violence/activities in Birbhum, Nadia and Murshidabad districts, which forced the district administration to make a formal plea to bring these districts under the ambit of LWE-affected areas.

Just like West Bengal, Orissa is yet another state where Maoists could fully exploit the sentiments of tribals and other backward sections on the issue of allotment of land to multinationals for mining or industrial purposes. The strategy of Maoists is to make further inroads into these sections by declaring solidarity and support to various resistance movements against multinational corporations (MNCs) and other groups which plunder the rich natural resources in the name of development and industrialization. Such movements are now active against POSCO's ₹55,000 steel plant in Dhinkia (about 100 km from Paradeep port); Vedanta's bauxite mining project at Niyamgiri (Kalhandhi district) and TATA's steel plant in Kalinganagar district. PPSS[11] and

Bisthapan Birodhi Janamanch (against Kalinganagar project) are two major movements having considerable mass support, especially from tribals and indigenous population. Another equally important movement is the Chasi Mulia Adivasi Samiti that was in the forefront of various struggles to retain the physical control of the land and defeat the move to transfer it for big business/MNCs.

Despite a long history of insurgency and the presence of a mosaic of ethnic/tribal movements strongly espousing 'subnationalist' trends, LWE could not make much headway in the North East, except in Assam, Tripura and Manipur where they have certain pockets of influence.

In the case of Assam, the LWE movement was greatly influenced by parliamentary ambitions. The Indian People's Front (IPF)/People's Democratic Front (PDF) floated by CPI(Marxist–Leninist [ML]) Liberation played a pivotal role in this direction. In fact, the PDF initially launched in Karbi Anglong district in 1985 provided revolutionary democratic orientation to the tribal peoples' aspirations for autonomy and considerably contributed to the protection of their rights and privileges. The PDF made their maiden entry into the parliamentary arena by winning one seat in Assam Assembly in 1985 elections. The PDF subsequently transformed into the Autonomous State's Demands Committee (ASDC) in 1987 continued to demonstrate their mass support by winning four seats in Assam Assembly in 1990 elections and five in 1996, besides one seat each in Lok Sabha and Rajya Sabha. ASDC also captured majority in Karbi Anglong District Council and also unseated the Congress in the neighbouring North Cachar Hills district in 1996. The Front also played an active role during the Assam movement on foreigner's issue. However, with the changing political scenario in the tsate, ASDC is gradually eroding its political clout and Left-extremist proclivities.

Moreover, a section of tea-garden labourers and plywood workers of the state particularly in Upper Assam have their roots in Maoist-infested areas in West Bengal, Jharkhand and Orissa. Thus, their representative organizations like United Reservation Movement Council of Assam (URMCA) maintained militant postures on a number of issues. Similarly, Assam Jatiyatabadi Yuba Chatra Parishad (AJYCP), a militant indigenous outfit strongly espousing the cause of Assamese, maintained linkages with LWE outfits. The arrest of Kanchan, the CPI(Maoist) state secretary of

West Bengal in 2010, and Chila Roy, an operative of Kamtapur Liberation Organization (KLO), indicated the attempts of Maoists to establish linkages with sections of United Liberation Front of Assam (ULFA) and KLO, for which a central leader in charge of North East played a crucial role. The Adivasi National Liberation Army (ANLA) of Assam and Santhali Tiger Force active in the tea belts of western and northern Assam districts are other two tribal outfits which are trying to establish contacts with Maoists, especially of Jharkhand for training of cadres and so on. In this backdrop, the statement made by Assam chief minister, Tarun Gogoi, in April 2010 that the Maoists are trying to set up bases in Assam with the help of ULFA assumes considerable significance.

In Manipur linkages were established between the CPI(Maoist) and the Revolutionary People's Front (RPF) of Manipur as early as in 2008 and the meeting of their representatives emphasized better coordination at various levels. However, in April 2010 the CPI(Maoists) declared solidarity with the labourers from Bihar and Jharkhand in Manipur who were given ultimatum to leave the state by Manipuri rebels. Even a delegation led by a member of the Tirhut Sub-Zonal Committee of Maoists visited Manipur and later gave an ultimatum to Manipuri students studying in Bihar, Jharkhand, West Bengal and Uttar Pradesh to leave those states. In Tripura, the heartland of CPI(M) in the North East, the outfits like Amara Bengali which came into existence in late 1970s had extremist profile.

Such activities in the North East helped the Maoists to expand their Strategic United Front by establishing linkages with militant/ revolutionary outfits in the region. Their strategy is to actively involve in various ethnic and 'sub-nationalist' issues and thereby consolidate their bases there. The spread of LWE or their extension organizations in the area, now in the midst of ethnic conflicts and protracted insurgency movements, would further vitiate the overall law and order and security scenario of the region with increasing number of human/civil rights issues.

The geographical proximity of Madhya Pradesh with LWE-infested areas in Maharashtra, Chhattisgarh and Andhra Pradesh led to the gradual increase in LWE activity, especially in districts like Balaghat, Seoni, Dindori and Mandela. The busting of the arms factory in Bhopal and the arrest of senior members of the Central Technical Committee in 2007 revealed that the border areas of the state (with Maharashtra and Chhattisgarh in particular) have been extensively used by the armed dalams as hideouts and for operations targeting security forces. The R&D units which operated from the state were one of the main sources for the supply of arms to the ultras in the neighbouring states. CPI(Maoists) are working out a plan to create a strategic exit route from Chhattisgarh to Madhya Pradesh for the swift movement in case of an emergency, especially in Abuj Marh.[12] They have identified safe havens like the forest areas extending from the Bhandara–Gondia–Balaghat junction in east Vidarbha to Pench National Park in Nagpur and Seoni districts via the Nagzira wildlife sanctuary. In 2010, areas of Balaghat have witnessed a large spurt in Maoist activity. Similarly, Sonebhadra district and eastern areas of Uttar Pradesh, bordering Madhya Pradesh registered an increase in Naxal violence during 2010. The presence of coal mafia and other criminal syndicates in Seoni–Sonebhadra belt coupled with the ineffective law enforcement in the area enabled Naxals to make steady inroads into this region. Sone Ganga Vindhyachal Zonal Committee, consisting of Chandauli, Sonebhadra, Mirzapur in Uttar Pradesh and Buxar, Rohtas, Bhojpur and Bhabhua districts in Bihar, continues to be one of the highly Naxal-affected regions.

The rapid industrialization in Punjab–Haryana belt coupled with the influx of workers from different regions has led to certain attempts to spread LWE groups in that area. Kobad Ghandy, a CPI(Maoist) Polit Bureau member, who was arrested from Delhi, was playing a pivotal role in co-ordinating their activities. The Maoists have their pockets in some districts of Punjab such as Malwa, Majha, Doaba, Dhuri, Barnala, Jalandhar, Ferozepur, Mansa and Bathinda. In the case of Haryana, presence of incipient LWE groups has come across from Yamunanagar, Narwana, Uchana, Kaithal, Kurukshetra and Karnal districts. The activities in these states were not armed-cadre based, but through front organizations floated by workers and peasants.

Though the South Indian states of Kerala, Tamil Nadu and Karnataka witnessed left-wing extremist activities during late 1960s and early 1970s, the movement could not make much headway in these states. On the other hand, the movement suffered reverses mainly due to the liquidation and arrest of prominent leaders. In the case of Karnataka, the 'encounter killing' of Rajamouli, the state secretary and the member of CC and CMC, in June 2007 was a serious organizational setback as Mouli was the chief architect of party's 'covert set-up' not only in Karnataka but also in the other two states. Earlier, in 2005, the police and Anti-Naxalite Force (ANF) shot dead party ideologue Saketh Raju and his associate Shivalingu who played the key role in building up the party in the state. Similarly, the killing of Gowtham (state committee member) and four others by the police in July 2007 further weakened the party. The arrest of Chandrashekhar Gorebal, Karnataka-state committee secretary of CPI(Maoist) in June 2010 was a serious setback to their move to expand their bases in the Western Ghats of Karnataka.

The situation was not different in Kerala and Tamil Nadu where LWE leaders and cadres were brutally hunted by the police, especially during the dark days of National Emergency. However, regrouping moves are in the offing mainly at the instance of designated central leaders familiar with the terrain of these states. Earlier in 2009, the Maoists in Karnataka had planned to organize the activities in Wayanad and Kannur districts in Kerala, Dashin Kannada, Dupe and Kodak districts of Karnataka and areas such as Gudalur in Tamil Nadu under a special zonal committee. Accordingly, secret meetings were organized in Kerala–Tamil Nadu and Kerala–Karnataka borders. Raja Mouli, before his killing, had frequent interaction with party leaders in these states. After his killing, Malla Raji Reddy alias Satenna (CC member who was in underground since long) took over the task of expansion and consolidation of the party in Kerala. However, Reddy and his associate Suguna were arrested by a special team of Andhra police from Angamali (Ernakulam district) of Kerala in December 2007. CPI(Maoists) attempted to establish a state committee in Kerala, but later dismantled this and brought Kerala under direct control of the CC. The arrest of Polit Bureau member Kobad Ghandy, who was co-coordinating party activities in southern states, also adversely affected the organization. Later, the Maoist spokesperson Azad was involved in organizing Maoist activity in the South Indian states. But the killing of Azad in July 2010 and the arrest of other leaders of the states had further adverse impact over the outfit.

However, the interstate tri junction of Kerala, Karnataka and Tamil Nadu, a focal point of Western and Eastern Ghats unique for dense forests was again in the Maoist radar during

February–March 2013, when movement of armed Maoists were reported from this belt. Despite a month-long joint commando operation (Thunderbolt) by Special Police Battalion and forest officials, no Maoist could be apprehended or their hideout busted. What the commandos/police could lay hand on were a bunch of printed pamphlets issued by one *jogi* on behalf of the Western Ghat Special Zonal Committee of Maoists denigrating 'imperialism' and their organized efforts to make inroads into the rich natural resources, the basic livelihood of the tribals and the underprivileged. Though the commando/police operation failed apparently due to lack of specific intelligence, the stark reality is that the Maoists have their long-term strategy of extending their Red Corridor to this tri junction for which South-west RB and the special zonal committees would mainly bank upon the support of sizeable section of Adivasi/tribal population in this area.

As part of operational strategy, the LWE groups have now attached considerable importance in strengthening parties in the urban centres with the dual objective of extending the people's protracted struggles to urban areas as prelude to the final stage of armed revolution and to establish safe hideouts for party cadres during stepped up anti-LWE operations by security forces. This strategy has been reiterated during the highly secretive CC meeting of the Maoists held in Orissa–Maharashtra border during February 2011, after a series of setback faced by the organization due to the arrest/encounter killing of senior leaders including Polit Bureau members like Azad, Krishenji and Kobad Ghandy. Their emphasis now is to strengthen their clandestine apparatus while continuing 'protracted guerrilla warfare' with more mass support. The Maoists have formulated their urban strategy based on their party document captioned 'Urban Perspective'. They strongly bank upon Mao's principles on revolution which underlines that

> Communist Party must not be impetuous and adventurist in the propaganda and organizational work. It should have well selected cadres working underground, must accumulate time and bide its time there. In leading the people in the struggle against the enemy, the party must adopt the tactics of advancing step by step, slowly and surely keeping to the principle of waging struggle on just grounds, to our advantage and with restraint and making use of such open types of activities or are permitted by law, decree and

social customs; empty clamor and reckless activity can never lead to success. (Mao on People's revolution)[13]

Based on such principles, the Maoists had assessed the scenario in India where urban centres, especially major cities and towns are the strongholds of reaction; enemy is most powerful with the solid support of police, army, state- apparatus and other counter-revolutionary forces which can very easily suppress people's forces and struggles. In such a scenario, the Maoists are not in favour of any short-term approach or direct confrontation with the enemy to produce 'quick results', but prefer long-term strategy, clearly a defensive one for protecting, preserving, consolidating and expanding party organization while mobilizing and preparing the broad urban masses for revolutionary struggles. They have identified three main tasks in this regard, namely (a) mobilize and organize the broad masses through mass organizations and movements and build the party; (b) build a united front mainly focusing on issues such as globalization, Hindu fascism and repression; and (c) military tasks which include sending of cadres to the country side, infiltration in enemy ranks, organizing the party in key industries, sabotaging actions in coordination with rural armed struggle, logistical support and so on. While PGLA and PLA perform the main military tasks, the urban movement may perform tasks complimenting the rural armed struggle.

In the recent past, some specific leads on the urban networking of Maoists have come across. A Maoist arms factory operating in the heart of Bhopal in MP with senior leaders of Central Technical Committee was unearthed in January 2007. This R&D unit of Maoists, engaged in manufacturing sophisticated weapons, functioned as a major logistical centre, supplying arms and accessories to CPI(Maoists) in various neighbouring states.

The Maoist document 'Urban Perspective',[14] which is considered to be the manual for urban work, describes the major urban corridors of India where Maoist activities are planned. Among them, the Ahmedabad–Pune corridor and the Delhi region has been two principal areas where the Maoists could expand its network considerably in the past few years. The arrest of Surya Devra Prabhakar in March 2010 disclosed the blue prints of the activities along Ahmedabad–Mumbai stretch with Surat, incidentally an industrial hub, as its headquarters. Around 11 important leaders of the urban network of Maoist organizations were arrested in the Surat police range in July 2010, including Kura Devender, a senior leader of CPI(ML) Janashakti; Sujata Swami, the wife of Mumbai area committee secretary of CPI(Maoist); Shakeel Pasha, secretary of Surat area committee and many others. A couple, in charge of Maoist activities in Delhi, Gopal Mishra and his wife were arrested in May 2010. They were responsible for recruitment of youngsters for the party cadre and leadership, in addition to running a trade union 'Mehnathkush Mazdoor Morcha' and expanding activities among workers in Noida and East Delhi. During the arrest of Sudip Chongdar, Bengal state secretary of CPI(Maoist) in December 2010, documents on the urban work of Maoists in Kolkata were seized, which included details of more than 200 workers of its city network.

Along with the expansion in urban areas, the Maoists in 2010 were successful in strengthening their Strategic United Front, which is a loose association of tactical and opportunistic partnerships aimed at achieving certain intermediary objectives. Unlike in the past when LWE had symbiotic clandestine relationships with political parties, the main feature of their current Strategic Front was the open linkages with parties or groups which outwardly oppose LWE in order to expand their support base exploiting the public sentiments. The best example was their relations with Trinamul Congress of West Bengal. The PCAPA[15] dominated by Maoist supporters had no reservations to collaborate with Tinamul workers on Nandigram and related agitations. The arrested Maoist leaders of West Bengal including Telugu Deepak, Madhusudan Mandal, Kanchan and many others confessed about their ties with Trinamul Congress as early as during Nandigram unrest. The Maoist leader Kishenji has openly supported TMC and has extended tactical support to her party in the West Bengal Assembly elections in May 2011 in which TMC has made sterling victory, ending over three and half decades of CPI(M) rule in the state. Though Maoists did not identify with any political party in Jharkhand, they had selectively supported candidates close to them during 2010 Jharkhand elections. Other important political group which maintains linkages with the Maoists is the Telangana Rashtra Samithi (TRS), now spearheading a movement for separate state of Telangana. This is also part of their regrouping strategy exploiting Telugu regional sentiments. On numerous occasions, Maoist front organizations, including the Revolutionary Democratic Front, allied with various other organizations over a wide range of issues like Kashmir problem, anti-Naxal operations, *Salwa Judum*, death of Maoist leader Azad, ban on Muslim radical outfits like Students Islamic Movement of India (SIMI), Sri Lankan operations against Liberation Tigers of Tamil Eelam (LTTE), Babri Masjid and so on. The organizations like PUCL, PUDR, Popular Front of India (PFI)[16] and radical members of Hurriyat Conference were seen associating with the Maoist United Front.

Certain demographic, socio-economic and developmental factors had contributed to the spread and consolidation of LWE movement in India. The 'Red Corridor'—mainly constituting parts of West Bengal, Bihar, Jharkhand, Uttar Pradesh, Orissa, Mahapatra, Madhya Pradesh, Chhattisgarh, Andhra Pradesh, and Karnataka, is considered to be the bastion of LWE and has some unique features. Thirty-three districts spanning eight states of India are identified as the worst affected by LWE or Maoist violence. The largest chunk belongs to Jharkhand (10), followed by Chhattisgarh (7), Bihar (6), Orissa (5), Maharashtra (2), Madhya Pradesh (1), Andhra Pradesh (1) and Uttar Pradesh (1). West Bengal has experienced an upsurge in LWE in recent years particularly in its western and southern districts of Purulia and Midnapore, bordering Jharkhand and Orissa.

These states/areas, especially of Eastern and Central India, are most backward and suffer from greater levels of poverty, illiteracy, lack of development and exploitation. For example, except Maharashtra, the per capita Gross Domestic Product (GDP) for these states for the financial year 2010 remained less than the all-India average (1100). Though the GDP for Maharashtra (1563) was higher than the all-India figure, the reality is that the LWE-affected districts like Gadchiroli, Gondia and Chandrapur are reeling under acute poverty and economic backwardness, coupled with the active presence of coal and mining mafia. The GDP/per capita index of other 'Red Corridor' states like Bihar (340), Uttar Pradesh (488), Madhya Pradesh (575), Jharkhand (649), Orissa (702), Chhattisgarh (804), West Bengal (876) and Karnataka (1070) are economically comparable to poor African and Asian countries like Ethiopia, Tanzania, Democratic Republic of Congo, Zambia, Mozambique, Bangladesh and Vietnam.

An interesting statistical observation is yielded by the comparative rates of growth in per capita incomes of the nine LWE states (Karnataka excluded). Except for West Bengal, Jharkhand, Madhya Pradesh and Uttar Pradesh, per capita incomes in the other states have been growing at rates faster than that of national per capita income. Per capita incomes in Chhattisgarh, Bihar and Orissa grew at averages of 17.5 per cent, 13.2 per cent and 13.3 per cent, respectively, during 2003–2004 to 2007–2008, a period when national per capita income grew by 12.4 per cent. Such faster growth in incomes should have dented poverty and challenged LWE in these states, which it clearly did not. This is probably because the beneficiaries from the higher growth incomes have only been a limited few. This is a major anachronism in our economy and development where wealth accumulates in particular areas or a microscopic section of the society and does not trickle down to the most backward and needy sections.

Such a skewed pattern in percolation of incomes has further accentuated the income divide within the states. Wide gaps surface not only between regions and states, but also within states and districts. These gaps accentuate the existing inequalities and widen the chasm between endowments and abilities to access across populations and societies. The more unfortunate part is the phenomenon of lower-income groups witnessing prosperity in close proximity and yet being unable to be a part of such prosperousness. The residents of Hazaribagh district in Jharkhand, for example, or Sambalpur in Orissa, are not oblivious of the higher living standards in Ranchi and Jamshedpur (Jharkhand) or Bhubaneshwar and Cuttack (Orissa), respectively. Nor is the average tiller from Purulia of West Bengal ignorant about the better life lived by his counterparts in Burdwan, barely a couple of hundred miles away! Existence of such trends and 'general psyche' will hardly abate LWE, but will only sharpen class conflicts between the haves and have-nots giving further fillip to LWE/similar movements.

The literacy rate of these states also remained low as compared to all-India average and percentage in other states. Barring Maharashtra and West Bengal, all the states have adult literacy rates lower than the national average. Bihar (63.82 per cent) has the lowest literacy rate among the 35 states and Union Territories (UTs) of India. The other LWE-affected states, namely Jharkhand (67.63 per cent), Andhra Pradesh (67.66 per cent), Uttar Pradesh (69.72 per cent), Madhya Pradesh (70.63 per cent), Chhattisgarh (71.04 per cent), Orissa (75.35 per cent), Karnataka (75.6 per cent) and West Bengal (77.08 per cent) figured 32, 31, 29, 28, 27, 26, 25 and 20 positions, respectively, out of 35 states/UTs in adult literacy rate. Madhya Pradesh's Alirajpur district has the lowest literacy rate of 37.22 per cent as also the LWE-affected Chhattisgarh's Bijapur district where the literacy rate is 41.58 per cent. The female literacy rate of these states was comparatively low. The low literacy rate of LWE-affected states/districts throws light to certain crucial factors closely intertwined with the general governance of these state. The rampant commercialization of educational sector and pathetic condition of schools, developmental aberrations and the all-pervasive bureaucracy mercilessly ignoring the genuine issues of illiterate/semi-literate people, particularly the tribals and other marginalized sections and so on are some of the facets of these states/areas. All these factors substantially contributed to the growth and consolidation of LWE movement.

Another noticeable feature of these areas is the vast tribal/backward population and abundance of India's natural resources. There are about 160 districts that fall under the so-called 'Red Corridor' that cover almost 1/5 of total forest area in the country. Tribals, Dalits and backward sections constitute the major chunk of the population. The tribals in India are around 8 per cent of the total population. Over 83 per cent of the tribal population is concentrated in the states of Madhya Pradesh, Orissa, Rajasthan, Gujarat, Maharashtra, Chhattisgarh, Jharkhand, West Bengal, Andhra Pradesh and Karnataka. Except Rajasthan and Gujarat, areas of other tribals-dominated states fall under the Red Corridor. Significantly, the LWE has its main strongholds in the tribal belt of these states. Around 550 odd tribes, having different culture, dialects, customs and traditions, constitute the tribal population. The major tribes of the LWE belt include Ho, Oraon, Kol, Santhal, Gond, Munda, Kuria, Koya, Konda, Chenchus and Lambadas.

As rightly pointed by Arundhati Roy,[17] these tribal people of central India have a big history of resistance that predates Mao Zedong by centuries. They rebelled many times against the British, against the zamindars and the moneylenders and forest encroachers. The rebellions were cruelly crushed, many thousands were killed, but the people were never conquered. Even after independence, they retained this legacy of rebellion which, in many respects, could be easily exploited by the left-wing extremists through their catchy slogans, commitment and dedication to the cause. Thus, the tribal people were at the heart of the first Naxalite uprising in Naxalbari village of West Bengal. Since then, the LWE operations and activities are inextricably intertwined with tribal uprisings/support. Unfortunately, the efforts by the state to wean away the tribals from the influence of LWE groups and to assimilate them in national mainstream could not meet with any major success due to a confluence of factors.

First and foremost were certain provisions in Indian Constitution. The Constitution ratified colonial policy and made the state custodian of tribal homelands. Overnight, it turned the entire tribal population into squatters on their own land. It denied them their traditional rights to forest produce; it criminalized a whole way of life. Though the Scheduled Tribes and Traditional Forest Dwellers (Recognition of Forest Rights) Act, 2006, has been enacted after a lot of debates and controversies, the implementation of the Act, especially in LWE-affected states is tardy. There are many ground-level difficulties for the effective implementation. The main issue is the conscious move of Forest Department to dominate the Forests Rights Committee (FRC) by nominating the members of Joint Forest Management (JFM) body to FRCs in contravention of the provisions of the Act. The heart of the matter is that the Forest Department, for which the Reserve Forest is a milch cow, continues to maintain their stranglehold by sidelining Gram Sabhas, FRCs and so on, on the issue of implementing this Act. The counter-Naxalite operations, especially 'Operation Green Hunt' in Orissa have also come in the way of the implementation of the Act, as demarcation of landholdings of Gram Sabhas, processing of applications of claims and so on could not be undertaken due to Naxalite threat. In many tribal areas of Madhya Pradesh, Chhattisgarh, Orissa and so on clashes occurred between Forest Department officials and tribals on the issue of distribution of pattas (title deeds) and on ensuring 'community rights' on forest resources. Taking cue from the past experiences of Integrated Tribal Development Projects (ITDP) and so on, much could not be expected from legislations like Forest Rights Act, especially in view of approach of bureaucracy and highly politicized local self-governing institutions like Panchayats and Gram Sabhas.

On the other hand, the continued threat of 'displacement of tribals' from their traditional homeland for dams, irrigation projects and mines in the name of development has intensified resistance movements by tribals, which to a great extent have been exploited by Naxals. Of the tens of millions of displaced people, more than 45 per cent are tribal people and the states of Chhattisgarh, Jharkhand, Orissa, Andhra Pradesh and West Bengal accounted for the largest number of displaced tribals by virtue of the fact that the tribal/rural belt of these states have more than 85 per cent of hydroelectric projects in the country.

It is an anachronism that the most recent expression of threat to tribals emanates from the abundance of natural resources in their traditional abodes. For example, the tribal/rural belt of Orissa provides 60 per cent of total bauxite produced in the country; 25 per cent of coal; 28 per cent of iron ore; 28 per cent of manganese and 93 per cent of nickel. The case of Jharkhand is more impressive. The state supplies 30 per cent of total coal, copper and iron core produced in the country; 60 per cent of graphite and 93 per cent of pyrite. Similarly, Andhra Pradesh, Maharashtra (particularly the coal belt of Chandrapur), West Bengal, Madhya Pradesh and Karnataka have rich natural resources like coal, graphite, copper, manganese and so on which ironically are located in tribal-dominated areas or its precincts. The globalization and liberalization coupled with free-trade agreements have opened these areas/resources for MNCs and big Indian corporates. These MNCs/corporates, in collusion with the corrupt political leadership in various states, are engaged in exploiting these natural resources purely on corporate capital lines without paying any heed to the basic issues of tribals or indigenous population. Over the past five years or so, the governments of Chhattisgarh, Jharkhand, Orissa and West Bengal have signed hundreds of memorandums of understanding (MOUs) with corporate houses worth several billion dollars, majority of them a secret, for steel plants, sponge iron factories, power plants, aluminium refineries, dams and mines. The tribal people must be moved in order to translate the MOUs into real money. Thus, new battle fronts were opened at places like Nandigram, Singur, Lalgarh (West Bengal), Dhinkia, Niyangiri

(Orissa), Baniladile, Lohandiguda (Chhattisgarh) and so on where tribals and indigenous people with the support of Maoists and pro-Maoist organizations built up strong resistance movements which gave an impetus for Maoists to seriously pursue their tactics of United Strategic Front for broadening their mass/support base. The politicization of the issue also worked to the advantage of Maoists, especially in states like West Bengal where they could get mileage from Nandigram–Lalgarh movements effectively carried out by TMC with their main aim to politically embarrass the CPI(M)-led Left Front government.

In fact, the tribal population in the country, especially in Maoist strongholds faces serious challenges which even question their very identity and existence. On governmental level, there is much rhetoric on the need of bringing them to 'national mainstream' from their present 'cultural museums' through developmental and welfare programmes. For that purpose, the central and state governments are keen to allocate substantial funds. The Planning Commission has formulated an Integrated Action Plan (IAP) of ₹13,000 crores for the speedy development of 60 LWE-affected districts in the country. In the selection of these districts, more emphasis has been given to economic backwardness, presence of tribal population and forest coverage, besides continued Maoist activities. The main focus is the development of social infrastructure such as primary education, basic health, sanitation, drinking water and road connectivity, for which funding will be made through local, Panchayat, block and district levels. The scheme envisages that in the first two years, the state governments should work to strengthen the systems to enable them to meet certain conditionalities. The plan document underlines that these conditionalities are not merely the strict implementation of the Panchayats (Extension to Scheduled Areas) Act (PESA), the Forests Rights Act (FRA) or the Centre's flagship schemes such as Mahatma Gandhi National Rural Employment Guarantee Programme (MNREGP), but include other tasks like consolidation of Panchayati Raj institutions, strict ban of liquor contractors from other states, streamlining of administration and so on.

The Planning Commission proposes to involve civil-society representatives in the monitoring mechanism of the schemes to plug loophole during implementation. Conceptually, the scheme really is laudable, but we should not forget the reality that more ambitious projects/schemes for the development of tribals and Adivasis undertaken by the state governments in the past did not bring any noticeable development among the target groups, as bulk of the allocated funds were siphoned off by contractors, government officials and grassroots level political intermediaries. In fact, such large-scale malpractices and malgovernance, especially in tribal/rural blocks of Andhra Pradesh, Chhattisgarh, Jharkhand and Orissa gave a fillip to Maoists to orchestrate their propaganda against administration and state apparatus. On the contrary, the schemes/programmes launched by Maoists such as community farming, digging of ponds/irrigation canals, nurseries/primary schools, village roads and so on, with the participation of tribals/locals, helped to strengthen their support base. Moreover, the actions of Maoists such as 'public trial' of corrupt officials and 'dispensation of ready justice' have further popularized the Maoists in tribal pockets. In the present context, Maoists are bent upon defeating the government's developmental programmes in their areas of influence, particularly tribal belts. In fact, the horrific annihilation of an entire company of the Central Reserve Police by Maoists in Chhattisgarh during April 2011 was the fall out of 'clear, hold and build' doctrine of the Union Government.[18] The above strategy was that the central forces deployed in the area would displace the Maoists and thus pave the way for civilian development programme. Such counter-insurgency strategies have not only ended up in jeopardizing the lives of police/central paramilitary personnel, but also led to horrendous atrocities against the tribals/local population, accentuating their further alienation from the main stream.

Just like tribals, the dalits in certain states are greatly influenced by LWE movement due to a plethora of socio-economic and political factors, especially their naked exploitation by the rich landlords and other influential sections. The SCs/Dalits constitute about 17.5 per cent of the total population in the country. The major Dalit concentrations are in 17 states, namely the Punjab (28.95 per cent); Himachal Pradesh (24 per cent), West Bengal (23 per cent), Uttar Pradesh (21.2 per cent), Haryana (19.4 per cent), Tamil Nadu (19 per cent); Uttarakhand (17.9 per cent), Tripura (17.4 per cent), Rajasthan (17.2 per cent), Orissa (16.5 per cent), Karnataka (16.2 per cent), Andhra Pradesh (16.2 per cent), Bihar (15.7 per cent), Madhya Pradesh (15.2 per cent), Jharkhand (11.8 per cent),

Chhattisgarh (11.5), Maharashtra (10.2 per cent) and Kerala (9.8 per cent). Except Bihar and Jharkhand, the left-wing extremists could not make any decisive influence among Dalits in other states.

The reasons were obvious. In other states with substantial Dalit population, the process of politicization cum resurgence of Dalits started many decades back leading to social transformation/social engineering which, to a great extent, could counter the exploitation of these sections. The North Indian states, especially in Uttar Pradesh, the implementation of Mandal recommendations led to the growth of a new elite and middle class from among the intermediate castes including Dalits. As rightly pointed out by Kancha Illaiah, 'The post-Mandal period, on the one hand, conscientized the OBCs, on the other, it began to homogenize SC, ST and OBCs, at least politically if not socially, and led to the bahujanisation of this social base.'[19] Moreover, the Bahujan Samaj Party (BSP) in Uttar Pradesh has really made a big impact among the Dalits in the state. The BSP emerged at a time of ferment among untouchable groups in North India. It has kindled the desire for emancipation among Dalits. Green revolution, changes in labour relations, increase in non-agricultural occupations and thus a relative decrease in economic dependency on the landowners, politicization of groups of untouchables and increased class struggle from above created a new situation. The BSP succeeded in expressing and enhancing this movement among low-caste people, mainly because of its anti–upper-caste agenda. The Dalit agenda of BSP coupled with Mandalization also influenced the Dalits in other states like Madhya Pradesh, Orissa, Rajasthan, Haryana and Uttarakhand. Such social and political resurgence among Dalits considerably checkmated the growth of Left and left-wing extremist forces in these states. In states like Rajasthan the SCs/Dalits were traditionally better placed in social and economic status and Left ideology could not make any impart among them. Moreover, the Marxist approach towards the resolution of the Dalit question, the tactics of entering into opportunistic electoral alliances even with the forces engaged in war of attrition with the Dalits and so on are totally contradictory to that of revolutionary communists. Though, CPI(Maoists) has decisive strength in states like Chhattisgarh, Jharkhand, Orissa and so on, they draw their main strength from tribals/Adivasis. Moreover, a clear demographic division exists in these states between tribals and Dalits with the latter getting well organized under the banner of mainstream political parties and well placed in socio-economic ladder as compared to the former.

In West Bengal and Kerala, the implementation of a number of progressive legislations in the areas of land reforms, tenancy rights, and education and so on by the Left party–led governments, especially of CPI(M), improved the socio-economic status of Dalits and other underprivileged sections. The formation of Dalit organizations on political lines and the emergence of a number of Dalit leaders at hierarchical level of mainstream parties substantially contributed to the Dalit resurgence which to a great extent could checkmate the moves of left-wing extremists to make inroads into these sections. In three other southern states, namely Karnataka, Andhra Pradesh and Tamil Nadu, similar political and social factors influenced the Dalit movement, detrimental to the growth of Left forces, especially left-wing extremism. The Dalit movement in Karnataka, symbolized by the Dalit Sangharsh Samiti (DSS) was known for its militancy as manifest by its agitational programmes and non-participation in parliamentary politics. As Leftists are very weak in the state, they could not influence DSS or other bodies which maintained their independent identity. Similarly, in Andhra Pradesh, except Mala–Madiga differences on the issue of reservation, the Dalits remained united with clear political perception. The presence of strong Dalit NGOs and organizations also played a key role in improving the socio-economic conditions of Dalits. On the other hand, in Tamil Nadu, Dravidian movement has played a progressive role in Dalit assertion. It could strike an effective alliance between backward communities and SCs under the umbrella of Dravidian politics. It secured a political space for the downtrodden masses in the state structure. It effectively challenged Brahmanism as an ideology. Its progressive role resulted in education and upward mobility of the downtrodden. The formation of Dalit parties like Puthia Thamizhagam (New Tamil Nadu) by Dr Krishna Swamy and other Dalit movements played a crucial role in Dalit-resurgence in the state, much to the disadvantage of Leftist forces.

The case of Bihar was entirely different. Though LWE movement started in the state in early 1970s on the strong ideological pillars of Maoism and protracted armed struggles, its spread and consolidation in 1980s and 1990s, especially in Central Bihar was more on the lines of a reactionary movement or philosophy predominantly influenced by caste tension and conflicts. The process of consolidation was more in areas where challenges by antagonistic classes were most pronounced. There were repeated conflicts/confrontations between the upper-caste landlords and Dalits since 1970s on a number of issues such as payment of minimum wages, abolition of *begari* system, implementation of the Land Ceiling Act, redistribution of the land held beyond ceiling limits and equal control over the village commons and the water bodies, such as *ahars* and *pynes* for agricultural purposes in favour of marginal farmers and *bataidars*. Such conflicts/killings occurred in Pipra and Parasbigha Nonhi and Nagwan, Belchi and Arwa that embroiled the entire south central and west central Bihar in 1970s and 1980s and culminated in Bathe in 1997 and later in Senari. By 1980s, the animosities and conflicts took serious nature and a deep polarization in caste and community consciousness occurred. On the one hand, the entire phalanx of the Dalits were deemed Naxalites; on the other, the upper castes progressively banded together, closing ranks, not only among the richer landowners, but along caste lines that embraced every rung of the social ladder down to the poorest of their caste men.

This led to the formation of 'caste *senas*' (private armies) by almost all major castes in the state to counter the Naxalites. Thus, the powerful castes such as Bhumihars, Kurmis, Yadavas, Rajputs, Pathans and Brahmins formed their own *senas* which ironically were backed by powerful political leaders belonging to these castes cutting across party lines. Besides, local landlord groups had, of course, used indirect state symbolism from the very beginning, exploiting the local power structure, such as the police constable, the chowkidar and the *dafadar*, to create an impression of lawfulness and indirect state support to their cause. To add to this was a highly controversial decision in 1986, during Bindeshwari Dubey's tenure as chief minister, to arm the landlords against the Naxalites. Thousands of licenses were issued to those who wanted them and could afford to buy them. The enormous and growing arsenal of licensed and illegal arms eventually came to be loaned out to the *senas* in their fight against the Naxalites.

Thus, the private armies of upper-caste landlords which operated with the patronage of the state apparatus on the lines similar to the *Salwa Judum* of Chhattisgarh government resorted to large-scale atrocities against Dalits in the name of countering LWE. The Dalits rallied and formed guerrilla squads under the CPI(ML) Party Unity and the CPI(ML) Liberation (mainly in Central Bihar) and the MCC in the south Bihar districts of Aurangabad, Palamau and Hazaribagh strongly retaliated with killings and violence creating a reign of terror in the larger areas of the state. The police became the targets of Naxalite attack in many places in view of their nexus with landowners and their patronage to caste *senas*. Inevitably, the police posts became objects of Naxalite retaliation, reinforced the unity of purpose and the character of confrontation, both among the *sena* and the police. The police force was detailed, on request, under officers of the same caste and class as the landowners and progressively became tools of systematic repression, contributing in no small measure to the spread of Naxalism in the area. The viciousness of the conflict was highlighted by the MCC-sponsored Baghaura–Dalelchak massacre[20] of 54 Rajputs in the Madanpur region of Aurangabad. This massacre was in retaliation to a series of smaller massacres of Dalits by the Rajputs. In the meanwhile, the Party Unity and Liberation squads were encountering many other heavily armed and politically connected caste army formations. While the attacks by the Party Unity and Liberation groups instilled terror among the landowners and their caste allies, the killing of Dalits only fed the desperation of these castes, increasing the influence of Naxalites. By the 1990s, most of the *senas* had been buried under the Naxal assault.

Truly speaking, these conflicts were moulded by caste factors and not by a class ideology. Moreover, the major gains were accrued to various political parties and not to the actual groups engaged in the conflict. However, certain unhealthy trends such as Naxalites offering protection to individual landowners in some regions in lieu of huge payments crept into the movement, leading to internecine conflicts mainly between the Liberation and Party Unity. Greatly influenced by such discernible trends, the Liberation group made to strike a balance between its underground activities and overground constitutional politics, including participation in elections. On the other hand, MCC, which all along opposed to all constitutional processes and was wedded to the idea of armed struggles, joined hands with PWG and formed CPI(Maoists) who have now become the leading LWE movement in Bihar and Jharkhand. The Maoists in Bihar continue to draw their main strength from Dalits, besides backward sections like Kurmis and Yadavas.

A case study of Chhattisgarh, now worst affected by LWE would demonstrate as how the Maoists built up their movement by exploiting the issues of tribals. The state was formed on 1 November 2000 by carving out backward/underdeveloped areas of Madhya Pradesh with the declared aim of accelerating the pace of development of backward areas. Around 44 per cent of the total land area of the state is forest which is 12 per cent of the total forest cover in the country. Out of 18 districts, 8 districts in northern and southern regions have sizeable forest cover. Around one-third of the total population are tribals who are mainly confined to Durg, Raipur, Rajnandgaon, Bilaspur, Surguja, Raigarh and Bastar. The prominent tribes are Gonds, Kanars, Muria, Kawars, Bhuriya, Baiga and Halbas. The forests are the mainstay of more than 80 per cent of the people who are engaged in agriculture. The state is rich in mineral resources which include coal, iron ore, bauxite, lime stone, dolomite and precious stones like diamond. Chhattisgarh is the only state which produces tin in the country. Though Bhilai Steel Plant was established many decades ago, industrialization is at a very low pace in the state.

One main issue which agitates the people, especially the tribals, from before the formation of the state is the steady depletion of the forest. This was largely due to encroachment, illegal felling of trees, mining activities, launching of industrial and other big projects. The depletion of forest areas has adversely affected the livelihood of tribals as they heavily depend on forest produce or forest-based jobs like plucking of tendu leaf, collection of mahua flowers and so on. The state produces around 20 per cent of the total tendu leaves produced in the country. Added to this is the steady exodus of non-tribals to tribal-dominated areas which has resulted in subtle changes in the demographic profile of the areas jeopardizing the social, economic and cultural interests of the tribals? The best example is Bastar area.

Planned development, especially the social infrastructure of the state, particularly the tribal blocks had been neglected for decades when the state was part of the undivided Madhya Pradesh. Ironically, the successive governments of Madhya Pradesh, greatly influenced by the powerful upper caste and business lobby, treated the tribals and backward sections as mere vote bank and exploited them from time immemorial. Such policies of the democratic establishments sow the seeds of LWE, which spread like a wild fire and engulfed larger areas of the state (now comprising Chhattisgarh), especially during the last one decade. It was in early 1980s that the PWG of Andhra Pradesh initially established their foothold in the area as part of their strategy to build an ideal base for their underground 'guerrilla army'. Initial bases were established in Bastar and Gadchiroli areas (bordering Chhattisgarh and Maharashtra). The PWG cadres organized tribal people demanding a hike in the price they were being paid for Tendu leaves (which are used to make *beedis*). At that time, traders paid 3 paisa for a bundle of about 50 leaves. The strike organized by them was successful and the price was doubled to 6 paisa a bundle. After a series of agitations and strikes during the last three decades, the tribals now get a price of one rupee per bundle of Tendu leaves. But the real success for the Party was to have been able to demonstrate the value of unity and a new way of conducting a political negotiation. But the irony is that strong collusion exists between contractors and political leaders/middlemen in Tendu-leaf tenders and they earn lakhs every season out of this business.

The Party's next big struggle was against the Ballarpur paper mills. The government had given the Thapars a 45-year contract to extract 1.5 lakh tonnes of bamboo at a hugely subsidized rate. The tribals were paid 10 paisa for a bundle which contained 20 culms of bamboo. A long agitation, a strike, followed by negotiations with officials of the paper mill in the presence of the people tripled the price to 30 paisa per bundle. For the tribal people these were huge achievements. Other political parties had made promises, but showed no signs of keeping them. People began to approach the PWG asking whether they could join in. Meanwhile, the excesses and atrocities in the form of arrest and humiliation of tribals, sexual exploitation of their women, destruction of their crops, forceful eviction from land and so on committed by Forest Department officials could be effectively exploited by PWG, which mobilized the tribals and built up a strong movement against Forest Department. The PWG support emboldened the tribals to take over forest land and cultivate it. This led to constant conflict between tribals and Forest Department officials. Such conflicts reached a flashpoint when attempts were made in 1986 to evict 60 villages of Bijapur for the establishment of a National Park there. The organized tribal revolt under the patronage of PWG ultimately forced the Forest Department to shelve the eviction drive which was perhaps the most decisive factor that led to the further growth and consolidation of PWG to more and more areas. Thus, between 1986 and 2000, the PWG redistributed 300,000 acres of forest land. With PWG making steady inroads into more and more sections of the people and virtually controlling the administration in vast areas, the police and paramilitary forces stepped in opening another saga of 'fake encounters', killings and bloodshed.

The merger of PWG with MCC in 2004 gave further impetus for the outfit to strengthen their organizational set up in Chhattisgarh. The united body has spread its influence across a 60,000 sq. km stretch of forest, thousands of villages and millions of people. An elaborate structure of Janatana Sarkars (People's governments) administers these areas. Each Jantana Sarkar is elected by a cluster of villages whose combined population can range from 500 to 5,000. It has nine departments: Krishi (Agriculture), Vyapar-Udyog (Trade and Industry), Arthik (Economic), Nyay (Justice), Raksha (Defence), Hospital (Health), Jan Sampark (Public Relations), School–Riti Rivaj (Education and Culture), and Jungle. A group of Jantana Sarkars come under an Area committee. Three area committees make up a division. There are ten divisions in Dandakaranya region. Side by side, the Maoists fortified their guerrilla set-up by creating a core operational zone (Dandakaranya Special Zone) centred on the dense forest of Abujhmad in the Bastar division. A special armed force of around 5,000 was also built up, equipped with assault rifles, mortar and a range of Improvised Explosive Devices (IEDs). They are supplemented by people's militia of around 20,000, equipped with all types of indigenous weapons. The growth and consolidation of Maoists coupled with the formation of guerrilla set-up had led to steady increase in Maoist violence since 2004. For example, the state which recorded 55 incidents of Maoist violence in 2002, compared to 117 in Bihar and 157 in Jharkhand, showed a steep increase of 352 incidents in 2004; 385 in 2005; 715 in 2006; 583 in 2007; 620 in 2008; 529 in 2009 and 625 in 2010. The causalities in human lives and damages to governmental/public properties were equally horrendous. For example, during the period 2005–2009, a total of 1,350 persons (458 civilians; 473 SF Personnel and 419 Maoists) were killed in Maoist-related violence. Besides causing serious set-back to the state economy through constant attack of the economic establishments, their massive extortion mainly from iron and coal mining companies, infrastructure project contractors, government officials and Tendu-leaf businessmen and so on, they were to the tune of over ₹2,000 crores annually.

Another equally important task of Maoists was the creation of revolutionary consciousness among the tribals, notably women. The party, in1986, set up the Adivasi Mahila Sanghathana (AMS) which was later transformed into the Krantikari Adivasi Mahila Sangathan (KAMS) and has now over 90,000 enrolled members. It could well be the largest women's organization in the country. Besides building up revolutionary fervour among women, the KAMS organized campaigns against the Adivasi traditions of forced marriage and abduction and many superstitions in tribal society jeopardizing the interests of women. More significantly, KAMS formed the main women recruiting base of PLGA and a large number of KAMS activists joined PLGA and turned as potential fighters of the movement. Overtly, KAMS became a formidable frontline force which on many occasions rallied thousands of women and organized protest campaigns against the excesses/atrocities by police and *Salwa Judum* in the name of counter-insurgency operations. It is estimated that women now make around 45 per cent of PLGA cadre.

The policy of Chhattisgarh government to patronize 'non -state actors' like *Salwa Judum* in their counter-insurgency operations was one of the major reasons for the mounting Maoist-related violence. The genesis of *Salwa Judum* in many respects was similar to the formation of private armies in Bihar by landlords and caste forces to counter Left extremists in the state during 1980s and 1990s. In fact, the *mukhiyas* (village heads) were most benefitted out of the land redistribution in Chhattisgarh area at the behest of LWE. The *mukhiyas*/big landlords lost much of their clout when the movement began to turn their attention to issues of equity, class and injustice within tribal society. Mahendra Karma, one of the biggest landlords in the region and at the same time a member of CPI, rallied a group of *mukhiyas* and landlords and started a campaign called the Jan Jagran Abhiyan (Public Awakening Campaign) in 1990 with a view to safeguarding the interests of big landlords. This movement backed by the then Madhya Pradesh Government let loose a reign of terror in forest and village areas to intimidate the tribals and supporters of LWE. The strong retaliation by LWE, killing the prominent landlords behind the movement, resulted in fading Jan Jagran Abhiyan.

Mahendra Karma on joining Congress Party made futile efforts to revive the movement in 1998. However, the politics in the state, especially the schism in the state unit of Congress worked to his advantage. Two major developments that occurred in the state in 2005 also favoured Karma's attempts to revive the movement in a new form. The first one was the installation of Bharatiya Janata Party (BJP) government. The second, and the more important one, was the signing of two MOUs by the government—one with TATA Steel and the other with ESSAR Steel to start their major projects at Bailadila, and Lohandiguda, respectively. The central government vigorously pursuing their globalization agenda and economic reforms and the state government in line with their developmental agenda made all efforts to implement the MOUs. Inspired by the blanket support by the power centres in New Delhi and Raipur, Mahendra Karma's efforts to float *Salwa Judum* fructified in June 2005. The rest was history.

Unlike the Jan Jagran Abhiyan, the *Salwa Judum* was a ground-clearing operation, meant to move people out of their villages into roadside camps, where they could be policed and controlled. Raman Singh, the state CM, announced that as far as his government was concerned, villagers who did not move into camps would be considered Maoists. So in Bastar, for an ordinary villager, he had only two options—either move out of his own home or to carry the label of a LWE activist and face the atrocities perpetrated by the state machinery or *Salwa Judum*. The first village the *Salwa Judum* burnt on 18 June 2005 was Ambeli. Between June and December 2005, it burned, killed, raped and looted its way through hundreds of villages of South Dantewada. The main centres of its operation were the districts of Bijapur and Bhairamgarh, near Bailadila. These were also Maoist strongholds, where the Jantana Sarkars had done a great deal of work, especially in building water-harvesting structures. The Jantana Sarkars became the special target of the *Salwa Judum's* attacks. Hundreds of people were killed in the most brutal ways. About 60 thousand people moved into the camps, some voluntarily, others out of terror. Of these, about 3 thousand were appointed as Special Police Officers (SPOs) on a salary of 15 hundred rupees. Many other dislocated people made their way to Andhra Pradesh and Orissa and joined as migrant workers. But tens of thousands fled into the forest, where they still remain, living without shelter.

The formation of state-sponsored *Salwa Judum*, the stepped up counter-insurgency operations by an array of central and state forces such as Chhattisgarh Armed Force (CAF), the Central Reserve Police Force (CRPF), the Border Security Force (BSF), the Indo-Tibetan Border Police (ITBP), the Central Industrial Security Force (CISF), Greyhounds, Scorpions, Cobras so on and naturally the counter-offensive by Maoists through ambushes, bomb blasts, reckless killings and attack of Slawa Judum camps virtually plunged the state into a civil war like situation. Every day passed with spine-chilling bizarre incidents of cold-blooded killings, arson and looting of villages, rape and molestation of women, ambushes and bomb blasts. Thus, in September 2005, 22 CRPF personnel and two police men were killed in a landmine blast in Dantewada district, whereas on the Republic Day of 2006, the Maoist guerrillas attacked the Gangalaur police camp and killed seven people and on 17 July 2006 another *Salwa Judum* camp at Erabor was attacked, 20 people were killed and 150 injured and on 13 December 2006 they attacked the Basaguda 'relief' camp and killed three SPOs and a constable. The most audacious of them all was the attack of the Rani Bodili Kanya Ashram (a girl's hostel that had been converted into a barrack for 80 Chhattisgarh police personnel) by the guerrillas in March 2007 in which 55 policemen and SPOs were killed. The state also witnessed major incidents of violence in 2010, such as killing of 75 CRPF personnel and a policeman of Chhattisgarh police in Dantewada district; bus blast by an IED in the same district resulting in the death of 44 per-sons, including 28 civilians and 16 SPOs; and killing of 27 CRPF personnel in an ambush in Narayanpur district. Meanwhile, the so-called 'biggest anti-Naxal operation' in Gachanpallia village deep in the forests of Dantewada district during September 2009 turned to be fake. Later, it was proved that at least 12 out of 30 killed in this operation were innocent civilians with no links to the Maoists. It was in the backdrop of such serious omissions and commissions adversely affecting the lives and properties of the civilians that the apex court and the NHRC issued specific directions/recommendations to Chhattisgarh government to dismantle *Salwa Judum* and to rehabilitate the tribals/other backward sections who were the victims of the violence/atrocities by *Salwa Judum*. While these directions are yet to be fully complied by the state, the ghost of *Salwa Judum*, discreetly patronized by the state apparatus, still haunts the tribals and poor people.

Over four-decades-old LWE movement in the country vis-à-vis the present status of the organization brings out certain factors which are indicative of its future in the Indian context. One crucial factor is the continued faith of the large chunk of Indian masses on democratic institutions, despite their total degeneration due to money and muscle power. A series of scams and scandals such as 2G Spectrum, Commonwealth Games, Adarsh Housing Society and so on that have recently surfaced are only the tip of the iceberg of a vicious circle of corruption and malpractices that have engulfed the Indian polity and system that have become rotten and nauseating. The irony is that the people continue to tolerate politicians and bureaucrats who have become epitomes of corruption and political manipulations. Majority of the people, influenced by caste, communal and political forces hardly pay any heed to the voice of Left Radicals or other movements which oppose the degenerated system and their corrupt and opportunist representatives at the helm of affairs. In this backdrop, certain questions pertaining to LWE are relevant. Whether conditions ever existed historically or strategically for armed struggle since the genesis of Naxalbari movement? If so, what prevented Naxalites to resort to such struggles? If not, whether they tried to work out alternate strategy to create conditions conducive for such armed struggles in pursuance of their ultimate goal of capturing power? How far the revolutionary groups could succeed in creating such conditions by forming mass or extension organizations? In fact, such questions and polemics on them led to sharp division in the Left revolutionary movement in the country.

Despite poverty and exploitation of overwhelming majority of the people by a microscopic minority backed by the state apparatus, the overall conditions in the country were never favourable for any armed struggle as envisaged by Mao. The bitter experiences of Telangana armed struggles (1946–1951) and the subsequent armed peasant movements in Srikakulam and Naxalbari (1960s and 1970s) demonstrated this truth that these movements were unable to effectively confront the might of the Indian state or its superstructures. The highly adventurist line of Charu Mazumdar advocating for the 'annihilation of class enemies' attracted comrades in many states like West Bengal, Bihar, Andhra Pradesh, Orissa, Tamil Nadu, Kerala and so on where 'Naxalite action' against feudal landlords and police stations created a reign of terror which led to most repressive measures by police and paramilitary forces. The movement naturally withered away in the wake of such operations. However, comrades from Tamil Nadu, Kerala, Uttar Pradesh, Bihar, Karnataka, Orissa and West Bengal met and set up All India Coordination Committee of Revolutionaries (AICCR) which was later renamed as All India Coordination Committee of Communist Revolutionaries (AICCCR). 'Allegiance to armed struggles' and 'non-participation in elections' were the two main agendas of the organization. This concept of armed struggle and the relevance of mass movement led to intense ideological differences within the movement.

The ideological line of AICCCR was first questioned by T. Nagi Reddy and D.V. Rao of Andhra Pradesh who formed APCCCR in1969. They gave emphasis on mass revolutionary line and preparation for sowing the seeds of armed struggle. Both deferred armed struggle and even opposed the armed squad resistance line of Chandra Pulla Reddy in 1973. This section fought relentlessly against the Charu Mazumdar line of 'active boycott' as a strategic line for the Indian revolution and stressed that in certain stages 'participation in elections' could be used as a tactics. In 1969, T. Nagi Reddy aptly put their line in words as:

> We [Naxalites] can go in for armed struggle in a really large area and still sit in parliament in other areas when armed struggle is not going on. If we had been carrying on the working class struggles in the revolutionary way during these 16 years, we could probably also have used the parliament, even if agrarian revolution was taking place in other areas. India has many different organizational revolutionary requirements. As for the future we must wait and see how things develop, how successful is our organization's work and how effective is the co-ordination of all these struggles. Then we must consider the various tactical possibilities open to us.[21]

Thus, the crux of the strategy was the issue of armed struggle for the seizure of power. While Charu Mazumdar stressed that the party should centre all its work from the very beginning on the armed struggle for the area-wise seizure of power, Nagi Reddy tried to theorize the spontaneous course of development of the Telangana armed struggle into a line. He argued that the peasants must first be mobilized to struggle for land. Following this, an armed resistance struggle to defend this economic gain must be developed. This resistance struggle should be developed into the struggle for political power; something like the 'phase theory of people's war'.[22] The essence of this line is the view that the masses can be mobilized for the struggle to seize power only in phases—struggle for land, armed resistance to defend gains and then the struggle for power. In opposition to this, Charu Mazumdar stressed the development of class struggle to the highest level by arming the masses with the politics of the area-wise seizure of power.

Despite such differences, AICCCR went ahead with its efforts to broad base the movement by rallying more communist revolutionaries to their fold. Thus, a new party, namely CPI(ML), after dissolving AICCCR was formed in May 1969 with the declared aim of vigorously pursuing Charu Mazumdar's 'armed struggle line'. However, a major group led by Kanhai Chatterjee did not join the new party because of their tactical differences with Charu Mazumdar on the concept of armed struggle and method of party formation. They formed MCC which all along followed a different revolutionary line. The revolutionary rhetoric created by CPI(ML) in 1969–1970 period with lot of violence and bloodshed in their major pockets was short lived when the state apparatus adopted repressive measures against them and put hundreds of workers behind the bars. The protagonists of Srikakulam struggles suffered major setback when their leader Panchadri Krishnamurty and six others were killed in police action. However, the movement continued in Andhra Pradesh till 1975 and attracted a number of intellectuals, civil rights activists and artists/literary figures who stood throughout with the left-wing extremist movement in the state.

The differences on the question of armed struggle continued to plague unity in CPI(ML). This became more vocal after the death of Charu Mazumdar in Calcutta jail during July 1972. The post-Charu era was marked by the narrow perceptions of individual leaders and serious polemics on the exact Maoist revolutionary line conducive for the 'protracted peoples struggle' in the Indian situation. This also led to a phase of 'course correction' or 'rectification process' which was clearly reflected during the deliberations of the Durgapur (West Bengal) meeting of the party (1974) in which the Central Organising Committee of CPI(ML) was reconstituted and renamed as CPI(ML) Liberation with Jauhar (Subrata Dutt) as general secretary. With the formation of Liberation, the tactical line of participation in parliamentary exercises had come to the open.

In fact, the declaration of National Emergency in 1975 and the repressive measures adopted against the LWE elements influenced the strategy and tactics of various groups. The CPI(ML) Liberation's new line in 1976 highlighted that armed guerrilla struggles would be continued along with the efforts to form a broad anti- Congress democratic front even by including non-communist parties. By 1977, Comrade Kanu Sanyal, the strong proponent of armed struggle also abandoned the doctrine of 'dedicated armed struggle' and accepted parliamentary practices as part of Naxalite strategy. But the MCC pursued an independent line mainly in Bihar. Party representatives from West Bengal and Andhra Pradesh kept away from the Central Organizing Committee which was ultimately dissolved in May 1977. These developments further deepened the crisis in the movement and accelerated further splits leading to the formation of CPI(ML) (Unity Organisation) in Bihar under N. Prasad's leadership PWG in Andhra Pradesh under: Kondapally Seetharamaiah (1980). PWG also discarded the line of total annihilation of 'class enemies' as the only form of armed struggle and emphasized the need of floating mass organizations.

Meanwhile, the Kerala State Committee of CPI(ML) in 1979 formed Central Reorganizing Committee (CRC)–CPI(ML), which upheld the 'proletarian revolutionary line of Comrade Charu Mazumdar' as one of its basic positions, but emphasized that 'Armed struggle is the main form of struggle and all other forms of struggle should be complementary to it.' The position taken by Kerala comrades diverged from the 1970 line of the CPI(ML) in two important aspects. The more obvious one was its proposal to develop mass struggles into political struggles in order to prepare the ground for initiating armed struggle. This contradicted Charu Mazumdar's well-known opposition to making economic or partial struggles a precondition for the initiation of armed struggle. It also contradicted Lenin's refutation of economism and the Leninist stand that economic struggles cannot be developed into the political struggle for power. The second was contained in the assumption that the armed struggle could be initiated only after uncovering and sharpening the contradictions. New interpretations were given on the exact revolutionary line, military line, political power and so on by applying and interpreting Marxism–Leninism–Maoism in bits and pieces in the name of tackling 'new questions' and breaking away from 'dogmatism'. Strangely, these polemics and ideological debate were undertaken by Kerala comrades without working out any practical strategy in pursuance of their line or for strengthening armed revolutionary line in the state. Thus, these polemics had downgraded to the status of mere intellectual debate and discussion by a set of leaders who failed to give any practical move or orientation for armed class struggles in Kerala. The Andhra State Committee of CPIML opposed the political line of CRC (CPML), whereas the detractors of this line within CRC floated Dissident-CRC-CPML which subsequently became defunct. By the end of 1991, the CRC-CPI(ML) was liquidated. And the hitherto 'unrecognized' potential of parliamentary elections for 'broad political mobilization' was finally discovered. Ultimately, the proponent of this line, K. Venu, ended up as a Congress-supported candidate in the 1996 State Assembly Elections—politically mobilized to serve the Indian ruling classes. But, the enlightened voters of Kerala flatly rejected him.

With the formation of PWG, the LWE movement in the country began to polarize mainly between the Marxist–Leninist line of CPI(ML) Liberation and the PWG line of armed struggle. The Liberation group branded PWG-liners as 'left adventurists' whose isolated actions of killings and other depredations adversely affected the spread and consolidation of left-wing extremist movement in the country. On the other hand, the PWG interpreted the line of CPI(ML) Liberation as 'revisionist' damaging the revolutionary fervour of the LWE movement. The other major groups which endorse the line of Liberation include: CPI(ML) led by K.N. Ramchandran and the CPI(ML) New Democracy groups. The Liberation which entered in the electoral politics of Bihar in 1989 under the banner of IPF, comprising other groups like CPI(ML) New Democracy, CPI(ML) Unity Initiative and

CPI(ML) S.R. Bhaijee sent the first Naxalite member to the parliament. One major feature of these groups is that they have All India Trade Union Centres or platforms uniting peasant organizations. However, their style of functioning is not in consistent with that of building revolutionary mass resistance but they display reformist tendencies. True that the 'New Democracy Group' still leads mass agitations, particularly in Punjab, Andhra Pradesh and Uttar Pradesh, but powerful rightist deviationist tendencies by embracing the path of participation in elections are reflected. It is significant that at one time the same organization, then known as the Chandra Pulla Reddy Group, was the strongest group in India, which asserted secret party functioning. Later they built mass organizations and struggles and expanded to the urban areas but sowed the seeds for capitulationism by almost resorting to total open functioning. The groups like the CPI(ML) led by K.N. Ramchandran (earlier known as Red Flag Group) have virtually become reformist, abandoning the path of revolutionary resistance and resorting to total open functioning. They go out of the way to condemn the military actions of the CPI(Maoist) and assert that India is a neo-colony. On the other hand, PWG and MCC which had been vigorously pursuing their line of armed struggle through confrontation with the the state apparatus, liberating areas and forming 'guerrilla zones' and establishing Jantana Sarkars merged in September 2004 and formed CPI(Maoists) who have now become the vanguard of LWE movement in the country. The Maoists who are committed to 'wage people's war for the establishment of people's government' totally rejects parliamentary exercises like elections.

There are numerous other organizations which engage to some degree in armed struggle, the most prominent one is CPI(ML) Janashakti (Rajanna Group) having their main bases in Andhra Pradesh and Maharashtra. Other groups and individuals whose line is in between that of the CPI(ML) Liberation and the CPI(Maoist) also exist. The newly christened CPI(ML), formed in January 2005 with the merger of the CPI(ML) Red Flag and the CPI(ML) Sanyal group, is one such group. Another middle force is the Communist Party Reorganisation Centre of India (ML) which was formed in 1994 under the leadership of Harbhajan Singh Sohi. This organization defers armed struggle, but also combats open functioning and participation in elections. It staunchly defends the CPI(Maoist) as Communist revolutionaries, defending their work in Chhattisgarh and Lalgarh but defers with their military line. The struggles it has launched in Orissa and Punjab are an abject lesson to the revolutionary camp in the struggle for mass preparation for revolutionary mass resistance, and the correct relationship of the mass organizations with the party. A remarkable aspect of this trend is that it rejects both 'active boycott' or 'participation' as correct tactics in the present situation. Earlier in 1970s, Sohi struggled for the mass revolutionary line by floating organizations like the Punjab Students Union and the Naujavan Bharat Sabha. He played a key role in the formation of the Unity Centre of Communist Revolutionaries of India (UCCRI-ML) in 1975. It played a major role in the formation and functioning of the anti-repression and anti communal front and also built up of mass revolutionary resistance against the Khalistani terrorism.

Earlier in December 2007, Prime Minister Manmohan Singh, while addressing a conference on internal security attended by chief ministers of all states, cited Naxalism as the lone biggest threat to nation's internal security. Much water has flown through Ganges since the statement by the prime minister. The intensity of the threat had become more severe during 2009–2010 when the graph of Naxalite violence including casualties to security personnel and civilians showed a steep ascendancy in states like Chhattisgarh, Jharkhand and Orissa. A closer analysis of these trends would demonstrate that LWE is the greatest challenge to human/civil rights in the country. A number of human rights bodies and NGOs like Amnesty International, Human Right Watch and Asian Centre for Human Rights have highlighted the naked violation of human rights arising out of the depredations of left-wing extremist groups and the counter-extremist operations by state apparatus through deployment of security forces and civilian militia such as *Salwa Judum*. The Human Rights Watch, India Report 2009, highlighted this peculiar scenario especially in Chhattisgarh as:

> In Chhattisgarh, government security forces and State-government-backed vigilantes called the Salwa Judum are responsible for attacking, killing, and forcibly displacing tens of thousands of people in armed operations against Maoist rebels. The Naxalite rebels retaliate in a brutal manner, abducting, assaulting, and killing civilians perceived to be Salwa Judum supporters. The government has

chosen to view those who do not join the Salwa Judum as Naxalite supporters.[23]

The situation was not different in other Naxal-affected states like Jharkhand, Orissa or Bihar where civilians continue to be caught in the crossfire between Maoist insurgents and government security forces. The loss of human lives in such crossfire was a matter of serious concern not only for human rights activists but also for all who believe in rule of law and due process of law. According to the statistics compiled by the Institute of Peace and Conflict Studies[24] more than 14,300 people have been killed since the start of the left-extremist violence in 1980, of which more than half died in the last ten years. Year-wise statistics compiled by the institute for the period 1989–2010 showed the total casualties as 10,875 (civilians 5,982; SF Personnel 2,097; and Naxalites 2,796) (Table 3.2). Thus, it is clear that the worst victims were the civilians.

Meanwhile, *South Asia Intelligence Review* highlighted that the leftist insurgency had cost more than 4,500 lives in Andhra Pradesh alone since 1990. Considering the death toll during the first phase of the movement (1967–1980), especially in Naxalbari, Srikakulam and so on, the overall death toll in Naxal-related

Table 3.2:
Deaths Related to Violence

Period	Civilians	Security Forces	Insurgents	Total
1989-01	1,610	432	1,007	3,049
2002	382	100	141	623
2003	410	105	216	731
2004	466	100	87	653
2005	524	153	225	902
2006	521	157	274	952
2007	460	236	141	837
2008	399	221	214	834
2009	586	317	217	1,120
2010	713	285	171	1,169
TOTAL	5,982	2,097	2,796	10,875

Source: The Naxal-Problem, IPCS Conference Report, March 2012 (quoted from Naxalite-Maoist insurgency, Wikipedia).

incidents/operations was around 20,000 which, no doubt, is more than the human casualties suffered by the nation in the conflicts with China and Pakistan.

The heavy toll in human lives was only one aspect of the tragedy. Equally serious were the other human rights issues and violations such as 'fake encounters/ encounter killings'; custodial violence; atrocities against civilians, especially women; reckless killing of civilians by Maoists branding them as 'police informers'; illegal detention and false prosecution against activists; displacement of people in the name of counter-insurgency operations and so on. The special Acts/Legislations enacted by the Centre and affected states to effectively deal with the problem gave draconian powers to the police and security forces which, on many occasions, misused them and created major human rights issues. Ironically, the human rights groups in the West used such misuses for anti-India bashing in various international forums. For example, the US State Department, Country Report on Human Rights Abuses, always highlighted such issues. Its report for 2002 observed:

> In Andhra Pradesh, the Disturbed Areas Act has been in force in a number of districts for over 4 years. Human rights groups allege that security forces have been able to operate with virtual impunity under the act. They further allege that Andhra Pradesh police officers train and provide weapons to an armed vigilante group known as the 'Green Tigers', whose mission is to combat the Naxalite group in the state. Little is known about the size, composition, or activities of this group. Court action in cases of extra judicial killings is slow and uncertain.[3125]

Similarly, *Salwa Judum*, another armed vigilante group in Chhattisgarh, came under bitter criticism by human rights groups for gross human rights violations in the name of counter-insurgency operations. 150,000 tribals from the remote villages of Chhattisgarh had been displaced and became homeless for months, living at road sides and relief camps in perpetual fear and terror. The ban on Maoists during June 2009 by the government also led to discernible trends, especially the conscious efforts by police and intelligence agencies to implicate and detain persons who were involved in various philanthropic activities among tribals and poor sections of Naxal-affected areas. A unique example was the prolonged detention and trial of Dr. Binayak Sen

of Chhattisgarh on the flimsy grounds of possessing Maoist literature and so on.

The serious flaws in counter-Maoist operations have created a
number of human rights issues including the killing of security
forces personnel in ambushes, bomb blasts and so on. Vijendra
Singh Jafa, an expert in such operations observed, 'Indian
counter-insurgency strategy and tactics have remained fundamentally conservative and traditionally influenced substantially
by accounts of British experiences'.[3226] On many occasions, state
responses have consisted of pumping in forces for conventional,
ground-holding operations with a view to displace guerrilla
forces, maintaining high force levels over sustained periods of
time and using their presence to push forward with developmental and political initiative to deprive of Maoists their acceptance
in the particular area. A typical example was the highly controversial Operation Green Hunt, a paramilitary offensive launched
by Government of India in November 2009 against rebels in the
'Red Corridor'. More than 20,000 personnel belonging to police,
CRPF, ITBP, BSF, SSB and special police units were deployed in
the operational area, besides the cadres of *Salwa Judum* militia in
Chhattisgarh. Neither the *Salwa Judum* with undisciplined and
untrained irregulars nor the paramilitary forces alien to the area,
unfamiliar with the terrain and customs and traditions of the local
population, helped to counter the Maoist threat.

Other factors also contributed to the failure of the operation
and large number of casualties to the Special Force (SF) personnel
on ground. The first and foremost is the dearth of specific actionable intelligence which is vital for the success of any counter-
insurgency operation. Neither the central and state intelligence agencies are successful in this regard nor the operational
forces have their own intelligence set-up to fill this vacuum.
Unfortunately, the central paramilitary forces which are deployed
in different states/areas to meet internal security exigencies have
never seriously thought of building up their own intelligence
apparatus. Whatever efforts these forces made were in the direction of setting up intelligence cell to spy on those personnel having differences with senior formations. Secondly, the lack of
co-ordination between the central forces and state police which
lead to serious tragedies like ambushes by the ultras resulting in
heavy casualties to personnel in the field. This has what happened

in Chhattisgarh, especially the 6 April 2010, killing of 76 SF per-sonnel, consisting of 74 CRPF men and two police personnel in an ambush by Maoists in Dantewada district. Thirdly, the high handedness of the forces particularly against the civilian popula-tion open a Pandora's box of issues which ultimately precipitate the hatred and anger of indigenous population against the forces. In fact, terrorizing a population into submission and ensuring that the cost for individuals and communities who support Maoists is intolerably high can work only in a more monolithic and authori-tarian state. In a state like India, the terror can and always will be limited in scope and scale. The result of simply creating more resentment and fear will only help the Maoists.

Keeping aloof the polemics on the relevance of population-cen-tred counter-Maoist operations, the need of the hour is to rectify the major flaws in such operations and work out a foolproof strat-egy to effectively to counter the Maoist threat. The first and fore-most task is to strengthen the state police set-up in the affected states, as these forces familiar with the terrain and demographic features are the best bet to successfully deal with the threat. The best example is the state of Andhra Pradesh where the state police particularly 'Greyhounds', despite allegations of human rights violations, could break the backbone of the Maoists. The condi-tion of police in other affected states is not much conducive to launch protracted operations against the Maoists due to a variety of factors. The case of Chhattisgarh, the citadel of the movement is a typical example the police–population ratio of Chhattisgarh is 103:100,000 as against 131 per 100,000 of all-India average. Moreover, a large number of posts at middle and cutting-edge levels remain vacant, adversely affecting the operational effi-ciency of the force. No doubt that merely hiring more personnel will not solve the problem. What is required is well-trained, prop-erly equipped and highly motivated personnel. The state Police is now lacking such personnel. This was manifest when Solicitor General Gopal Subramaniam admitted in supreme court dur-ing 2008 that the Chhattisgarh government was finding it diffi-cult to find recruits to the police. He further added: 'policemen are not ready to step into the forest'. Another equally important aspect was the unwillingness of young, dynamic and profession-ally competent personnel to join in the elite counter-insurgency units modelled on the lines of Greyhounds. Ironically, instead of overcoming such bottlenecks through well-planned manpower-development strategy, the state government adopted shortcuts, such as recruitment of SPOs from the ranks of *Salwa Judum*, bringing more discredit to the entire law enforcement machinery in the state. More distressing was the findings of Human Rights Watch that the state government recruited children under the age of 18 as SPOs who were extensively used in counter-Naxalite combing operations. Another vital area is proper training, especially in guerrilla warfare and use of weapons. Instead of depending on army's School of Jungle Warfare in Variegate for imparting training in jungle warfare, the state should start its own institutions and regularly impart training to selected police personnel. Similarly, instead of treating weapons as a decorative piece during ceremonial parades and so on, the personnel should familiarize with the use of all types of weapons for which there should be regular firing practice and so on. The intelligence capabilities of the state police by properly blending 'hum-int' and 'tech-int' need to be strengthened, especially in the light of the repeated failure of central intelligence agencies in catering tactical/operational intelligence during counter-Maoist operations. Needless to mention, the intelligence agencies bereft of accountability on their functioning or the inputs furnished by them are of little use in major counter-insurgency operations.

4

Left-Wing Extremism and Human Rights in Andhra Pradesh

In the backdrop of the pan-Indian scenario of the left-wing extre-mist movement, a detailed empirical study has been under-taken on the genesis, growth and consolidation of LWE in Andhra Pradesh in order to ascertain the extent of human rights violations arising out of the movement. Interrelated issues such as violation of human rights of marginalized sections like tribals and rural poor were also examined.

For more than three decades (1970–2000), the state of Andhra Pradesh witnessed extreme form of left-wing extremist violence. The spread of political extremism in Andhra Pradesh had two-fold impact on the protection and promotion of human and civil rights. On one hand, it led to extreme forms of human/civil rights violations due to the depredations of extremists and counter-extremist operations by security forces, but, on the other hand, it had accentuated social transition with increased awareness on the rights and privileges of the rural poor and the marginalized sec-tions. Take for example, Telangana armed struggle (1949–1952), the first revolutionary movement of peasants against exploita-tion by big landlords and demanding 'land to the tillers'. Despite witnessing ruthless suppression, infamously known as 'Sardar Patel measures', that led to the killing of around 6,000 persons, the above struggle accelerated the process of social transforma-tion in many parts of Andhra Pradesh. In fact, the Communists, as part of their strategy, carried forward the legacy of Telangana struggles by floating peasants' and agricultural workers' unions which to a great extent played a major role in safeguarding the interests of small-scale farmers and farm workers.

Similarly, the genesis of LWE, initially in the northern districts of Andhra Pradesh, viz. Srikakulam, Vizianagaram, Vizakapattanam, East and West Godavari districts, during the late 1960s and later to the entire Telangana region since the middle of 1970s can be mainly attributed to socio-economic factors such as poverty, unequal distribution of land, low wages, caste and gender oppression, oppressive behaviour of village elite, especially against marginalized sections and maladministration by local self-governing bodies. The socio-economic milieu and developmental scenario of the state in many respects signalled the dangers of a 'soft state' that spawns the 'unholy nexus between the law maker, the law keeper and the law breaker' that fits into the account of Gunnar Myrdal in his classic work, *The Asian Drama: An Enquiry into the Causes of Indian Poverty*.[1] The situation was graver in Andhra where the powerful Reddys and Khammas, who maintained considerable sway over the state machinery, had virtually defeated land reforms. It was not a question of land reforms alone, even minimum statutory wages were not paid to farm workers; nor were they treated as human beings in many parts of the state where feudal landed gentry treated them as mere slaves. More than that, the law enforcement machinery had to remain as silent spectators of the oppression and exploitation of underprivileged sections by the rural elite and landed gentry. The dispensation of justice to such unfortunate victims, on many occasions, was a myth.

The case of Telangana was unique in any respects. Though Telangana area is very rich in water and other natural resources, poverty and exploitation prevailed in the region to a great extent. The common adage, 'poverty amidst plenty' is rightly applicable to the area. History, politics, economy and administrative set-up greatly contributed to this anachronism. Historically, most part of the erstwhile princely state of Hyderabad was divided among *jagirs*, *samstans* and big landlords who possessed anything between 50 to 200 acres of land. After the liberation of the state from Nizam's rule, the newly formed state abolished the *jagirs* and *samstans* and initiated steps to free the tenants from the clutches of landlords. Unfortunately, there had been failure in the real distribution of land on account of several factors such as the reluctance of political executive to antagonize the powerful caste lobby, defects in the land reform policy and the real intent thereof. Thus, the gap between the rich and poor increased.

The various provisions of land ceiling laws that were common to all regions of the state did not satisfy the hope and aspirations of the large majority of people in Telangana region. The poorest strata of the society were forced to work as daily wagers or annual or seasonal farm labourers on conditions similar to bonded workers. The most striking form of feudal oppression was *vetti* or *vettichakiri* (beggar)—the forced unpaid labour which the working people of low castes had to perform and give as 'gift' to the *dora* (landlord). All types of public land were in the hands of *dora*s or those who were totally subservient to them. The 'patwari' records were unfathomable and the record of 'patta' (title deeds) and public land were most confusing. The revenue officials, influenced by rural elite, never tried to settle such issues. Around 75 per cent of agrarian population in North Telangana was landless or owned less than 2.5 acres of land.

The condition of tribals was most depressing. The tribal-land alienation was a major issue in which the influential non-tribals occupied sizeable percentage of fertile and irrigated land. The development of agency areas (dominated by tribal population) with the formation of Integrated Tribal Development Agency (ITDA) has become a myth as lion's share of the allotted funds for ITDA for various schemes went into the pockets of local officials, political intermediaries and contractors. The contractors, their agents and corrupt forest officials exploited the poor peasants and tribals engaged in 'Tendu-leaf plucking' during the agriculturally lean season by denying them minimum wages or collecting regular commission or bribe. Added to these was the traditional social domination through the caste system, through which the upper-caste elites maintained supremacy over Dalits and tribals. It was in such a socio-economic milieu interwoven with land issues, caste factors, social oppression and exploitation of weaker sections and apparent failure of government agencies to ensure development that Telangana region became a citadel of left-extremist groups.

The state was an experimental ground for various left-wing extremist groups which followed the different strategies and tactics leading to the split and formation of a number of groups. During the peak years of LWE (1970–2000), there were 16 left-wing extremist groups in Andhra Pradesh. However, five of them were more active. These groups were:

1. PWG (now known as CPI [Maoists]): PWG was formed in Andhra Pradesh on 22 April 1980 by Kondapalli Seetharamaiah, one of the most revered ideologues of left-wing extremists in India. It strictly adhered to the strategies and tactics employed by Mao Zedong during the Great March[2] and vigorously pursued a revolutionary line of the elimination of class enemies for which the formation of secret mass organizations had been emphasized.

   PWG witnessed its 'ebb and flow' stages in Andhra. Just as the pan-Indian scenario, successive state governments adopted different strategies to tackle the problem. In 1982–1983, the former Andhra chief minister, Shri N.T. Rama Rao described Naxalites as 'true patriots who had been misunderstood by the ruling classes'. He de-escalated anti-PWG operations, not only winning their electoral support, but also opening the way for the escalation of extremist violence to unprecedented level. His successor M. Chenna Reddy of Congress returned the compliment in 1988; N.T. Rama Rao (hereafter NTR) replayed the gambit in 1994. On each occasion, Naxalite violence showed an upward trend which to a great extent could be reversed during the stepped up anti-Naxalite operations undertaken by the state governments headed by former chief ministers, Shri Chandra Babu Naidu of Telugu Desam Party (TDP) and Late Shri Rajasekhara Reddy of Congress. In 1997, Koratala Suryanarayana, a senior leader of Communist party (Marxist) had succinctly put this trend as: 'the political parties which have been in power in the State for the last three or four decades have been trying to utilize or use the services of these extremist groups either to come to power or to perpetuate their power'.[3]

   These factors had considerably contributed to the growth and consolidation of PWG and later CPI (Maoists) in Andhra and neighbouring states. As PWG, it had its roots in all the districts of Andhra with its strongholds in Telangana districts (Adilabad, Nizamabad, Karimnagar, Warangal,

Khammam, Mahabubnagar, Nalgonda, Medak and Ranga Reddy). As early as 1990s, the outfit had declared its stronghold districts in North Telangana as 'Guerilla Zone' and divided the rest of the state into four 'struggle areas'. The strategy of PWG was to promote the Guerilla Zone into 'liberated areas' and 'struggle areas' into liberated zones in phases. They had further consolidated their position through unity with MCC, having their strong bases in Bihar, Jharkand and so on. The newly formed group rechristened as CPI(Maoists) had become a major threat to the internal security of the nation through their repeated depredations against security forces and destruction and sabotage of governmental assets and so on. Their formation of a Compact Revolutionary Zone (CRZ) from the forest tracts of Adilabad (Andhra Pradesh) to the border of Nepal, traversing through the forest areas of Maharashtra, Orissa, Chhattisgarh, Bihar, Jharkhand and so on has led to the entire area being vulnerable from security and law-and-order angle.

PWG/CPI(Maoists) have developed fraternal links with revolutionary Communist groups from other countries. They took a leading role in the formation of a Co-ordination Committee of Maoist Parties and Organizations in South Asia (CCOMPOSA),[4] in which revolutionary communist groups from Nepal, Bangladesh and Sri Lanka are prominent members, besides other left-wing extremist groups from India. Internationally, the group which established fraternal links with Revolutionary International Movement (RIM) has been getting good response as manifest by the participation of PWG/Maoists representatives in an international seminar organized by the Workers Party of Belgium (WPB) in Brussels. The PWG/CPI(Maoists) managed to get the moral support of other Marxist–Leninist Maoist parties from Brazil, Chad, Mexico, Nepal, Philippines, Senegal, USA, Turkey and so on, on a common slogan, 'the people's war being led by the working class in India'.

The major front organizations of PWG/CPI(Maoists) include: (*a*) Rytu Coolie Sanghams (Peasants and Agricultural Labourers Union); (*b*) Singareni Karmika Samakhya (SIKASA) which is active among coal miners; (*c*) Radical

Youth League (youth wing); (*d*) Radical Students Union (students wing); (*e*) Progressive Democratic Students Union (students wing); (*f*) Progressive Organization of Women (women' s wing); (*g*) Revolutionary Writers' Association, alias VIRASAM (literary front); and (*h*) Jana Natya Mandali (cultural wing).

2. CPI(ML) Janasakthi: It was formed in 1992 with the merger of seven CPI(ML) groups. It has its strong bases in the districts of Nizamabad, Karimnagar, Warangal, Khammam, Nalgonda, Mehaboob Nagar (all in Telangana region); East and West Godavari (Coastal Andhra); and Kurnool (Rayalaseema). In the middle of 1990s, Janasakthi had split into three groups, named after respective faction leaders, viz. Kurra Rajanna, N.V. Krishnaiah and Veeranna. The Rajanna faction who criticises the 'mass line strategy' is strong in Telangana and Rayalaseema regions, whereas N.V. Krishnnaiah (hereafter NVK) faction had its pockets of influence in the coastal districts. Veeranna faction is almost defunct. Rajanna faction is more inclined towards 'guerrilla warfare'.

3. CPI(ML) New Democracy: It was initially formed in 1988 by Yatendra Kumar and had its main pockets of influence in the districts of Nizamabad, Karimnagar, Warangal, Khammam, Mehaboob Nagar (all in Telangana region); and East and West Godavari, Srikakulam, Guntur and Prakasam (Coastal Andhra). It followed the strategy of 'revolutionary mass line' and advocated for moderate violence, but concentrated more on mass mobilization programmes focusing on issues of common men. New Democracy acknowledges the relevance of parliamentary democracy and is willing to associate with mainstream Communist parties and like-minded CPI(ML) groups in carrying out joint struggles and agitation programmes on mass issues.

4. CPI(ML) Phani Bagchi: It had its pockets of support in the districts of Nalgonda, Ranga Reddy, Karimnagar, Warangal, Khammam (all in Telangana region); East Godavari (Coastal Andhra); and Kurnool (Rayalaseema). This group is committed to armed struggles and indulges in violence.

5. CPI(ML) Praja Pratighatana: It is a breakaway group from CPI(ML) Phani Bagchi and had its pockets mainly in parts of Telangana area. This group is also committed to the path of violence.

The internecine conflicts and fratricidal killings between the major CPI(ML) groups have added new dimensions to the human rights arising out of LWE, apart from their moderate to large-scale violence and depredations against civilian population, security personnel and government/semi-government officials. This also manifested that LWE was one of the major areas/source for human/civil rights violations in the country.

The unabated violence by LWE groups and the counter measures by the police and other security agencies continued in the state during 1980s and 1990s. Over 4,000 people died in the violence and conflicts between the police and LWE activists. Official statistics say 1,204 persons were killed by PWG in the state during 1990–1996, when there was large-scale violence by LWE. Human rights activists recorded 854 encounter killings by police during the same period. As per the statistics on encounter killings compiled by the Andhra Pradesh Civil Liberties Committee (APCLC), there were 335 such killings during the period 1966–1977 and 1,168 encounter killings during 1977–1996, with maximum number of killings (256) in 1992. The official statistics (statement of DGP, Andhra Pradesh) also showed that 1,316 extremists and 33 policemen were killed in 1,432 encounters which took place during the period 1968–1997. Equally distressing were the casualties and human rights violations caused at the instance of LWE groups. The total number of persons killed by them from 1968 to 1997 as per police records was 2,046. These included 307 policemen/home guards and 69 other government servants killed during the period of 1981–1997. The above statistics clearly manifest the seriousness of human rights issues arising out of LWE.

The LWE groups were instrumental for the extensive damage to public and private properties such as government vehicles, Andhra Pradesh State Road Transport Corporation (APSRTC) buses, railway stations, rail bridges, very high frequency (VHF) wireless stations, cinema halls, private buildings, police stations and so on. As per the official figures for the period 1992–1997, the total damage was to the tune of ₹953,323,000 with maximum damage (₹442,365,000) in 1996. Besides, cultivable land worth several crores was lying fallow mainly in Telangana districts as extremist groups had forcibly occupied them from landowners, but could not start cultivation due to legal entanglements. This had either created a decline or stagnation in agricultural production in Telangana districts. This was only one side of the adverse impact on the economy. On the other hand, developmental activities came to a total standstill in LWE-affected areas of Telangana for decades when the extremists had declared a virtual blockade of state-sponsored developmental or other activities in these areas. Keeping apart other socio-economic and political factors, the LWE factor had also adversely affected the overall development scenario of Telangana region.

The anatomy of LWE, their depredations and human rights violations manifest certain clear trends. First, just as in other states, PWG/CPI(Maoists) had been able to sustain high militant and violent profile in Andhra Pradesh, as can be clearly seen from the case study on LWE violence in the state during the peak period of violence (1994–1997). Out of 703 murders, PWG and its fronts were responsible for 544 (77.3 per cent), while all other groups for 159 (22.7 per cent). Similarly, out of 4,011 violent incidents during the same period, PWG was involved in 3,112 (77 per cent) and the others in 599 (23 per cent). This also demonstrated PWG's total adherence to their revolutionary violent line and their striking power in contrast to other LWE groups.

Second, Telangana was bloodied from violence of LWE and of internecine fights between different groups. Caught in this bloody war were the people, especially the poor, the Dalits and tribals. The nine Telangana districts, namely Adilabad, Karimnagar, Nizamabad, Khammam, Medak, Mehaboob Nagar, Warangal, Hyderabad and Nalgonda showed high intensity of extremist violence, in which people of the region were virtually sandwiched in between the wanton killings by LWE groups and the repressive policies of the state. A district-wise analysis of such killings/injuries by the extremists and police during the period 1980–1997 showed that extremists killed 1,038 persons with maximum casualties (453) in Karimnagar district. In the case of grievous injuries to persons due to extremist violence and police operations as well as in the destruction of properties, Karimnagar remained at the top.

Third, though the prominent LWE groups like PWG were ideologically committed to violence and unconstitutional means in pursuance of their ultimate goals, the 'social reformist role' played by them in a society dominated by feudal, oppressive and exploitative forces need closer analysis. Perhaps this role, coupled with the active association of a large number of sincere and ideologically committed intellectuals without any personal agenda and ambitions with the movement during late 1970s and 1980s, enabled it to create much goodwill and mass support among the marginalized sections of the society, particularly tribals and rural poor. The movement at that time was instrumental in bringing out a sea change in the rural economy and in the plight of Dalits and Adivasis. They could considerably demolish the feudal oppression which impeded the raising of capital by the landless labour. The left-wing extremists were able to curb the practice of *vetti* (forced labour), indiscriminate levying of taxes and collection of *dandaga*—surplus yield from the landless. Significantly, they catalyzed the enactment of land legislations which to a great extent contributed to the distribution of surplus land to the landless and tribals.   ,

On the social plane, the people belonging to SC/ST and backward classes unfurled the flag of self-respect and thereby initiated the process of social resurgence of Dalits, tribals and backward sections. Through the tactics of Praja Courts[5] and 'ready justice', they helped to create deterrence on the corrupt practices of a section of forest officials and local government officers, especially in rural and tribal development departments. They had also undertaken a number of developmental and welfare schemes such as safe drinking water supply schemes; repairs to irrigation tanks; establishment of farmers' co-operative societies to supply quality seeds, pesticides and fertilizers; and construction of hospitals and school buildings in rural areas, for example, in districts like Nizamabad, the secret of mass support to the outfit was such developmental/welfare schemes, neglected by the successive state governments. The construction of rural roads of about 120 km, linking Nizamabad and Karimnagar districts; laying of about 13 km stretch of village road between Manala village of Kammarpalli Mandal and Rudrangi at a cost of about ₹35 lakhs; distribution of about 400 acres of surplus land (forcibly occupied) to landless poor; forest management by fully protecting the interests of tribals in around 18,000 acres of forestland; construction/repair of irrigation tanks in Gandhari Mandal and Sirikonda; holding of medical camps and free distribution of medicines and digging of bore wells and so on were such schemes undertaken by them with the support of local masses. Properly understanding such ground-level strategies of left-wing groups is highly imperative for the local self-governing bodies and government departments to chalk out counter plans and schemes to wean away the poor and marginalized people from their stranglehold. But such an approach was found lacking among these sections that totally negate the developmental and welfare oriented activities of LWE groups in rural areas. Perhaps, this was part of the strategy of administration/local governments to cover up their own omissions and commissions.

Over the years, many unhealthy influences had crept into the left-extremist movement in the state. The entry of a number of 'lumpen elements' into the organization, large-scale extortion of money from landlords and its misuse for personal ends, moral turpitude of leaders and cadres, tactical flaws in the form of wanton killings and depredations, destruction/damage of public/private properties, personality clash among cadres, induction of large number of immature and uneducated youth into the movement and so on had disillusioned sizeable number of committed leaders/cadres, who had either left the organization or surrendered before authorities. The so-called Tactical Counter-Offensive Campaign (TCOC) by the Maoists in 'struggle areas' sometimes got boomeranged when innocent tribals and civil population were the victims. The killing of Congress leader C. Narsi Reddy and eight others in the state on 15 August 2005 was one such typical incident. The Maoist-hit team had fired with automatic weapons on a meeting where a national flag was unfurled and innocents were killed. The ultras subsequently apologized but the deep resentment among the public about the indiscriminate killing had long-term adverse impact on the outfit. Such tactical lapses had occurred in contravention to the ideological line of Maoists that revolutionary cadres would not target civilians but only 'class enemies'.

In fact, the Maoists had heavily paid to such lapses which could be successfully exploited by police and other security agencies through their systematic operations. Special mention should be made of 'Greyhounds'—the Special Task Force of state police which had won the accolades from all corners for their professionalism and competence in anti-Naxalite operations in Andhra Pradesh. The success of 'Greyhounds' could be mainly attributed to the fact that this specialized force functioned beyond the contours of conventional organizational structure and set-up in police with highly committed and motivated personnel who were offered liberal incentives and facilities. Moreover, they had built up their own intelligence network through a process of assimilation with local population and utilizing potential surrendered cadres, instead of blindly depending on half-baked intelligence generated by organized intelligence agencies at the centre and in the state. Such police strategies had paid rich dividends to police who could get an upper hand by late 1990s in their operations against Maoists, Thus, a number of top leaders of the Maoists including three Central Committee members and many underground 'dalam leaders' were liquidated. Simultaneously, police leadership had seriously addressed developmental and people's issues in the affected areas which forced the administration to take more concerted efforts to initiate developmental and welfare-oriented schemes in Maoist dominated areas. In many respects, the police played the role of a 'facilitator' in the developmental process which was totally derailed due to the lethargy, fear and indifference of the district administration.

The police success had created much desperation among the cadres, which was manifest in the form of indiscriminate killing of civilians branding them as 'police informers' or use of landmines and explosives against police and other agencies. It was this widespread, all-consuming violence that used to take a few lives daily in the state which prompted former Justice M.N. Rao of Andhra High court to seek solution to it. In his judgment in June 1996, he observed:

> Despite its magnitude and menacing dimensions, the problem we think does not admit of any solutions. A Peace Commission with representative character inspiring confidence in all sections of the society including Naxalites and police and backed by the State power and consent, we believe, can bring about immediate cessation of police encounters and violence by Naxalites and then only in the resultant peaceful atmosphere, a meaningful search for permanent solution is possible.[6]

It was in line with the instructions of the High Court that an independent initiative, viz. Committee of Concerned Citizens (CCC) headed by retired IAS officer, S.R. Sankaran and consisting of prominent human/civil rights activists was constituted in order to arrest the escalation of violence and large-scale violation of human rights arising out of LWE. However, the Committee could not achieve any specific result because of the different stand of Maoists and the police, as the former were not prepared to deviate from their strategy of revolutionary struggles and the cult of violence whereas the latter were against the suspension of their operations against the ultras. The dialogue exercise in the state was continued by the Congress governments, but had been reversed on 17 August 2005 after the assassination of Congress Minister C. Narsi Reddy on 15 August 2005, while attending Independence Day function. In fact, the recalcitrance from the part of extremists on one hand and law-enforcement agencies on the other, created major stumbling block in peace negotiations to defuse large-scale violence perpetrated by extremist groups. Ironically, states like Chhattisgarh, Jharkhand, Orissa and parts of West Bengal are still bleeding due to Naxalite violence because of such deadlocks in the process of negotiations.

5

Human and Civil Rights of Marginalized Sections

From human and civil rights angle, it is pertinent to clearly recognize those marginalized and oppressive communities in our society which are the worst victims of human rights violations. In the present Indian context, different parameters are used to describe these sections on the basis of their socio-economic backwardness, living conditions or discrimination meted out by them in the society. Some commonly accepted parameters include: illiterate or semi-literate, landless and shelterless sections, especially of unorganized sectors devoid of any viable skills and knowledge that fetch marketable capital; bonded/child labourers; victims of caste/communal conflicts, development paradigms and human rights violations; and under trials and socially untouchables.

Taking these parameters into consideration, we can identify Dalits, tribals/Adivasis, poor women and children as the marginalized sections on whom day to day human rights violations take place. Dalits and Adivasis/ tribals comprise about one-fourth of India's population. Dalits constitute 16 per cent and Adivasis 8 per cent. About 80 per cent of Dalits and 92 per cent of Adivasis live in rural areas. Dalits continue to face wide-ranging economic and social disadvantages, day-to-day humiliation and degradation, denial of justice and violent atrocities in India. By and large the Dalit condition is marked by high incidence of poverty, low education, limited employment opportunities and marginalization in all spheres of public life. These deprivations are compounded by diverse types of violence that they are subject to.

The Planning Commission document, Development Challenges in Extremist Affected Areas (2008)[1] brought out certain important factors on the present condition of Dalits, Adivasis, women and other marginalized sections in Indian society. The proportion of SCs below the poverty line is around 38 per cent which is higher than the corresponding poverty ratio for the population as a whole (around 26 per cent). Similarly, the proportion of STs below the poverty line was 47.3 per cent in rural and 33.3 per cent in urban areas, which was again much higher than the poverty ratio for the population. The Dalits who were deprived of proper educational facilities for decades still remain educationally backward. This has adversely affected their employment facilities. Moreover, the incidence of landlessness is more among SCs as compared with other caste groups/communities. These facts indicate that the persistently high poverty of SC households is closely associated with low levels of ownership of capital assets like land, low levels of education and considerably lower diversification of avenues of employment.

Another crucial aspect is political marginalization. Conceptually and constitutionally, the Dalits like other sections have the political right to exercise their franchise. This naturally has contributed much to Dalit empowerment and in improving their status. Ironically, in many states, Dalits have been deprived of this right because of the dominating influence of money and muscle power in elections. The hard reality is that the reins of power have remained with the dominant sections of society, whether it be the upper castes or in recent years the middle castes. A major fallout of this political marginalization is the social discrimination and human rights violations. In the matters of residence, food, clothing, marriage and employment, Dalits continue to face many kinds of discrimination. Even untouchability, the most blatant form of social discrimination against Dalits, persists in many forms. A recent study[2] of untouchability in 565 villages in 11 states identified no less than 63 types of untouchabilities practiced in many villages of the country. Same is the case with human right violations. Large-scale human rights violations, crimes and atrocities have been perpetuated against the SCs in the rural areas. These pertain to civil rights (right to vote, right of access to public places, and so on), social rights (freedom of movement, access to education, and so on), economic rights (ownership of property, change in employment-operating businesses, joining labour unions, and so on) and political rights (participation in democratic governance). Dr. Ambedkar, the architect of Indian Constitution had rightly cautioned this contradiction as:

> We are entering into a life of contradictions. In politics, we will have equality. In our social and economic life we will have inequality. In politics, we will be recognizing one man, one vote, one value. In our social life, we shall by reasons of our social and economic structure continue to defy the principle of one man, one vote, and one value. If we continue to deny it for long, we shall do so by putting our political democracy at peril. We should remove this contradiction at the earliest possible moment or else those who suffer from inequality will blow up the structure of political democracy which this assembly has laboriously built up.[3]

Ironically, even after six decades, these contradictions still persist due to a plethora of socio-economic and political reasons and act as the breeding ground for organized discontentment and struggles by Dalit-tribal groups. The genesis of discontent among Dalits lies in the age-old, caste-based social order that condemns them to a life of deprivation, servility and indignity. The Constitution of India and various legislative and policy measures have created entitlements to undo this structure of oppression. But the traditionally privileged classes have had an undue influence on the process of implementation of these measures as a result of which these safeguards failed to safeguard the genuine interests of Dalits. The all-pervasive bureaucracy, predominantly dominated by the upper- and middle-class elite, remains insensitive to the plight of these sections and, on many occasions, defeats the governmental policies and programmes meant for their upliftment.

The plight of the tribals is also not much different. There are over 84 million tribal people in India. They are present almost in all states/union territories and located mostly in hilly and forest areas. The architects of the Constitution, being conscious of the distinct identity of the tribal communities and their habitat, provided certain articles exclusively devoted to the cause of the tribal people, including Articles 244/244A,[4] 275(1),[5] 342,[6] 338(A)[7] and 339.[8] Following these provisions in the Constitution aimed at ensuring social, economic and political equity, several specific legislations have been enacted by the central and state governments for the welfare and protection of tribal people and their tribal domain. In the seventies, a serious attempt to focus on the tribal population in the planning process was made in the form of a Tribal Sub-Plan strategy. The process of bringing all tribal-majority areas under the Fifth Schedule of the Constitution was also taken up. The 73rd and the 74th amendments to the Constitution of India, followed by the Provisions of Panchayats (Extension to Scheduled Areas) Act, 1996, popularly known as PESA, brought in a new model for self-government in the Fifth Schedule areas of the country. Despite the plethora of development plans, programmes and activities initiated in the tribal areas, the majority of STs still live in conditions of serious deprivation and poverty.

The tribal people have remained backward in all aspects of human development including education, health, nutrition, and so on. Apart from socio-economic deprivation, there has been a steady erosion of traditional tribal rights and their command over resources. In general, the contradiction between the tribal community and the state has become sharper, translating tribal areas into open conflict in many areas. Almost all over the tribal areas, including Nagaland, Manipur, Tripura, Assam, Jharkhand, Orissa, Chhattisgarh, Maharashtra, Andhra Pradesh and Kerala, tribal people seem to feel a deep sense of exclusion and alienation that has been manifesting itself in different forms. Even states like Kerala where there were radical land reforms as early as in late 1950s, have recently witnessed Adivasi/ tribal struggles demanding restoration of alienated tribal lands. The *Report of the Expert Group on Prevention of Alienation of Tribal Land and its Restoration* (Ministry of Rural development, Government of India, October 2004) pointed out that the socio-economic infrastructure among the tribal people is inadequate, thereby contributing to their disempowerment and deprivation. Such deprivation and neglect have led to serious malnutrition/starvation deaths, death of new born babies and dreaded diseases among tribals in many of their hamlets in Kerala.

Apart from poverty and deprivation in general, the causes of the tribal movements/struggles are many. The most important among them are absence of self-governance, forest policy, excise policy, land-related issues and multifaceted forms of exploitation, cultural humiliation and political marginalization. Land alienation, forced evictions from land and displacement also added to unrest. Failure to implement protective regulations in scheduled areas; absence of credit mechanism, leading to dependence on moneylenders and consequent loss of land; and often even violence by the state functionaries added to the problem.

In the famous report of the commissioner of SC/ST in 1988 (28th Report).[9] he attributed the violence related to both Dalits and STs to three causative factors. One, unresolved land disputes related to allotment of government lands or distribution of ceiling surplus lands to SC/ST persons. Two, tension and bitterness on the account of payment or underpayment of prescribed minimum wages. Three, resentment of upper castes over the manifestation of awareness among the SCs and STs about their rights and privileges, as enshrined in the Constitution and various other laws related to their welfare. These factors substantially contributed to the naked violation of human and civil rights of these sections.

All these factors were exploited by left-wing extremist groups to increase their support base among Dalits and Adivasis. The Expert Group which minutely studied these aspects in Naxalite-dominated states of Andhra Pradesh, Bihar, Chhattisgarh, Jharkhand and Orissa observed: 'The main support for the Naxalite Movement comes from dalits and adivasis'.[10] On the basis of the empirical studies of selected number of Naxalite-infested and developed districts in these states, the Expert Group identified the following parameters for the spread and consolidation of LWE in these states, especially among Dalits and tribals: (*a*) High share of SC/ST population; (*b*) low levels of literacy rates; (*c*) high level of Infant Mortality rate; (*d*) low level of urbanization; (*e*) high share of forest coverage; (*f*) high share of Agriculture labours; (*g*) low level of per-capita food grain production; (*h*) low level of road length per 100 sq. Km; (*i*) high level of rural households without banking facilities; and (*j*) high share of rural households without specific assets.

The findings of the Group in respect of the condition of women are also of much relevance when we analyse the human rights scenario of this marginalized section in Indian society. The report highlighted:

> The subjugation of women is another important aspect of the deeper maladies that afflict rural India and contribute to popular

unrest. In spite of formal equality with men under the law, Indian women continue to face wide-ranging disadvantages, whether it is in terms of property rights, workforce-participation, educational opportunities, and access to health care or political representation. India has some of the worst indicators of gender inequality in the world, including a very low female–male ratio, a major gender bias in literacy rates, and a low share of women in the labour force. Gender related development indicators such as maternal mortality rates and sex-selective abortion also shed a sobering light on the predicament of Indian women.[11]

Some real-time statistics give a true picture of the condition of women in India. As per Human Development Report 2006[12] by United Nations Development Program (UNDP), India's gender development index rank is 96 out of 136 countries for which the data exist. Similarly, the Human Development Report 2006[13] in a statistical appendix titled, Gender Empowerment Measures shows that the women workers in India on an average get only 31 per cent of the wages given to the men. The gravity of the situation could be properly appreciated if we realize that there are only four countries behind India out of 171, that is to say, Pakistan (29 per cent), Sudan (25 per cent), Swaziland (29 per cent), Tunisia (28 per cent) and Saudi Arabia (15 per cent) in this ranking. A number of factors—traditional, social, economic and political— have contributed to this situation. Basically, the Indian society, by and large, is yet to overcome traditional patterns of gender inequality and female subordination due dominating influences of archaic conventions, customs and practices. Imagine a society that attaches sacrosanctity to the inhuman practice of 'Sati' or 'devadasi system' or 'honour killing'[14] in 21st century! These are the acute forms of human rights violations which no civilized society can ever imagine. Such atrocious practices and the economic and social disadvantages of women in Indian society reflect a whole gamut of patriarchal norms and practices such as patrilineal inheritance, patrilocal residence, the gender division of labour, the gender segregation of public spaces and the discouragement of widow remarriage. The recent sad saga of brutal rapes, killing and molestation of women and infant girls in many states and the apparent failure of state superstructures to safeguard the life and dignity of women amply demonstrate the plight of Indian women in the present millennium.

The proper empowerment of women is the most effective weapon to check the increasing incidence of human rights violations against women in a patriarchal society. Certain global and national developments have recently taken place in this direction; the most significant being the intervention of United Nations. The UN General Assembly in July 2010 voted unanimously to create a UN entity for gender equality and employment of women named UN Women (UNW).[15] The new entity is meant to accelerate the progress in meeting the needs of women and girls worldwide. It aims to create a vibrant ethos, a valiant instrument to accelerate gender equality and women's empowerment and bring to a close discriminatory disparity. More significantly, the UN resolution has called for the appointment of an undersecretary general to head the UNW and the establishment of an executive board to provide intergovernmental support to and supervision of its operation. This move should be radically supported by every country and India should not lag behind in this task.

Similarly, the Millennium Development Goals Summit at the UN[16] held in September 2010 identified gender equality as a priority area in the development process. Within our country, the National Policy for the Empowerment of Women, 2001, was a landmark development in institutionalizing the gains of women's movement in the country. The objectives and goals of the above policy include the creation of an enabling environment for women through economic and social policies; active protection of rights; equal access to decision making and social sector needs, strengthening institutional support systems and legal machinery, and forging partnership with civil society. It is noteworthy that the policy incorporates all the concerns and issues that women's movement and NGOs have engaged over the past three decades: domestic violence, rape, poverty, conditions of work, employment, representation, support and solidarity networks, health, nutrition, credit, child care, education, housing, the adverse impact of globalization, property rights and so on. The implementation of this policy would definitely contribute to the empowerment of women and protection of their rights.

Just like women, the rights of children, especially of rural and poor background seldom figure prominently in country's agenda. Moreover, in India the general awareness about the rights of children among the adults and children is limited. A study report[17] in 1994 by Maheshwar Madan Lal revealed that overwhelming majority of children in India never asserted their rights and were ignorant of their fundamental rights due to lack of education. Similarly, the percentage of awareness among adults on these rights varied from 10 to 15 per cent, which is really a matter of concern in protecting these rights.

The above trend of increasing violation of human rights of children clearly reflected in the evaluation reports of various international bodies such as the UNICEF, Amnesty International, and International Commission on Human Rights, Commonwealth Human Rights Initiative and so on. Such violations go unabated, despite the fact the Government of India had ratified a number of UN conventions and declarations such as the Convention on the Rights of Child in 1992[18] and 1989[19] protecting the rights of children. The very basic right to life of children is violated in a number of situations such as communal and ethnic conflicts. While the adult fringe elements of different religions wage bloody riots, the children are often caught in the crossfire, raped, tortured or murdered because of their religion.

Another equally distressing trend is the denial of primary or elementary education to children. Over 60 million children are still out of schools, despite the government's ambitious plans such as 'Sarva Siksha Abhiyan'. The plight of girl, Dalit and indigenous children is more disturbing. In many rural and tribal-dominated areas, elementary education is a taboo for these sections in view of discrimination and social untouchability. Children of lower castes are subjected to discrimination at an early stage. The children in armed conflict or in terror/extremist-affected areas are the worst victims of excesses and violations. In many such areas, they are recruited as members of 'private army/suicide squad' of terror groups or enrolled to state-sponsored vigilante groups like *Salwa Judum*. There are over 500,000 conflict-induced internally displaced people, out of which majority are children.[20]

The problem of child labour is yet another serious threat to childhood. But the irony is that many children, their parents or teachers or civil society at large in rural and urban areas, are unaware of the rights of children. There is an urgent need to sensitize the people on these rights and main areas of violation. The people from all walks of life should be made aware of the best interests of children. For that purpose, civic action groups such as parents' bodies, cooperatives, residents' associations, Self Help Groups (SHGs), women's groups, student organizations, youth clubs, voluntary bodies and political parties should play a pro-active role. It is pertinent to note that since 1996, the Supreme Court of India made proper rehabilitation of child workers a legal requirement, and subsequently NHRC had successfully pressed some local governments to act. The bodies like NHRC should adopt a proactive role in matters like child labour without wait-ing for the directions of judiciary or the government.

Ironically, the approach of the government in sincerely fight-ing child/bonded labour is not much healthy. This was revealed in an exhaustive research study undertaken by the 'Human Rights Watch' in 2003 on the subject, Small Change: Bonded Child Labor in India's Silk Industry.[21] One of the main finding of this study was that the Indian government failed to protect the rights of hundreds of thousands of children who toil as virtual slaves in the country's silk industry. The reality is that child labour in the country with an alarming number of over 60 million is not con-fined to one particular sector or industry but rampant in almost all major areas of activity/industries such as carpet, glass and bangles, brass vessels, matches and fireworks, printing, textiles, hotels and restaurants, poultry and goat farming and so on.

Moreover, it is a well-researched truth that there exists a vicious circle of poverty and child labour as well as illiteracy and child labour. There also exists a clear parallel between child labour and adult unemployment in many sectors, as the former constitutes the cheapest and most vulnerable work force. Thus, only a multi-dimensional approach meant for Education for All (EFA), poverty alleviation and employment generation with the active involve-ment of all concerned stakeholders alone will help to contain child labour in Indian society. Such an approach should inevita-bly consist of awareness building and consciousness raising, com-munity participation, alternative and viable economic and social rehabilitation and enforcement of national and international legal instruments in relation to children. It is significant to note that Millennium Development Goals of UN envisage a paradigm shift on child rights protection with the active involvement of other agencies like UNICEF, UNDP, UNESCO, World Bank and ILO by linking up child labour with education, poverty alleviation and employment generation. Let us hope that such initiatives would definitely help to eliminate child/bonded labour from Indian society.

The above analysis of the general condition of major marginalized sections in the country leads us to one major finding that the development paradigm pursued since independence did not help to resolve discontent among marginalized sections of society. The Expert Group rightly observed:

> This is because the development paradigm as conceived by the policy makers has always been imposed on these communities, and therefore it has remained insensitive to their needs and concerns, causing irreparable damage to these sections. The benefits of this paradigm of development have been disproportionately cornered by the dominant sections at the expense of the poor, who have borne most of the costs. Development which is insensitive to the needs of these communities has invariably caused displacement and reduced them to a sub-human existence. In the case of tribes in particular it has ended up in destroying their social organisation, cultural identity, and resource base and generated multiple conflicts, undermining their communal solidarity, which cumulatively makes them increasingly vulnerable to exploitation.[22] (*Development in Extremist Affected Areas: An Expert Group Report to the Planning Commission*).

The report also rightly identified that the disturbing aspects of socio-economic context that prevails in large parts of the country may contribute to the political developments including the growth of LWE. Our empirical study in Andhra Pradesh has corroborated these findings, especially the social and economic backwardness of the marginalized and the rampant human rights violations of these sections.

The Dalits in Andhra Pradesh constitute 16.19 per cent of the total population. Out of which, 70 per cent of the Dalits are in the Telangana region of the state. Out of 69 subgroups of Dalits, Madigas (with 18 communities, predominantly in Telangana); Malas (25 communities), mainly in Coastal Andhra and Rayalaseema; Rellis (12 communities in Coastal Andhra); and Adi Andhras (4 communities) are prominent by nomenclature. The intercommunity conflict among Dalits, especially between Malas and Madigas is a major factor that works against the overall development of Dalits in the state. The Malas, who are the most advanced, enjoy 70–80 per cent of the reservation facilities extended to SCs in government jobs as well as admission in educational institutions, despite the fact that Madigas numerically outnumber them. This apparent contradiction which was endorsed by Shri K. Ramachandra Raju Commission in1993,[23] which probed into the socio-economic status of major SC groups (Madigas and Malas) vis-à-vis the extent of reservation facilities enjoyed by them, had opened a new controversy in the state, adversely affecting Dalit unity.

The Dalits are the backbone of state's rural economy as their overwhelming majority is engaged in agriculture or allied occupations. Despite their significant role in rural economy, they are the most deprived, underprivileged and exploited sections in the society. Micro-level studies conducted in Chittoor and Nalgonda districts revealed that some of the causative factors for the general unrest and violation of human rights of Dalits in the country, such as unresolved land disputes, non-payment of minimum wages and reaction of upper castes against Dalit resurgence were found applicable in the case of Dalits in the state as well. Naked violation of human rights of these sections still prevail in the rural areas in the form of untouchability, widespread practice of separate cups for Dalits in tea stalls; restrictions on using footwear, shirts or *talapaga* (headgear), tilak or ornaments; forced caste-related jobs such as disposing dead animals/manual scavenging; different types of bonded labour; the denial of minimum wages and so on. In some parts of Telangana, the *doras* (landlords) legitimized their superior position over Dalits by superimposing and maintaining caste-based inequality. Caste perceptions played a significant role in establishing the new power structure in which they control the economy, politics, society in general and the people.

Among the various causative factors, Dalit resurgence initiated during 1970s at the instance of Dalit Mahasabha was the most crucial one that led to a series of human rights violation against Dalits, particularly in Coastal Andhra Districts of Krishna, Guntur, Prakasam, West and East Godavari. The Dalits, especially the younger generation, were not prepared to be content to bemoan their fate, but demanded land, economic betterment, education, employment and above all social equality and dignity. This had sharpened the rift between Dalits and 'rural elite' who with their political clout and socio-economic advancement tried to contain the resurgence of Dalits. The outcome was organized mass attacks against Dalits wherever their self-assertion was widespread and a mass phenomenon as in the Krishna and Godavari basins of Coastal Andhra.

The massacre of Dalits at Karamchedu (Prakasam district) in 1985 and Chundur (Guntur district) in 1991 by upper castes belonging to Khamma and Reddys, respectively, was the culmination of such efforts of self-assertion of Dalits and intolerance shown by the privileged castes. A case study of Chundur massacre clearly demonstrated the above facts. Chundur, the Mandal headquarters was located about 15 km from Tenali town (Guntur district) with an area of 18 sq. miles and having a population of 5,800, with almost equal strength of Dalits and upper castes. The most dominant among the upper castes was Reddys (800 families), who owned most of the land, followed by Telaga (225 families), Brahmins (25 families) and Vysya (15 families). Among the Dalits, the largest group was Malas (401 families) followed by Madigas (100 families). Out of the nearly 2,400 acres of cultivable land in the village, the Reddys owned about 1200 acres; Telagas, 250 acres; the Brahmins over 100 acres; and Vysya about 65 acres. The Dalits owned hardly 90 acres. Except for about 100 acres that were given on tenancy to the Dalits, most of the land was in possession of upper castes. There were only few landlords in the village. Those villagers who possessed more than two hectares of land were only around 85, whereas majority of them (1,100) owned land less than one hectare. However, the upper-caste people of the village owned around 2,600 acres of land in the adjoining village.

The socio-economic development in the coastal areas, including Chundur, had been rapid. Canal irrigation, multiple cropping and increasing social wealth contributed to the transformation of Dalit occupations. The age-old *vettichakiri* (bonded labour) had given way to *rythukooli* (wage farm labour) which in turn had been replaced by a system of *kavuludhari* (tenancy) farming as a common mode of earning for Dalits. The extent of socio-economic transformation had also reflected in the fact that many of the Dalit women had given up menial house jobs in favour of work in agricultural fields and so on during late 1980s. Education was another factor which contributed to the resurgence of Dalits. There were three primary schools and one high school in the village. Nearly 3,000 people in the village, including a good number of women, knew how to read and write. The literacy among Dalits was also comparatively high: 15 Dalits had done post graduation, many of them were graduates and over 200 had passed matriculation. The better education had facilitated the Dalits to secure jobs in the railway, post and telegraph (P&T) and revenue offices. The mobility in geographical terms, with a rail line connecting Chundur with Tenali, had led to the broadening of Dalit perspective, leading to criticism and occasional challenge of caste dominance in the village. Added to this was their political clout with their representatives getting elected to Mandal Praja Parishad and Mandals as presidents? Over a period of time, there was an all-round change in the lifestyle, perception and attitude of Dalits that clearly reflected their self-assertion. This transformation was seen as a threat to the authority and superiority of 'rural elite' represented by upper castes. Thus, a minor incident like an educated Dalit youth stretching his leg on a seat occupied by an upper caste boy in a cinema hall led to the social boycott of Dalits, which later culminated into a carnage.

The post-Chundur period witnessed the emergence of active Dalit human rights NGOs, which strongly espouse the human rights issues through networking of NGOs in the Dalit front and action-oriented programmes to build up strong movement against violations of human rights. Their strategy is all-round attack on 'untouchability', which apparently is the root cause of 'Dalit paradigm' influencing the sociocultural exploitation of Dalits. Special emphasis was laid on playing a proactive role in Dalit issues, for which these NGOs were asked to recognise the struggles/movements by Dalits and indigenous population; actively get involved in these processes by sharing resources of information, infrastructure and finances; and finally become a part of liberation process.

Prominent Dalit NGOs in the state like National Campaign on Dalit Human Rights (NCDHR)[24] led by Paul Divakar of Chittoor have come out with plan of action for the resurgence of Dalits for fully safeguarding their civil and human rights. In a personal interview with the author, he explained the action plan of NCHDR for Dalit empowerment in Andhra. The salient features of this plan include: (a) transformation from target groups to action groups through which the present system of tailor-made development programmes for Dalits, which defeats the concepts of self-determination, leadership, need and priorities, should be changed; (*b*) Dalit participation in power (including network groups and NGOs) so that they can play a decisive role; (*c*) overcoming disabilities of caste that adversely affect self-confidence, positive self-image and balanced perspective should be overcome through serious measures; (*d*) specific training for human resources development of Dalit groups for improving positive self-image, the norms and values of non-exploitative community; (*e*) linking up, developing and sustaining macro-linkages in order to involve in major Dalit issues and problems through networks and so on; (*f*) viable geopolitical movement with a view to break the narrow geographical barriers that have resulted in efforts not reaching the threshold effect; (*g*) research on Dalit issues and topics, especially sound intervention strategies to protect interests; (*h*) atrocity monitoring cells to effectively monitor Dalit human rights violations; (*i*) projection of Dalit issues at national and international level without any bias or prejudice; and (*j*) bringing a Dalit perspective in both government policies and NGO–donor interventions . Through such proactive and affirmative campaigns/programmes, the NGOs and Dalit organizations envisage the total transformation of Dalits, which would not only put an end to their socio-economic exploitation, but may also enable them to play a crucial role in the political field with their numerical strength of over 16 per cent of total population in the state.

NCDHR strongly espoused the question of caste discrimination in total variance with the official line of NDA government during the meeting of UN Committee for the Elimination of Racial Discrimination (CERD) held in Geneva[25] in August 2002. The argument of the government was that the concept of race in India, as recognized by the Constitution, is distinct from caste and the two are mentioned separately as prohibited grounds for discrimination. Thus, the international community should not equate caste issues concerning Dalits with racial discrimination. Through this stand, the government tried to cover up the hard reality that the discrimination in the form of untouchability, worse than racial discrimination in many countries, is all pervasive against Dalits in the Indian society. The plight of the large majority of Dalits in India reminds us of the sad note of James Baldwin, the African-American writer in one of his popular works, *Letter to My Nephew on the One Hundredth Anniversary of Emancipation*:

You were born where you were born and faced a future that you faced because you were Black and for no other reason. The limits of your ambition were, thus expected to be set for ever. You were born in a society spelt out with brutal clarity in as many ways as possible that you were a worthless human being. You were not expected to aspire to excellence; you were expected to make peace with mediocrity.[26]

In their hearts of hearts, the overwhelming majority of Dalits aspires that untouchability and other forms of discrimination based on descent practiced in India should be equated with or included in racial discrimination and other related intolerance. The attempt of NCDHR was to project such a line before the international community, especially before the human rights NGOs and thereby mobilize opinion in favour of Dalit issues in India.

The Dalit dilemma in Andhra Pradesh and, for that matter, for whole of India needs to be properly tackled for improving the country's record in human rights field, as Dalit population in India are the worst victims of rights violations. The Bhopal Dalit Declaration of 2002[27] was a major landmark in the direction of finding viable solutions in improving the condition of Dalits, as also their human rights scenario. The Conference posed two major questions: Is it possible to adopt the American model by developing diversified assets, capital, entrepreneurship and skills as Americans had done by giving a share to African-Americans in all kinds of national assets? Is it possible to create a democratic civil society which would strengthen political democracy by creating conditions of social equality that become the backbone on national development?

While examining these two questions in the Indian context, it is an established fact that whether in agriculture or industry or other vocations, bulk of the creative labour power comes from Dalits. If this power is properly harnessed with the provision to own capital, it will definitely give a boost to our economy. The Bhopal Declaration made it clear that without a share for the liberalized private capital for Dalits, the state and civil society are bound to crack. In other words, the newly mobilized Dalits can be given access to the gains of market economy. Through this process Dalits can, in the long run, socially and economically empower themselves. The state has a crucial role to play in this regard. For example, the huge revenue generated by the state through massive disinvestment of public sector units, otherwise not earmarked for any specific purpose other than containing inflation or for other populist schemes, should be allocated for social causes including Dalit upliftment. Some of these funds could be used for general investment in primary education, health and housing, especially in rural areas where there are sizable Dalit population. Similarly, portion of these resources could be used to set up an entrepreneurship fund for qualifying Dalits, as in the case of such special funds earmarked for qualifying women in some states. Third, it could provide money to Dalits in the form of scholarships and grants which could be redeemed at suitable qualifying private institutions, especially in sunrise sector. Similarly, a true political democracy based on social equality and social justice could be established only by demolishing caste-oriented practices and discrimination encouraged by various religions in the name of spirituality and religiosity which creates wrong images in the civil society. The increasing incidents of 'honour killing' of high-caste teenage girls who marry Dalit youth by their own parents, the sacrosanctity attached to such gruesome practices by their caste/community and the indifference of political set-up to sternly deal with such dastardly acts are reflective of the reality that a political democracy on egalitarian lines is still a myth in Indian context. In that process the biggest casualty is nothing but human rights of Dalits.

Just like Dalits, the tribals in Andhra Pradesh are the worst victims of human rights violations. Out of the estimated 50.24 lakhs tribal population in Andhra (around 6.6 per cent of the total population) comprising 33 communities, two-third live in the hilly and scheduled areas of Srikakulam, Karimnagar, Warangal, Khammam, West and East Godavari districts and Adilabad. Mahaboob Nagar and Karimnagar are other two districts with major tribal population. The prominent tribes of the state are Gonds, Lambadas, Chenchus, Koya-Konda, Yanadis and so on. There are around 6,000 notified tribal villages in Andhra known as 'scheduled areas' under a special order in 1953. These areas are governed by the provisions of the Fifth Schedule of Indian Constitution in order to protect their rights and privileges as well as the cultural identity. The tribal-dominated districts were once the citadels of left-wing extremist movement, which indicates the socio-economic backwardness of the area coupled with massive exploitation and violation of fundamental and human rights of the tribals for many decades.

As in the case of Dalits, the human rights violations of tribal community in Andhra are closely intertwined with the land issues and their increasing loss of identity. For the overwhelming majority of tribals, the land and forest are their main sources of livelihood and deprivation of these sources virtually makes them helpless to survive in the fast changing socio-economic set-up in which their only alternative is to forgo their indigenous character and cultural identity. Once they compromise with their indigenous culture, they easily become victims of exploitation such as organized trafficking in women, illicit brewing of liquor, drug peddling and so on at the instance of non-tribals and their agents.

The extent of land alienation prevalent in the tribal belt of the state is phenomenal and it is true of all districts where there are sizeable tribal populations. At onetime the entire cultivable land was held by tribals in the tribal belts located in the far flung, underdeveloped remote areas of hilly tracts. Now, the tribal land-holding has drastically come down and is to the tune of around 6 lakhs acres in the scheduled areas, taking into consideration the legal titles (patta) held by them. The extent of land illegally occupied by non-tribals through 'benami' transactions or falsification of revenue records and so on is not fully traceable. In fact, over 55 per cent of the land in scheduled areas comprising Srikakulam, Karimnagar, Warangal, Khammam, West and East Godavari, Adilabad and parts of Mahaboob Nagar districts is owned by non-tribals, who constitute 48 per cent of the population in the areas. The land alienation in sub-plan areas is even more devastating and there is no effective legal protective cover. The tribal land has been alienated mainly through 'benami' transfers, acquisition for developmental projects and long-term tenancy for the cultivation of commercial crops.

The process of displacement of tribals in their homeland and interrelated socio-economic issues constitute one of the major areas of human rights violations. This has been accentuated by other factors such as gradual process of deforestation, commercial exploitation of forests for the urban needs of the elite and the export of forest-based raw materials. At present, there are 10 major and medium forest-based industries in the state and their raw-material requirements are met with an agreement with the government authorizing to cut the forests. Neither the availability of forests nor the potential and use are taken into consideration. Added to this are the problems of illegal felling of trees and large-scale organized mining activities that go unabated because of the nexus between the forest/mining department officials and business/smuggling syndicates backed by powerful political leaders. Another major issue of decreasing access to forest resources for the sustenance of tribal communities is the increasing state control over the forest resources. Irony is that in certain tribal belt of Telangana, the tribals cannot even lay their hand on some herbs and plants categorized as rare medicinal plants! Such issues have created a loss of livelihood and survival of tribal communities, severely affecting their access to timber, fuel wood, minor forest produce and fodder needs.

On the other hand, in the search for alternative areas for subsistence and livelihood, the tribals are subjected to extreme exploitation and naked violation of their basic rights. Tendu-leaf collection is an important source of exploitation in tribal/forest areas. Apart from abysmally low wages, the tribals are forced to give a substantial part of their collection as portion of customary payment to the contractors, besides the bribe to the forest officials. Another area of exploitation/harassment is country liquor (arrack sector). In Andhra, the contract for brewing country liquor is auctioned off to the highest bidder every year in what is called excise auction. Over the years, the 'toddy/arrack business' has grown up by leaps and bounds with the emergence of powerful liquor barons who run their own 'private armies' to smoothly run their business in many districts. Because of the steep hike in the price of liquor, many tribal hamlets are engaged in brewing their own liquor through a process known as 'Ippa sara' (liquor made out of Ippa/Mahuva flowers). The 'private armies' of liquor contractors in certain districts like Visakhapatnam and Karimnagar resort to the constant raid of tribal hamlets and torture of the tribals engaged in such activities. Besides, the police and excise officials, influenced by liquor barons, raid such hamlets and torture tribals in the name of illegal brewing of liquor.

In many cases, developmental projects do not reach the tribal population, but only deplete their sources of livelihood and increase their miseries. For example, a check dam across Pendilipadagu stream in Bhimavaram village of Addatigala

Mandal of East Godavari district led immediately to the process of leasing land to non-tribals in view of improved irrigation facilities. Thus, much of the benefit of the check dam went in favour of non-tribals. Similarly, a reservoir in the river Maddigeda (major tributary of Yeleru river in East Godavari district) was constructed in 1982 at Addatigala at a cost of ₹3.98 crores with the main objective to provide irrigation water to tribal lands, but its benefits are now mainly reaped by non-tribals; a bulk of Yeleru river water from the tribal areas of East Godavari district is being canalized to Vaizag Steel Plant.

Another area of concern is the displacement of tribals through construction of big dams. The state has almost two dozen major dams. Official data in respect of six of these dams indicated that these dams together had displaced around 5.5 lakh persons, majority of them are tribals. To cite an example, the famous Nagarjunasagar dam had displaced 5,098 families of which 36 per cent belong to Lambada tribe. Similarly, in the case of Srisailam Project, 80 per cent of the 20,728 displaced families belonged to tribals and other backward castes, with 75 per cent having no land at all. In the case of Polavaram dam, over 30,000 families with an estimated population of around 130,000 were displaced, 45 per cent of these displaced persons were tribals. The rehabilitation and resettlement of displaced tribals have been neglected in majority of cases, as a result of which the plight of these sections had been aggravated. In many instances the newly developed rehabilitation centres/colonies are bereft of basic amenities like power, drinking water and so on, whereas the resettled tribals are devoid of any viable job or occupation as source of their livelihood. The result is that many among them become vulnerable to social/criminal evils like illicit brewing of liquor, prostitution, child labour and so on.

The 'neo-cultural' invasion of the indigenous culture, values and traditions of the tribals by systematically demolishing their existing institutions (family and community) and values (equality and equal status for women) should be interpreted as a major onslaught on their cultural/human rights. This leads to unhealthy influences in the tribal community such as exploitation of tribal women by non-tribals, increasing number of 'unmarried mothers' and 'orphaned children', lack of community bonds and social evils like dowry system and moral conflicts.

Another matter of serious concern is devaluation of tribal values and division of tribal community on religious/belief lines leading to intra- and inter-tribe conflicts and tensions. Such issues are the breeding grounds for easy subversion of tribals, growth of extremism and militancy and spread of ideologies like secessionism or separatism or their further alienation from the mainstream. One of the most distressing trends is the organized efforts by fundamentalist and revivalist groups to use illiterate and poverty-stricken tribals as potential tools in perpetrating violence against members of other community/castes during communal riots or ethnic conflicts. The leaders of these fringe groups ingeniously subvert the minds of poor tribals and create cleavages within the community, highlighting the alleged social or economic disparities. The venom unleashed by these elements through such orchestrated campaign and propaganda, sometimes with the tacit support of the administration and law-enforcement agencies, precipitated into hatred and vengeance and led to macabre killings, looting and rape of innocent people.

The study revealed that the human rights of tribals can be safeguarded only through their planned sociocultural and economic development. The policy of the government that tribals should be brought to mainstream would be materialized through the implementation of such a development strategy focusing on their all-round development. Ironically, government's efforts in this direction could not meet with any major success. No doubt, the government is spending crores of rupees for the socio- economic, cultural and educational advancement of these communities for which agencies like Integrated Tribal Development Agency (ITDA) had been constituted as early as 1970s. Apart from government agencies, nongovernmental bodies like International Fund for Agricultural Development (IFAD), a UN specialized agency based in Rome, which seek to combat hunger and rural poverty by increasing food production and income and improving health, nutrition and educational standards had also stepped into the field of tribal development in the state as early as 1990s. IFAD had sanctioned ₹770 million for four tribal districts for a period of seven years (1991–1998) with an additional sanction of ₹1.85 billion crores to five more tribal-dominated districts. The pertinent question is where did all these funds go? Many social researchers are unanimous in their view that if 50 per cent of the total funds sanctioned/spent by the governments and NGOs since 1970 had gone to the actual beneficiaries, the scheduled areas of the state and people thereof should have become the most advanced. But the tragedy was that only less than 5 per cent of these funds reached these most ignorant and marginalized sections. (According to the empirical study of one Hyderabad-based NGO, around 2 per cent of the developmental funds only reached these sections.[28]).The anachronism of this developmental pattern and the fate of the tribals were well focused in the words of a local tribal leader as: 'When roads are there, there are no culverts, when culverts are there, roads are washed off. Then, what to speak of public conveyance? There are primary health centres, but no doctors or medicines. There are schools in the villages, but no teachers. There are bore wells, but no water. ITDA offices are here and there, but no officials'.[29]

An action plan at the instance of state and well-organized NGOs—instead of stereotyped developmental schemes by various state departments—alone can help to mitigate the problems of tribals. According to authentic studies, over 93 per cent of tribals in the country are engaged in agriculture and allied activities, more than two-third being cultivators. These Adivasi/tribal farmers are subjected to myriad forms of exploitation by the highly interlocked non-tribal axis of power that dominates the land, land lease, labour, credit and input markets. The exploitation of tribals by this powerful axis through exorbitant rate of interest on loans, forced sale of their output to the creditors at a throwaway price and last but not the least bonded labour to the creditors/rural elite is so intense that majority of the tribals lease out land in distress on most unfavourable terms, which ultimately reaches the hands of landed gentry. What is the solution to overcome this tribal predicament? Two aspects are important. First, the constitutional right of tribals to own and possess their land should be fully protected. Second, state-sponsored efforts to improve the productivity of their agriculture-based ventures should be taken. For that purpose, massive public investment is required in tribal areas for specific watershed and micro-irrigation programmes with renewed thrust for dry-land agriculture, use of high-yielding varieties of seeds and optimal land-use planning. Huge stock of foodgrain lying unused in FCI godowns should be put to urgent use to finance such projects. The income generated as a result of such investment will lead to increased offtake from Public Distribution System (PDS), lowering the burden of food subsidy. Every effort should be made to save income through Self Help Thrift Groups (SHTG), linked to Public Sector Undertakings (PSU) banks, whose outreach along with that of PDS should be greatly extended to tribal hinterlands. The government's new subsidy scheme of direct payment to the beneficiaries through banking channels should be vigorously pursued in respect of tribals so that rampant corruption and malpractices in the PDS in tribal blocks could be minimized.

Another equally important task is active involvement of tribals in forest reforms whose success depends largely on the proactive and sincere approach of tribals. This naturally demands a major shift, away from the current bureaucratic style of functioning of Forest Department, especially of the JFM programme, towards a genuinely community forest-protection initiative under the leadership of the Gram Sabha or other local self-governing bodies. The state with the active involvement of NGOs should promote alternative technologies of energy and housing that would reduce dependence of local communities on forest for fire wood, timber for constructions and so on. State-sponsored co-operatives of landless tribals should be formed for processing and marketing of various non-timber forest produce. However, the success of these programmes depends on the progressive empowerment of tribals, so that they can effectively take over the leadership of the development process. Here comes the crucial role of grassroots level NGOs. They must assist in preparing a group of local youth who are technically empowered to manage these schemes. They would also function as watchdogs ensuring accountability of the state and NGOs working in that area and build networks that are pro-tribal, pro-women and pro-poor, so that a new leadership can be provided to local self-governing bodies.

Such initiatives are vital in the case of empowerment of women and safeguarding their basic rights. The Left parties in 1960s and 1970s built a strong women's movement in Andhra, which was given a new direction by women autonomous groups that spearheaded historic 'anti-arrack movement'[30] in 1990s. Yet the ground-level human rights scenario pertaining to women in the state was far from satisfactory as revealed by the study. The landed gentry in many parts of rural Andhra piously followed the feudal culture that regarded women as an object of pleasure and as commodity. However, the regional and mainstream parties that were in power, from time to time, outwardly preached for gender equality and empowerment of women. Though some cosmetic measures like a bill giving equal property rights to women and a university meant exclusively for women and so on had been initiated, plight of majority of women, especially in rural areas continues to be one of exploitation, gender inequality, denial of opportunities and so on.

As any violence against women is interpreted as violation of human rights (Vienna Declaration, 1993), extent of such violence/violations are high in the state. A case study[31] in respect of offences/atrocities against women (1991–1997) clearly demonstrated the above trend. During this period, there were 2,955 murders; 4,917 rapes; 14,261 molestations; 3,321 kidnapping/abduction; 363 dowry murders and 2,153 dowry deaths. Almost all these offences showed an upward trend during this period, despite the concerted efforts by police to curb the offences against women. The rural tribal or Dalit women were the victims of rape in more than 70 per cent of the rape cases. The increased awareness among women/public on the existence of laws preventing offences against women, coupled with their readiness to approach police, mainly contributed to the increased number of cases of harassment, dowry, abetment of suicide and bigamy. This was indicated by many samples during the course of the study.

One distressing trend was the violence perpetrated by law-enforcing agencies against women, particularly in Telangana districts. The incident of rape of Ms Ramejebee[32] and the murder of her husband (1979), gang rape of Parvathamma (1983)[33] and last but not the least the abduction and gang rape of Hussainee Bee (1998) exposed that law-enforcing agencies are not free from the influences of feudal and colonial culture which treated women as mere 'commodity'. Such isolated cases of atrocities against women by the protectors of law had been used as a powerful propaganda weapon by extremists and other groups to discredit police.

The growing violence against women is only one side of the rights' violations. There are other areas of violations such as sexual exploitation, prostitution, female foeticide and so on, which reflect the low status of women in the society and the failure of civil society to protect their rights. Traditions, superstitions and obscurantist practices and customs also play a major role on the exploitation of women. In the remote villages of Telangana, parents still dedicate their prepubescent daughters to goddess Yellamma. Unmarried girls dedicated to village deities, forced to remain unmarried throughout their life, for no fault of their own, take up the age-old profession of prostitution and end their lives in utter agony and misery. They are known by different names— devadasis in Nizamabad; yoginis in Medak; basvis or basvinis in Kurnool bordering Karnataka. Their total number is in between 5,000–6,000.

No government can eradicate such social evils which are inter-linked with poverty, customs and traditions. Added to this is the 'social sanction' accorded to such practices by the community. Many voluntary organizations had come forward to rehabilitate these hapless women. For example, Sanskar Plan International, an NGO based at Vani in Nizamabad district, was successful in the rehabilitation of around 2,000 yoginis in that district by launching a special drive at a cost of around ₹1.20 crores. Subsequently, they extended their programmes to Medak district to rehabilitate over 1,000 yoginis there. One major handicap of NGOs working in this sector is the lack of powers as the governments do not empower the NGOs to take up such issues. The state government had their own programmes like Jeevan Jyothi launched in 1995. As per this programme, ₹10,000 would be deposited in the name of every identified victim in the nearest bank with the provision that she could utilize the interest amount for livelihood. But the reality is that social evils like prostitution cannot be eradicated through financial help alone. What is needed is creation of awareness among victims, proper rehabilitation through alternate employ-ment and financial help and acceptance of the victims by civil society. For that purpose, joint programs/campaigns by the gov-ernment and NGOs are necessary.

The children especially from rural and poor background are subjected to different types of right violations. Denial of basic pri-mary education, child/bonded labour and sexual exploitation are some common areas of right violations pertaining to children. The study unfolded these issues in Andhra Pradesh.

The State accounts for the highest number of child labour in the country, one of the worst forms of human rights violations in any civil society. According to official statistics, around 1,700,000 children are working in Agriculture, manufacture and processing, consumer, live-stock and forestry, trade and commerce, transportation, mining and quarrying. The maximum number of child labour is in Hyderabad/Ranga Reddy district followed by Mehaboobnagar. In Yedira village at Jarcherla centre in Mehaboobnagar district, the feudal practice of children working as 'cattle grazers' under landlords for 2/3 years to clear the debts of their parents ranging from ₹2,500 to ₹4,000, had been in practice for many years.

Poverty alone is not the sole factor for the child labour in the State. Rao (1980) through his study on the extent of child labour particularly in the Agricultural sector showed that certain traditional practices in rural areas prompted many families to send their wards for labour to the land lords for getting favours from the latter for the tenancy of lands, irrigation water etc. Low wages, unorganized nature of child workers and their limitations to bargain with their employees for better conditions are other facets of child labour in agrarian sector. Rani & Singh (1983) in their study on child labour in 28 Restaurants and other commercial establishments in Warangal city also identified the poor wage structure, absence of any norms on jobs and above all the willingness of parents to send their children for any work-hazardous and non-hazardous- as the major trends in this sector. COVA, a Hyderabad based NGO in their study on child labour in the old city of Hyderabad (1996) however, identified poverty, illiteracy and more number of children in the family as the major factors for child labour particularly in Muslim community. Though majority of child workers earned income ranging from ₹300 to ₹800 per month neither they nor their parents complained about the low wages. Similarly around 28 per cent of children felt primary education as luxury for affluent classes and were not eager to have such education. In the course of interaction with child labours in Restaurants/commercial establishments etc in Hyderabad, Vijayawada, Warangal and Visakapattanam, such trends have been noticed. Many of them were proud of their mere earnings for their poverty-stricken families in the form of monthly wages and were less concerned on their future.

An inter-related issue is the case of street children—who run away from problems at home or born on the streets. The large cities like Hyderabad, Vijayawada, Guntur and Visakapattanam, account for the largest number of such children whose estimated strength is over 1.5 lakhs. Vijayawada alone has more than 25,000 such children. The rehabilitation of these children is an important agenda for NGOs and human rights groups. A number of NGOs are involved in the rehabilitation of child labour and street children. Sri Krishana Chaithanya Vidhyatharh Vidhyavaharh (SKCVV) started in Vijyawada during 1987 by Mathew Norton, once a drug addict from London, Navjyothi Balbhavan (Vijayawada) SIDUR, M.V. Foundation (both in Hyderabad) etc are some leading NGOs in the field. The State government had also initiated a program 'back to school' to deal with child labour. The children who have never gone to school or school drop-outs are picked up and taught lessons in 1067 social welfare centers. In 1997 under Dr Ambedkar Jayanti Scheme, around 42,000 children were covered with the help of 1,660 teachers and 385 social workers. The second phase of the project covered 105,000 child labours. such as ' back to school' or primary education through social education centers have limitations to effectively fight child labour especially when the sizeable section of these children have less inclination towards basic education. Such programs should be linked to financial incentives to child labours/families or vocational training which may enable them to takeup new jobs. Coordinated approach between the government and NGOs is needed for the success of such schemes. Meanwhile, the enforcement agencies should strictly enforce the various legislations banning child labour.

6

How to Tackle Left-Wing Extremism?

The study has unequivocally revealed that the LWE and the interrelated human/civil rights issues continue to be the most challenging task for the country in the present century. The political executive is fully aware of the seriousness of the challenge as manifest from the statements of the prime minster and senior ministers on a number of occasions. However, the crucial question is as how a permanent solution to LWE could be arrived at? Even at conceptual level, serious differences exist among political parties/ leaders, policymakers, police functionaries and senior bureaucrats. There is one strong school of thought that LWE threat should be treated as a basic law-and-order issue or a serious challenge to the internal security and as such it should be treated with an iron hand by fully utilizing the logistics and resources of the state and its superstructures. This school highlights the West Bengal experiment of early 1970s, when the first phase of this violent movement could be effectively contained or eliminated by resorting to such strong-arm methods. On the other hand, according to another school of thought, the Naxalite movement has to be recognized as a political movement with a strong base among the landless and poor peasantry and marginalized sections. Our empirical study of the problem in states like Andhra Pradesh proved that there is substantial ground-level basis for this argument. They argue that its emergence and growth needs to be contextualized in the social conditions and experience of people who form a part of it. Though its professed long-term ideology is capturing state power by force, in its day-to-day manifestation, it is to be looked upon as basically a fight for social justice, equality, protection and local development.

The union government in its status paper on LWE (2005)[1] had conceptually accepted the line of approach of these schools, while emphasizing the need of strongly dealing with Naxalite violence. Basically, it has to be recognized that no state could remain as a silent spectator to a situation of seizure of power through armed struggle when the Constitution provides for change of government through democratic process. The state has also the responsibility to safeguard the lives and properties of all citizens. Thus, the action plan of the centre inter alia included: (*a*) taking stern action against the Naxalites indulging in violence; (*b*) addressing the problem simultaneously on political, security and development fronts in a holistic manner; (*c*) effective interstate coordination in dealing with the problem; (*d*) prioritizing faster socio-economic development in the Naxal-affected or prone areas; (*e*) supplementing the efforts and resources of the affected states on both security and development fronts; (*f*) promoting local resistance groups against the Naxalites; (*g*) using mass media to highlight the futility of Naxal violence and the loss of life and property caused by them; (*h*) proper surrender and rehabilitation policy for the Naxalites; and (*i*) affected states will not have any peace dialogue with the Naxal groups, unless the latter agree to give up violence.

Not only that, the centre's strategy to deal with left-wing extremist threat could not meet with any major success, but also that its two aspects, namely promoting local resistance groups and no dialogue or negotiations with extremists till they unilaterally denounce violence evoked sharp controversy, especially at the instance of civil/human rights activists. The formation of state-sponsored groups like *Salwa Judum* in Chhattisgarh opened a Pandora's box of issues which ultimately led to the intervention of the apex court with a historic judgment to scrap the force. It is equally true that LWE or similar movements that are the offshoot of socio-economic and developmental issues cannot be permanently solved through state-sponsored oppressive or violent means or state vigilantism. For violence by the state will breed more violence and bloodshed by the weak, frustrated and helpless radical group. Long ago US President Eisenhower rightly observed:

Every gun that is made, every warship launched, every rocket fired signifies—in the final sense—a theft from those who hunger and are not fed, those who are cold and not clothed. This world in arms is not spending money alone. It is spending the sweat of its labourers, the genius of its scientists, and the hopes of its children.[2]

The Expert Group in their study on the development challenges in extremist-affected areas rightly commented on the wider implications of such strategy as:

Encouragement of vigilante groups such as Salwa Judum and herding of hapless tribals in make-shift camps with dismal living conditions, removed from their habitat and deprived of livelihood as a strategy to counter the influence of the radical left is not desirable. It delegitimizes politics, dehumanizes people, degenerates those engaged in their 'security', and above all represents abdication of the State itself. It should be undone immediately and be replaced by a strategy which positions an empowered task force of specially picked unresponsive officials to execute all protection and development programmes for their benefit and redressing people's grievances. This is the best strategy to eliminate the influence of radical left groups.[3]

Similarly, the centre's stand against process of 'negotiations' with the extremists has only made the entire issue more complex and complicated with stepped-up violence and depredations by the extremists, in which security personnel and civilian population suffered major casualties. This approach is inconsistent with the government's stand vis-à-vis other militant groups in the country like Naga rebels, ULFA, Bodo militants and the insurgents of J&K. In fact, negotiation approach is used the world over to tackle insurgencies democratically. It will cause the least possible injury to the people caught in the conflict. The government has more than once conveyed its willingness to hold talks with any group which is prepared to come to the negotiating table. Why a different approach to the Naxals? The doors of negotiations should be kept open.

The process of negotiations should not come in the way of the state's efforts in strengthening the law-enforcement machinery in the affected areas. Some of the suggested measures could be: additional police stations/outposts in the affected areas; filling up the police vacancies and improving the police–people ratio; sophisticated weapons for the police; training to the personnel in counter-insurgency, including protection of fundamental rights and human rights; incentive allowance for personnel posted in affected areas; and leadership of a high order for the forces deployed and ban on extrajudicial killing and 'encounter' killing. The ad hoc arrangements such as en masse recruitment of personnel or formation of state-sponsored special forces like *Salwa Judum* with policing tasks and powers should be dispensed with. While additional manpower is required to effectively man the extremist-affected areas, mere increase in the number of personnel without adequate resources or modern equipment and training will serve no purpose. On the contrary, such ill-equipped and professionally incompetent force will become a liability as the security of the personnel and safety of weapons become difficult in extremist areas. Instead of routine drill and weapon training, they should be imparted training in jungle warfare and enlightened on the conceptual, structural, organizational and strategic framework of major extremist groups operating in the area.

Besides, an effective intelligence network should be built up by the deployed forces for generation of real time or actionable intelligence, which the central or state agencies constantly fail to provide because of lack of professionalism and accountability. Moreover, these agencies are more concerned about the generation of half-baked or semi-reliable or totally unreliable intelligence, which are of little use for successful counter-extremist operations, but are useful to stake inflated claims or more funds and resources in the name of combating LWE. The concepts like setting up of a unified command of Naxalite-affected states or effective intelligence-sharing mechanism among the states at higher level would practically work only when the intelligence/law-enforcement machinery is developed on true professional lines. The basic logical question is how this so-called unified command or intelligence-sharing mechanism will work without any specific actionable intelligence or without a professionally competent, well-equipped and motivated force capable to confront the ultras in the field? Merely expanding the top of the pyramid of such agencies with new structures or mechanisms would only overburden the set-up and shake their foundations with little use to face the looming threat of LWE!

While seriously discussing such questions, the success story of Greyhounds in Andhra Pradesh is a role model for anti-Naxalite operations. In a nutshell, over the years, the Andhra police on its own has built up a highly professionalized and motivated specialized group by selecting the most ideal personnel from various branches of state police; imparting them training on jungle and guerrilla warfare, inculcating special traits like safety, speed and secrecy; and deploying them for the long-term task of dealing with Naxalites in their home turf. Significantly, a number of innovative schemes and incentives were introduced for the personnel and their kith and kin such as insurance policy for the personnel in field, out-of-turn promotion on achieving specific operational results, job guarantee to the dependents of the personnel if any killed in action, department's own co-operative, housing and educational establishments to meet the needs of the family members of the personnel deployed on duty and so on.

Drastic changes and innovations are imperative in strategic management and operational strategies. Hasty decision to deploy central forces alien to the area and not familiar with the topography and engaging them in counter-extremist operations should be avoided. Such ill-conceived decision led to the ambush and tragic killing of 76 CRPF personnel by Maoists in Dante Wada area of Chhattisgarh on 6 April 2010. Moreover, the omissions and commissions during anti-Naxalite operations would be easily orchestrated and propagated against the forces in action. At the same time, the police/paramilitary personnel engaged in anti-extremist operations should strictly adhere to the parameters of rule of law/due process of law and desist from any action amounting to harassment of civilian population, particularly women, children, tribals, Dalits and so on, in the name of combating extremism. The need of the hour is to professionalize and humanize the state police forces, which should be assisted by properly trained and sensitized central forces at the time of exigencies. However, militarization of central paramilitary forces by imparting training through army instructors and so on should be avoided as greater regimentation would accelerate the alienation of the forces from civilian population. It seems that more emphasis was given for such militarization efforts during the meeting of the chief ministers of the LWE-affected states convened by the centre during July 2010, in the wake of growing Naxalite menace in the country.

The centre has offered states (Chhattisgarh, Orissa, Jharkhand and West Bengal) more helicopters, logistics support and intelligence sharing, besides sanctioning about 16,000 additional SPOs, establishment/strengthening of 400 police stations in the affected districts at ₹2 crores a police station on an eighty–twenty (80:20) basis for two years.

We should remember that substantial funds have been allocated to various states under Police Modernization Programme with the main aim to equip and enrich police forces so as to combat major national security threats like extremism, terrorism and so on. No one can vouch for certainty that these funds have been properly utilized for improving the professionalism of the force or its infrastructure or logistics. Ironically, many state police forces have purchased modern vehicles, procured latest electronic gadgets and computers, constructed guest houses or hired apartments for operational purposes, which, in majority of cases, were unfortunately used by higher echelons in the force. Unless there is effective accountability and monitoring mechanism on the utilization of funds, the grand idea of developing our state police forces as elite, highly professional and competent force to effectively deal with serious national security challenges, like growing threat of LWE, will remain as an unfulfilled dream. The heart of the matter is that our police forces and intelligence agencies are not free from corruption and large-scale embezzlement of public funds in the name of sensitive and secret operations.

Any counter-extremist strategy blindly depending on guns and police weaponry will not help to bring permanent solution to Naxal threat. Instead, a holistic approach that lays emphasis on accelerated socio-economic development of the backward areas, specifically focusing on marginalized sections like Dalits, tribals and rural poor will help to contain the threat. Our study has revealed that these sections constitute the main sources of support for LWE in their major citadels like Chhattisgarh, Jharkhand, Bihar, Orissa and Andhra Pradesh. Sandwiched between the Naxals and security personnel in operation; they are also the worst victims of human/civil rights violations. Thus, a multipronged strategy should be worked out to ensure all-round development of these sections and to wean them away from the influence of LWE.

One cardinal truth is that the sad plight of the overwhelming majority of SCs/STs and other marginalized sections was not due to the dearth of constitutional mechanisms or legislations, but the result of omissions and commissions by various agencies/departments in the implementation of various programmes meant for these sections. Even police was not an exception to this trend. On many instances the law and order machinery failed to safeguard the life and properties of marginalized sections during caste–communal conflicts. Their genuine complaints were not properly looked into; nor was there effective dispensation of justice. The affected groups experience violence in their daily lives—SCs due to the caste-based social order and STs due to cultural dominance of the larger society. The incidence of atrocities is on the increase and the deterrence envisaged in the laws, specially enacted for this purpose, is not in evidence. This is because the implementation of important criminal laws—the Protection of Civil Rights Act and the SCs and STs (Prevention of Atrocities) Act—has been dismal.

Thus, the first and foremost task should be in the direction of the effective implementation of various protective legislations meant for these sections. The existing Constitutional provisions concerning their rights and privileges should be fully protected and more emphasis need to be laid down on the enforcement of various provisions under the Protection of Civil Rights and SCs and STs (Prevention of Atrocities) Act and other Acts and policy decisions governing their interests. Specific mention should be made about the Provisions of the Panchayats Extension of the Scheduled Areas Act, 1996, the National Rural Employment Guarantee Act, 2005, the Scheduled Tribes and Other Traditional Forest Dwellers (Recognition of Forest Rights) Act, 2006, and the National Rehabilitation & Resettlement Policy, 2007, which have a number of development/ welfare-oriented provisions ensuring the all-round development and social advancement of these sections.

Unfortunately, except NREGP, there are major bottlenecks in the effective implementation of other legislations. In the case of PESA, as the District Planning Committees have not been properly activated and not created in line with the provisions of PESA, original power of panchayats at each tier in the preparation of local plans including tribal sub-plan for economic development and social justice has been considerably diluted. Similarly, the bureaucracy backed by political intermediaries in the panchayat set-up still maintains an upper hand in policy and financial matters of the system, relegating the elected representatives of marginalized sections to background. Virtually, the elected representatives have no effective control over the officials. This is more glaring in rural and tribal areas where women representatives and those belonging to SC/ST communities are sidelined and ignored in all policy decisions. It should not be forgotten that it was the same bureaucracy that had abjectly failed in delivering good governance in the affected areas and was responsible for precipitating discontent and disaffection among the marginalized sections. Thus, the panchayats should be properly empowered with specific agenda and the bureaucracy should be made more accountable to the elected bodies of the three-tier panchayat set-up

Similarly, though the Forest Dwellers Rights Act[4] has been enacted with much fanfare, the progress in the implementation of the Act is tardy in many states like Andhra Pradesh and Chhattisgarh. Ambiguity still exists on certain terms/provisions in the Act such as 'other traditional rights', 'rights to minor forest produce' and 'primarily reside in and be dependent on forest or forest land' and so on. Moreover, there is a conscious move from the part of bureaucracy, especially the Forest Department, to interpret such ambiguous provisions detrimental to the interests of Adivasis/forest dwellers. The mining mafia is still active in many areas where unholy nexus exists among the mafia, the politicians and corrupt forest officials. Large tracts of the reserved forest areas are ravaged by this lobby for illegal mining, thereby depriving the forest dwellers their livelihood. Already tension between tribals and Forest Department has developed in many states on the issue of allotment of forest land and the complexion of JFM Committees. So long as such differences or controversies persist, the Act would fail to achieve its objective of removing 'historical injustice to forest dwelling Scheduled Tribes and other traditional forest dwellers who are integral to the very survival and sustainability of the forest ecosystem' (Recognition of Forest Rights Act 2006—Angul at angul.nic.in/tribal-act.pdf). Moreover, disaffection and dissatisfaction among them would grow, thereby aggravating social dissension and unrest.

No doubt, the National Rehabilitation & Resettlement Policy,[5] is a significant step in the present context when displacement of Adivasis/indigenous population for launching developmental projects has become a major issue causing discontent, unrest and tension arising because of the widespread forcible displacement. In fact, serious resistance movement has come up in states like West Bengal, Orissa, Chhattisgarh, Jharkhand, Andhra Pradesh, Maharashtra and Madhya Pradesh on this issue. LWE and other groups are engaged in organized efforts to exploit the discontent and frustration among the affected sections, particularly the Adivasis in LWE-dominated areas. Meanwhile, prominent NGOs in the tribal front, along with Indian Social Institute, have undertaken extensive research[6] on this issue and brought out a status paper on the displacement and rehabilitation of indigenous people due to the construction of projects, particularly major dams. There is an urgent need to implement rehabilitation and resettlement justly and with empathy to all by requiring authority/agencies/bodies to remove the trauma suffered by displaced persons.

An interrelated issue is the acquisition of land for major projects, especially in the wake of the formation of SEZ and the entry of large number of MNCs with their megaprojects. The Land Acquisition Act, which was enacted earlier, needs thorough revision and amendment so as to protect the interests of marginalized groups without hampering economic development. The general trend of acquiring large extent of land for 'public purpose' should be dispensed with. For that purpose, the term 'public purpose', as defined in the amended Land Acquisition Act, should be restricted to projects taken up for national security and public welfare implemented directly by the government. This, to a great extent, will help to check the liberal process of acquiring land by corporates and registered societies in the name of 'public purpose'. Similarly, adequate safeguards should be built into the law to protect poor and vulnerable sections in case of direct procurement by companies with the connivance of intermediaries and so on. There should be a mandatory provision for rehabilitation and resettlement of persons whose lands are procured by companies or other private interests. The acquired land remaining unutilized should be restored to erstwhile landowners. The definition of land should be amplified so as to include government, public, forest, panchayat land and community property resources, so that loss of using rights can be compensated. The determination of compensation should be based on replacement value, based on market value. The responsibility shall lie on acquiring authorities to ensure free and informed consent of the Gram Sabha in the acquisition of land. Any fraud or manipulation in acquisition process or procedures should be seriously dealt with and offenders should be brought to book.

The land-related issues was one of the main causative factors for the growth of LWE and interconnected socio-economic issues of marginalized sections. In states like Andhra Pradesh, the issue remained live for many decades and could be easily exploited by various Naxalite groups. Thus, urgent measures should be initiated to settle such issues. These should inter alia include: (*a*) effective implementation of land ceiling laws and the distribution of surplus ceiling land among the most vulnerable landless poor, and simultaneously, a review should be undertaken on the existing ceiling laws, taking into consideration the increased productivity of land due to better irrigation and technological facilities; (*b*) setting up of land tribunals or fast-track courts to expeditiously settle land ceiling cases; (*c*) amendment in the definition of 'personal cultivation' in the state tenancy law to eliminate absentee landlordism; (*d*) formulation of policy and legal framework to enable small and marginal farmers to lease-in land with secure rights on a formal basis and at the same time to protect them against reverse tenancy of medium and large farmers to corporate agencies; (*e*) modernization of the land-administration system, including a crash programme of updating of land records, computerization of textual and spatial records, and integration of the registration offices on priority basis; (*f*) regularization of all landless poor who have occupied government land; and (*g*) strict enforcement of laws prohibiting transfer of Adivasi lands to non-Adivasis and acquisition of land by non-Adivasis in Fifth Schedule area, also strengthening the protective measures against alienation of tribal land. This must be done as a priority national programme and action should be taken regularly to monitor its progress: (*a*) A time-bound survey is needed of all land under cultivation of SCs/STs culminating in (*i*) grant of title to those who do not have title and (*ii*) identification of land of STs alienated illegally, and restoration through Gram Sabhas by the powers vested in it under provisions of Panchayats/(Extension to the Scheduled Areas) Act (1995) and in an analogous manner in non-scheduled areas; and (*b*) taking over of the Bhoodan land still in the possession of donors or their heirs or temple, and the endowment lands beyond ceiling or the lands abandoned by mining projects or industrial activity and utilizing them for redistribution to eligible landless poor.

Just like land alienation, usury and indebtedness are the other major causes of acute distress and exploitation. Indebtedness among STs in Andhra Pradesh, Jharkhand and Chhattisgarh is particularly widespread on account of food insecurity, non-availability of production and consumption credit through public institutions, and corruption in the public-lending agencies. Laws to check indebtedness and regulate credit through private sources do not get implemented mainly due to the dominating role of moneyed class. This should be corrected through liquidation of all debt liabilities of weaker sections in cases where the debtor has repaid the principal amount. Similarly, effective steps should be initiated to strengthen grassroots level co-operative and other bodies for credit/loan facilities to small and marginal farmers and poorer sections. The revival and restructuring of the Large Area Multipurpose Cooperative Societies (LAMPS) and Primary Agricultural Cooperative Societies (PACS), with the specific targets of meeting all credit needs of the SCs and STs and weaker sections, should receive highest priority. Similarly, the cooperative banking structure, which is the most accessible to the poorer sections, should be urgently revamped and revitalized in the light of multitude of recommendations made in this regard, and the central legislation should enable member-controlled and member-dominated cooperative societies. There is also a need for widespread provision of grain banks managed by Gram Sabhas in tribal areas. Special provision of long-term loans for purchase of land by assetless, poor and resourceless families that are dependent upon agriculture for their livelihoods should be implemented. NREGA should be intensively implemented in the indebtedness prone areas.

For many decades, the extremist-affected areas that remained cut off from the mainland due to hilly topography and undulating terrain with concentration of tribal population were neglected. The failure to provide infrastructure and services as per national norms is one of the many discriminatory manifestations of governance there. These disparities, therefore, result in non-available/poorly provided services. It is high time that such disparities should be removed by speedy creation of infrastructure. Existing infrastructure should be rejuvenated and modernized with provision of adequate funds for their maintenance and upgrade. Fully functional services at par with the developed areas with personnel, equipment, facilities and funds for contingent expenditure should be created and provided for.

The first priority is elementary education for which adequate number of trained teachers should be provided for the schools in the remote areas. Side by side, technical/vocational training schools in line with the local needs should be started. Couple of residential schools should be opened to encourage basic education of girls in far-flung, remote areas.

There is need for a universal public health and nutrition system that is functional at the primary level of care. The first requirement in this task is to discontinue commercial vending of liquor and other intoxicants in terms of the excise policy for tribal areas (1974) and institutionalize control of the Gram Sabha over the preparation and use of traditional drinks. Health sub centres, primary health centres and community health centres should be started with adequate number of qualified medical professionals/paramedical personnel and regular supply of life-saving drugs to these centres. To overcome the chronic shortage of staff, special incentives or disturbed-area allowances on the pattern of the North-east should be introduced with effective monitoring system to ensure attendance of personnel.

Anganwadis should be provided on demand to SC and ST hamlets, which are the worst provided in terms of anganwadi centres in the country. With the help of ICDS, an effective nutrition chain meant for pregnant and lactating mothers, malnourished children and children studying in government primary schools and so on should be launched. Another area of concern is rural electrification. The emphasis should be on the uninterrupted power supply to poor households and not merely erecting electric poles or laying power lines by making huge investment. Ensuring rural road connectivity and safe drinking water facilities to all habitations in the affected areas are other two priorities that should be vigorously pursued by the administration. The co-operation and participation of local population are prerequisites to initiate such developmental and welfare schemes as the extremists are bent upon hindering such organized governmental programmes and schemes, apprehending erosion of their support base among the target groups.

On a closer analysis, it was found that dissatisfaction with improper governance, and often malgovernance, created anger among the suffering population. LWE heartland states of Andhra Pradesh, Orissa, Chhattisgarh, Madhya Pradesh, Jharkhand and part of Maharashtra are minimally administered. State intervention, both for development and for law and order, has been fairly low. These states/areas exhibited all the unique features of a 'soft state' (Gunnar Myrdal). In fact, there is a kind of vacuum of administration in these areas which is being exploited by the armed movement, giving some illusory protection and justice to the local population.

The basic steps required in this direction include establishment of credibility and confidence of government; keeping a continuous vigil for fulfilment of people's vision; effective protection, peace and good governance; rejuvenating tribal economy including social services; sustainable development with equity in tribal areas; holistic planning from below in scheduled areas; and negotiating crises by focusing on ending of confrontation. Basically, the entire administrative set-up should be reorganized with effective decentralization, in which the three-tier Panchayat set-up should have a decisive role. The state should take strong measures to eliminate corruption in various departments such as police, forest, revenue, health, education and PWD. The overall emphasis should be to tune up administration to the expectations of the common masses. The major deficiency of the absence of a justice administration system in rural areas, which adversely affect the marginalized sections in getting due justice from the part of administration, should be overcome. To overcome this bottleneck, a model of dispute-settlement mechanism and justice administration consistent with PESA, 1996, in Fifth Schedule areas should be worked out. A beginning can be made in this direction by quickly enacting the Nyaya Panchayat Law[7] by the centre with enabling provisions for the states to adopt. The properly constituted Nyaya Panchayats, by timely disposing of the complaints and grievances of the local population, can effectively neutralize the much-published 'people's court' and 'public trial' by Naxalites in their strongholds.

Mobilizing the support of the people is also absolutely essential to weaken the support base of the Naxals. The authorities should encourage civil society groups and NGOs in mobilizing such support. In states like Andhra Pradesh and Chhattisgarh, some surrendered cadres of LWE have started associating with local NGOs and were instrumental in taking up welfare–developmental programmes among marginalized sections. The major political parties are not playing their role in this regard. The representatives of these parties have virtually abdicated their responsibility. On the contrary, their present strategy is playing 'hide and seek' as part of their 'vote-bank politics'. They should adopt a co-ordinated approach by treating Naxalism as a 'national issue' posing a serious danger to democratic set-up and constitutional framework of the country. In order to play a constructive role in extremist-affected areas, committees comprising representatives of all major political parties should be formed at the district, mandal and village level involving poor sections of the masses to wean them away from the influence of the extremist groups.

7

Human Rights NGOs and Their Increasing Role

The NGOs are those organizations in civil society which are either formed to assist the needy/disadvantaged or to pursue a common interest and/or to take action on a particular subject or issue which causes disadvantage or is detrimental to the well-being of people or society as a whole.[1] Though NGOs are part of the total fabric of the organizations in the society, they are distinguishable from other groups by their focus on the disadvantaged, disadvantage or wider concerns on issues which affect peoples' well-being. While the governments generally deal with common matters/issues of the people and not specifically the disadvantaged, the NGOs directly or indirectly deal with the needs, problems and issues of the most disadvantaged in the society. Thus, NGOs operate at the interface between the government and its institutions on one hand, and civil society, more broadly, on the other hand.

The question of interface of NGOs with the government or its institutions leads to two different interpretations as 'institutional or intermediary NGOs' and the people or community NGOs. The former ones are usually formal, legally incorporated organizations closer to public institutional fabric, whereas the latter are characterized by their additional reliance upon the members themselves to control or/and undertake the work of the organization. The 'people's NGOs', which are closer to the fabric of civil society, are more potential in espousing issues such as human rights.

NGO Explosion in 1970s: Emergence of Human Rights NGOs

Towards the end of the 20th century, there was a virtual explosion of NGOs that are now involved in every aspect of human need and endeavour. The size of NGO sector varies widely across the countries. It is estimated that about 10 per cent of public development aid, worldwide, is now being channelized through NGOs. The UN over a decade ago the UNDP estimated that the total number of people 'touched' by NGOs in developing countries across the world is around 250 million. This covered about 20 per cent of 1.3 billion people living in absolute poverty in developing countries. Now, with a plethora of new issues such as climate change, environment, displacement, habitat and internal strife, there is a steady increase in number of NGOs world over.

The explosion of NGOs was due to a myriad of international and national factors such as the erosion in the 'concept of state sovereignty', 'globalization', shrinkage of the globe brought about by IT and communication revolutions, the end of cold war and so on. Many key issues and problems that were once national had transcended beyond continents and could no longer be solved at national level. They include concerns such as poverty, unemployment, environmental degradation, climate change, population explosion, spread of diseases such as HIV/AIDS, the regulation of MNCs, the control of drug trade/drug syndicates, humanitarian response to natural calamities/civil wars and, last but not the least, the creation of awareness among civil population on threats of different shades of global terrorism. There has been a paradigm shift in the role of government that it should be more of that of policymaker or 'facilitator' and less of a provider. In many underdeveloped and developing countries, the governments have turned to NGOs to do more of the providing. Privatization, decentralization and localization are parallel manifestations of the same general trend.

The NGO explosion of 1970s synchronized with enormous expansion in the number of NGOs concerned with human rights. Many factors contributed to this trend. The coup against Allende government in Chile and solidification of military dictatorship in the continent of South America gave rise to human rights organizations as 'human rights and solidarity groups' across the world, particularly in Europe and North America in the name of 'national liberation'. In fact, the seeds of 'social justice' were sown by Pope John's famous Vatican-II Declaration (1961)[2] and Declaration of Medelin Conference (1968).[3] They had sprouted and grown up in the minds of oppressed Christians, especially in Latin American countries like Nicaragua, EL-Salvador and so on, in late 1970s, when the concept of 'liberation theology'[4] had taken genesis with the active involvement of a section of Christian clergy and laymen. This led to the formation of a number of Christian Action Groups (CAGs) and 'activist groups' throughout the world. They became the vanguard for the protection of human/ civil rights of oppressed groups and ensuring social justice.

The developments in the socialist world were equally significant. The dissidents in the East Europe and USSR were given an enormous boost by the enactment and dissemination of Helsinki Final Act[5] of the Conference on Security and Co-operation in Europe in 1975 and the formation of Helsinki Watch Committee and Soviet Jewish Groups. Noted writers like Alexander Solzhenitsyn tried to break the iron curtain of many socialist regimes and blow the fresh air of freedom and civil rights in such societies through their legendary literary characters. Many Asian countries like Myanmar, erstwhile East Pakistan (now Bangladesh), Sri Lanka, Philippines, India, Vietnam and North and South Korea witnessed strong 'national liberation struggles' at the instance of ethnic and 'sub-nationalist groups' that gave an impetus to the formation of a number of civil rights organizations and 'activist groups', extending moral support and solidarity to these fighting groups. The UNDHR in 1948 and the enactment of a number of covenants and instruments such as ICCPR created more awareness among the comity of nations on civil society and civil rights. The human rights programme by the US-based Ford Foundation in 1970s for extending financial and other assistance to reputed human rights groups gave an impetus to the formation of independent NGOs, active in the human rights front. The selection of Amnesty International for Nobel Peace Prize in 1977 gave more credibility and recognition to NGOs and 'activist groups' vigorously espousing human rights cause world over. The end of

Vietnam War enabled the progressive Americans to redirect their energies to a broader range of concerns and humanitarian issues in different countries. All these factors had considerably contributed to the consolidation of human rights NGOs at international level.

With the emergence of prominent NGOs in the human rights field, UN Charter (Article 71) acknowledged the potential contribution that these NGOs can make in the fields of economic, social, cultural, health, educational and related matters by associating with organizations such as the Economic and Social Council. The role of NGOs had further increased when there was in practice a 'visibly discernible lack of commitment on the part of many governments either to protect human rights in their own countries or act for their protection at international level'.[6] Thus, Felice Sauer has aptly noted: 'virtually in every instance, NGOs have been a factor in documenting the human rights situation, thus confronting abusive governments and their sponsors at the Commission of Human Rights sessions'.[7]

The Resolution 1503 Procedure approved by the Economic and Social Council of UN in 1970 improved the status of human rights NGOs in supplying information to members of Human Rights Committee in their individual capacity. In 1993, the Committee formally recognized the role of NGOs by deciding that information sent by them to secretariat should be distributed to all members of the committee as official documents. Thus, the unquestionable role of NGOs in the protection and promotion of human rights had been upheld by the World Conference of Human Rights held in Vienna during 1993. The Vienna Declaration (Article 38) highlighted:

> The World Conference of human rights recognized the important role of NGOs in the promotion of all human rights and in humanitarian activities at national, regional and international level. It appreciates their contributions to increasing public awareness of human rights issues, to the conduct of education, training and research in the field and to the promotion and protection of all human rights and fundamental freedoms. While recognizing that the primary responsibility for the standard setting lies with the States, the Conference also appreciated the contributions of NGOs to this process.[8]

In this respect, the World Conference emphasized the importance of continued dialogue and co-operation between governments and NGOs. The approach was that NGOs and their members genuinely involved in human rights issues should enjoy the rights and freedoms as recognized by UNDHR and the protection of national laws. These rights and freedoms may not be exercised contrary to the purpose and principle of UN. Accordingly, NGOs should be free to carry out their human rights activities without interference of the governments in power provided that they should function within the framework of national law and UNDHR.

Functions of Human Rights and NGOs

Though Vienna Declaration presents an ideal situation of interface between the governments and NGOs, many states perceive them as a potential threat and adopt direct or indirect mechanisms to strangulate them. What are the reasons for that? A brief argument is that they speak 'truth to power'. If a government is repressive and violates international human rights norms, the power elites have every reason to view human rights NGOs as a threat to their legitimacy. These elites and their agents never cherish the truth being upheld by these NGOs, irrespective of any ideologies or vested interest. Many of these NGOs have made excellent contributions in a variety of fields closely connected with life, dignity, culture and livelihood of human beings, especially the underprivileged and marginalized sections.

One of the major tasks of Human Rights NGOs is fact-finding through information gathering, analysis and documentation. It is now generally accepted that intergovernmental human rights machinery depends heavily on the fact-finding reports of human rights NGOs. For example, UN Working Group on 'forced disappearances'[9] along with many governmental agencies rely upon NGOs and not the government themselves in respect of such data. The Working Group on Arbitrary Detentions, for example, reported in 1995 that 74 per cent of the cases that they took up in 1994 were brought up by international NGOs and another 23 per cent came from national NGOs, whereas contributions from all other sources were less than 3 per cent. The Special Rapporteur on Arbitrary Executions acknowledged the important role of NGOs in alerting the international community about summary executions in many countries. Many governments with 'cover-up agenda' on the human rights violations resort to unfair means to silence human rights NGOs branding that their activities would jeopardize national security or national ethos. UN and other international bodies could not do much to overcome such national issues.

At national level, though governments are charged with the investigation of allegations of human rights violations, there are only a handful of countries where the system of administration of justice, together with national institutions can be relied on to gather, analyze and act impartially on the real facts of human rights violations. The NHRC, India has clearly spelt out this discernible trend in the backdrop of conscious efforts by governments and its agencies to cover up serious human rights issues and violations. A typical example cited by the Commission was the genocide in Gujarat in 2002. Not only that the Gujarat government openly flouted the directions of the Commission but also tried to influence various governmental agencies and institutions to cover up naked violations of human rights like cold-blooded massacres, mass rape and fake encounter killings and so on. Moreover, there were conscious efforts to silence NGOs and civil rights activists/eminent personalities like Ms Mallika Sarabhai, Medha Patkar and so on, who tried to bring out real and unbiased facts on Gujarat pogrom. Despite such coercive and intimidation tactics by the government and its agencies, credit goes to noted civil/human rights activists such as Testa Setelvad in collecting and documenting specific inputs on the dastardly crimes perpetrated against innocent men and women in Best Bakery — Naroda Patiya incidents. Moreover, it was at the instance of such NGOs and activists that the apex court intervened in the whole issue and defeated the organized efforts of Gujarat government to bury the entire Gujarat episode under the carpet and thereby defeat the rule of law and due process of law.

Another significant activity of these NGOs is the denunciation of human rights violations at international and national levels. In the realm of power politics and international relations, the governments and political parties keep conscious silence on major human rights violations. Such approach was manifest, be it in Palestinian issue or US blockade of Iraq or naked violation of human rights in Pakistan or China. In such a scenario, the human rights NGOs play a crucial role in bringing such issues to international attention and mobilizing world opinion.

Lobbying at governmental and intergovernmental levels assumes considerable importance in respect of the major tasks of human rights NGOs. While recognizing their limitations or power, many of these bodies have successfully lobbied governments at national, regional and international levels in order to halt human rights violations. Many of these NGOs were successful in taking up such issues before international or regional bodies such as Inter-American Commission, Court of Human Rights, European Convention and Courts of Human Rights, African Commission of Human Rights, the Organization of Security and Co-operation in Europe and the European Parliament. In recent times, such lobbying has been started before international financial institutions like the World Bank, International Monetary Fund and World Trade Organization and so on with a view to influencing these bodies against extending financial aid/other assistances to those countries/agencies engaged in gross human rights violations. In fact, Amnesty International's intensive lobbying at international forum on human rights issues in India was one of the major contributory factors for the formation of NHRC in India during 1993. Similarly, ILO played a crucial role in influencing international trade and commerce bodies against promoting carpet/ silk industries in India which engage substantial child labour in contravention of the guidelines of ILO and so on.

Many NGOs provide protection to victims and potential victims under dictatorial regimes. One of the tactics adopted by Amnesty was the adoption of specific political prisoners by its subgroups and launching worldwide campaign for their release. Another strategy is to apply international humanitarian norms in the domestic courts to sue human rights violations. The 1998 decision of US Court of Appeals to the Second Circuit in the case of Filartiga vs. Pena-Irala[10] was a landmark victory in this regard. In this case, a New York–based NGO, Centre for Constitutional Rights (CCR) filed a case in New York in 1984 on behalf of Paraguayan activist and physician Joel Filartiga, accusing the inspector general of police, Asuncion, in the torture death of

Filartiga's 17-year-old son. This involved the application of Alien Torts Act as the basis for bringing a federal action for an alleged human rights violation of internationally recognized human rights law. Though the District Court refused to hear the case, on appeal the case was heard and decided in favour of Filartiga. Subsequent to this decision, US human rights groups lobbied for and saw a new law enacted, The Torture Victim Protection Act.[11] Recently, various international and national NGOs including Amnesty played a significant role in the release of Dr. Binayak Sen, a civil and human rights activist who was detained for more than two years by Chhattisgarh government on the alleged charge of collusion with CPI(Maoists) in the state.

Potential NGOs can provide considerable expertise to UN, international bodies and national commissions on human rights in the formulation and implementation of their programmes. They can participate in human rights norms-creating processes in a variety of ways such as participation in conferences, suggestions on draft articles for inclusion in norm-creating institutions, constructive criticism of articles during draft stage, conducting research on major issues and making specific recommendations and providing legal expertise and advice. In the case of Police and Prison Reforms, a few NGOs/civil liberties groups like PUCL have made significant studies which were appreciated by NHRC in its annual reports.

Prominent Human Rights NGOs

The major international NGOs with specific human rights concern are: (*a*) International League for the Rights of Men (established in 1942 and now rechristened as International League for Human Rights); (*b*) International Committee of Jurists (1951) and (*c*) Amnesty International. There are regional bodies like Human Rights Internet (HRI) in Canada, Indo-American Institute for Human Rights in Costa Rico, PUCL of India or those having broad mandate like Human Rights Watch Committee in New York or specific issue-based ones like Minority Rights Group (MRG) in United Kingdom. Commonwealth Human Rights Initiative (CHRI) is yet another major body which plays a crucial role in documenting various human rights issues in commonwealth nations and lobbying for protection of these rights at intergovernmental and international level.

The Amnesty International is the largest nongovernmental human rights organization in the world, formed in 1961 by the British Lawyer Peter Benenson with its international headquarters in London has now an estimated membership of 7.5 lakhs, spread over 165 countries. With around 500 well-trained and dedicated personnel at the headquarters, Amnesty maintain high standards in research, documentation and reporting on a wide range of human rights issues in almost all the nations. The country representatives also play a crucial role on the collection, collation and analysis of ground-level data for the use of Amnesty. The organization has been regularly publishing annual reports on human rights issues in different parts of world since 1972.

Besides, Amnesty also publish specific reports on different shades of human rights issues such as displacement and forced disappearances, problems of refugees and migrants, ethnic cleansing, environmental hazards and so on in various countries. Its special volumes titled, *Political Killings by Governments* (1983)[12] and *Torture in the Eighties* (1984)[13] evoked considerable criticism, especially by those regimes which regularly used draconian laws and instruments to suppress the genuine aspirations of common people. Several other publications of Amnesty made extensive data/documentation on various facets of human rights violations including reports on alleged encounter killings and custodial deaths in India. The Amnesty Report of 1992 focused on the problems of 'torture, rape and deaths in custody in India',[14] listing out 415 specific instances of human rights violations of above nature during the period 1985–1991. The report highlighted that large proportion of India's torture victims are suspected criminals, whereas torture had also been used as effective means to punish political activism and as a punitive reprisal for resistance to military or police operations. The report also cited the instances of torture in counter-insurgency operations in J&K, the North-east and the Punjab and listed out the events and incidents in order to substantiate their findings.

An analysis had been made citing some of the reasons which provided fertile ground for torture in custody, which inter alia included poor service condition of police personnel; political interference in police work; overloading of inadequate police personnel on crime detection, obsolete police training modules; lack of emphasis in the application of science and technology in police work; poor resources and public pressure to detect sensational cases at any cost and so on. One cardinal point highlighted by Amnesty was that the laws providing for the protection of human rights are substantial, but in practice, they do not work satisfactorily. The grievance-redressal mechanism is virtually a facade to protect the guilty for several reasons and there is inadequate arrangement for compensation to the victims of human rights violations.

A 10-point programme of action that was suggested by Amnesty to combat torture included:

1. Adoption of official policy to protect human rights for which proper guidelines should be issued to all agencies including police
2. Impartial investigation on all allegations of torture
3. Bringing all perpetrators of violations to justice and to award model punishment
4. Strengthening legal and other safeguards against torture
5. Informing detainees of their rights
6. Proper training to police and security forces to uphold human rights
7. Speedy compensation to victims
8. Medical treatment and proper rehabilitation of victims
9. Proper probe into the causes and pattern of torture
10. Strengthening of India's commitment to human rights at international level

Similarly, Amnesty's India Report of 1996, criticized TADA and highlighted that hundreds of 'prisoners of conscience' were languishing in Indian jails. In Indian context, Amnesty's reports discussed a wide range of human rights issues such as misuse of special legislations/Acts such as TADA/POTA, torture, ill-treatment of prisoners, custodial deaths, instances of rape and atrocities against women, disappearances, disgusting condition of correctional institutions, extra-judicial executions by security forces, deliberate/arbitrary killing of civilians, hostage taking by armed groups and so on. Though Amnesty appreciated the initiative of NHRC in raising public awareness on human rights and awarding compensation to victims, it observed that the mandate of NHRC remained limited in respect of human rights violations by the Armed forces.

Amnesty's consistent campaign on various human rights issues such as cause of 'prisoners' of conscience/illegal detention sometimes evoked controversies on the ground that the organization adopted anti-etablishment policies and maintained soft approach towards terrorism/extremism. In February 2010, Amnesty was in the centre of such controversy when Ms Gita Sahgal,[15] head of Amnesty's gender unit and daughter of famous novelist Nayantara Sahgal, came out with the concern that the organization was risking its reputation by making common cause with cage prisoners, framed by Mozaam Beg,[16] a former Guantanamo Bay prisoner, to highlight the plight of terror suspects in American custody. Sam Zarifi, Amnesty's Asia Pacific director, also expressed similar sentiments holding that the organization's campaigning did not always sufficiently distinguish between the rights of detainees to be free from torture and their views. The main allegation pertained to Mozaam Beg, an Afghanistan national, who was picked up by US in the post-9/11 American hunt of Al Qaeda/Taliban supporters. Beg, after spending three years in Guantanamo camp, was released in 2005, following a consistent campaign by Amnesty and other human rights groups against illegal detention and torture. However, the official line of Amnesty is that any suggestion of its international work with Mozaam Beg or cage prisoners has not weakened its condemnation of rights' abuses by Taliban or other similar-minded groups. Amnesty's dilemma over Mozaam Beg is the general scenario confronting human rights NGOs that vigorously use the services of ex-terrorists or surrendered LWE, who usually are never accepted by official agencies or the civil society at large.

One main criticism against Amnesty is that its perspective is biased towards the West. It does not investigate the human rights violations in the West as vigorously and extensively as in the case of third-world countries, despite the fact that more than 90 per cent of its staff are from West European and American countries. This approach is mainly on the hypothesis that the western world is more sensitive to human rights issues as compared to the third world. It is also stated that its pro-West bias is the result of its main sources of finances/funds that mainly come from the West. Unless such biases in its recruitment and perspective are rectified, Amnesty cannot be rightly claimed as 'international' or 'global'.

NGOs and CLM in India

The genesis and spread of civil rights groups and human rights NGOs in India can be largely attributed to the failure of the state and its agencies in protecting human rights or the abuse perpetrated by them and the dominant sections of the society through various forms of exploitation and oppression. Most of the civil liberties groups in India had been formed in direct response to the gross and systematic violation of rights by the state. They vigorously pursue a line of promoting and protecting the rights of individuals and groups, sometimes in direct confrontation with the state. Thus, the relations between the state and civil liberties movement/human rights NGOs remain strained if not hostile, as clearly manifest during the course of this research project.

The concept of human rights NGOs had developed during the British rule in India more or less parallel to the growth of constitutional government and parliamentary institutions. The Indian Civil Liberties Union (ICLU) formed in 1934 was the first civil rights/human rights organization in India. Its main aim was to oppose the British colonial regime which was engaged in naked violation of civil, democratic and human rights of the large majority of Indian masses except a microscopic minority close to the regime. Jawaharlal Nehru, its founder, envisaged the scope of civil liberties organizations/human rights NGOs as primarily preventing the government 'from becoming too autocratic'. Nehru pointed out:

> It is obvious that questions of civil liberties only arise when there is a conflict between the public or certain sections of it, and the executive government ... A democracy can only function properly if public opinion constantly checks government and prevents it from becoming too autocratic.[17]

The legacy of the civil rights movement as one opposed to the government was inherited by the civil liberties/human rights organizations after independence. Basically, this character of the movement was interpreted as 'anti-state'. This had led to the antagonism between the state and civil liberties movement. The new government which was engaged in nation-building process was faced with a mosaic of challenges from regional, ethnic and parochial forces jeopardizing the unity and sovereignty. The state had to use the civil service, army and the police—armed with repressive powers to contain these challenges. There were instances of police firing on peasants, political activists, students and trade union leaders. The government backed by the neo-colonial privileged social classes made organized moves to suppress the groups fighting for the rights of the traditionally oppressed and marginalized sections. The social and economic exploitation of the underprivileged sections have intensified. Coupled with these factors, the Naxalite uprising of late 1960 and the declaration of National Emergency (1975–1977) gave an impetus for the formation and consolidation of a number of civil rights organizations/human rights NGOs.

The civil liberties/human rights organizations in the country can be broadly classified into two: those arising out of the Naxalite movement and those inspired by National Emergency and the movement of Jaya Prakash. The organizations in the first category such as Association for the Protection of Democratic Rights (APDR) and Andhra Pradesh Civil Liberties Committee (APCLC) mainly focused their agenda/campaign on police brutality, especially against LWE. However, since the middle of 1970s, there was a major shift in their strategy. Instead of collecting information on police excesses through fact-finding missions and petition, the government adopted a more militant posture and mobilized the people in their 'struggles' mainly espousing the cause of Left radicals. On the other hand, civil rights organizations like PUCL formed in response to the naked violation of civil and democratic rights during the National Emergency adopted a liberal approach. Their aim was to uphold and promote civil liberties and democratic way of life by peaceful means in the country.

The above polemics in civil liberties movement has influenced the approach of these organizations towards Left-extremist movement and their violent depredations. The organizations like All India Federation of Organizations for Democratic Rights (AIFOFDR) interpret movements like the Naxalites as arising from socio-economic conditions. They believe that until and unless those conditions are changed, it is impossible to look at the question of Naxalite violence in isolation. Its declaration states that rights' abuses in India stem from the fundamental conflict between the ruling classes and the exploited masses. The state is depicted as the agent of the ruling classes, and all efforts by the state to alleviate poverty and exploitation are viewed as a form of deception. AIFOFDR and other democratic rights organizations thus do not have much faith in the constitutionally guaranteed rights or the legal system of the country. On the other hand, bodies like PUCL firmly uphold democracy and other constitutional bodies and denounce any form of violence or struggle that weakens democracy. The approach of PUCL leadership is that 'extremist groups are equally responsible for the violation of human rights through their depredations against civilians and police; destruction of public and private properties etc as in the case of police which resort to the killing of persons in fake encounters in the name of fighting extremism'.[18] The above differences in Civil Liberties Movement (CLM)/human rights NGOs open the sensitive issue of 'state violence' versus 'violence or abuses by armed opposition groups'. Some basic questions arise in this connection. Can the state violence be treated at par with violence by armed opposition? Should the human rights groups vociferously denounce such violence by armed opposition groups? Or should the human rights groups and activists treat the violence committed by armed opposition groups as irrelevant to their proclaimed mandates? Should they treat it as a problem that the government alone should handle under the laws of the land, subject to due process? What stand the international conventions and humanitarian law suggest in such matters?

While pondering over these issues, it should be noted that the state, as the legally constituted entity in control of the territory under its jurisdiction, has the sole legitimate right to use force to provide security, maintain law and order, and guarantee the protection of the fundamental rights of its citizens. Besides, it has different arms such as executive, judiciary and legislative and other agencies for streamlining its effective functioning. Many senior leaders of APCLC hold that the violence by extremist organizations or armed opposition groups is qualitatively different from state violence and the two types of violence cannot be equated.

They highlight that the state, through its lawfully constituted law-enforcement mechanisms, is responsible for the protection of the civil liberties of the citizens. The Cr Pc and the penal code are the means by which the state is legally entitled to deal with all such situations, including the violence by extremist groups. Under such a framework, the primary concern of human rights groups is to focus on protesting the human rights abuses committed by the state.

The international human rights law and conventions also attach more concern on the violation of rights by states. For example, the mechanisms of human rights law usually do not address abuses, ranging from terrorism to common criminality, perpetrated by actors other than the state. Human rights organizations have no international legal mandate to condemn non-state actors. Thus, such condemnation can be controversial. In contrast, activities of human rights groups against a state's violation of constitutionally guaranteed fundamental rights, or against laws that violate the essence of international human rights treaties, are viewed as legitimate, both by the state and by public opinion. Moreover, the ICCPR and other international human rights mechanisms were developed with the understanding that human rights law should be applied to restrain governmental action.

The International Human Rights NGOs such as Amnesty International and Human Rights Watch have seriously addressed the issue of violence by armed opposition groups in order to sensitize the human rights NGOs as to how the issue should be dealt with in the changing global scenario of terrorist violence. Amnesty International has indicated that 'groups in opposition to the governments that have acquired the characteristics of the governments' can meet the same standards mandated by humanitarian law with respect to governments. Here, the crucial question is how and when such a 'group' attains the characteristics of a government? According to the interpretation of Amnesty International, 'an opposition group' attains this status when they control people in its territory in a way similar to the exercise of governmental jurisdiction, able to implement procedures for the protection of human rights in the territory and is recognized by governments and international organizations. But in majority of cases such a scenario never happens as groups opposed to any established government and operating in their territory are never recognized by the government or international organizations. Thus, in actual practice the governments seldom apply the same standards of humanitarian law to such groups.

The Humanitarian Law that applies to the governments and 'armed opposition groups' is governed by the provisions of the Geneva Convention and Protocol II/Common Article 3 of the Geneva Conventions[19] and the Protocol Additional to the Geneva Conventions of 12 August 1949, and Relating to the Protection of Victims of Non-International Armed Conflicts (Protocol II).[20] The various provisions under the above conventions/protocol lay down that persons taking no active part in the hostilities, including members of armed forces laid down their arms and those placed *hors de combat* by sickness, wounds, detention or any other cause shall in all circumstances be treated humanely, without any adverse distinction founded on race, colour, religion or faith, sex, birth or wealth, or any other similar criteria and their life and person should be protected with personal dignity.

But what matters more in the case of human rights NGOs is the approach towards the violence perpetrated by armed opposition groups. This is all the more important in Indian context in which major violations of human rights, such as torture, kidnapping, hostage taking, extortion, killing and suppression of freedom of opinion routinely occur in many armed conflict situations. The reluctance of human rights NGOs or their failure to denounce certain type of violence by armed opposition groups adversely affects their legitimacy as unbiased observers. The repeated and vociferous criticism of the government on the human rights front, when seen in conjunction with their apparent silence on the abuses committed by armed opposition groups, meets with a hostile reception. The activities of the human rights groups would be construed as partisan and unfair, if not fundamentally misdirected, leading to an increasing loss of credibility and further marginalization, even with the victim groups. Often, the human rights groups are accused of being mere surrogates for different militant groups, more concerned with protecting the human rights of the militants than of the citizens.

On the other hand, such an approach and resulting image of human rights NGOs facilitate the state to justify their highhanded operations against extremist/revolutionary groups with public sanction. Even the activists of human rights/civil liberties organizations are targeted by branding them as 'fraternal allies of extremists'. A number of draconian legislations, such as National Security Act (NSA), Armed Forces Special Powers Act, Disturbed Areas Act, TADA/POTA and so on, would be enacted with unlimited powers to police, army or central paramilitary forces who operate in the affected areas. The civilian population who are sandwiched between these forces and the extremists would become the worst victims of human rights violations.

There are a number of situations that warrant human rights NGOs to adopt balanced approach in respect of their stand towards the depredations by revolutionary groups. For comprehensive discussion, we can broadly classify these activities as strategic/operational, ideological and sporadic/random. The first category include: Planned attack of police stations or other security establishments and butchering of duty and off duty personnel; killing of police/security personnel/ volunteers of state vigilantism like *Salwa Judum* engaged in operation against the armed opposition groups; cruel torture and summary executions of security personnel who fall into the hands of ultras; reckless killing of people suspected to be 'police informers'; extensive use of explosives/planned explosive devices against preselected targets like VIPs, security personnel on convoy, security establishments/camps and so on. The second category includes a broad spectrum of violence and depredations ranging from 'ethnic cleansing' or genocide of minorities to individual annihilation of 'class enemies'. In this process, many of these groups systematically annihilate innocent persons including women and children in the name of the colour of their skin or the belief or customs that they inherit from time immemorial. Their targets also include the so-called government 'collaborationists' or the erstwhile 'comrades-in-arms' who are seen as deviating from the 'true line'. There is no doubt that the human rights groups will have to take an unequivocal condemnatory stand on such acts even if they are perceived as pitting themselves against those, who in the ringing words of the UDHR, 'have recourse, as a last resort, to rebellion against tyranny and oppression'. Ambushes and sporadic strike of security posts or hostage-taking to end stepped up security operations and so on include the third category of violence which depends much on the ground-level exigencies of armed opposition.

There are many practical difficulties for human rights NGOs to arrive at right conclusions/stand in respect of the actions of armed opposition groups. Unlike in the case of state violence or violations, the operations or depredations of armed opposition groups are covert or clandestine, planned and executed by a set of leaders. Thus, collecting and collating reliable information on abuses by armed opposition groups is a herculean task. This dearth of information is further compounded by the fact that most reports of such activities that do exist in the media are heavily coloured by a governmental point of view, which routinely exaggerates the horrors of these activities, de-contextualizes them, and converts all political dissident activity, particularly when it involves violence, into crime.

For human rights communities, the concrete action plan and the strategy chosen depends upon the contingent circumstances, the actual ability of the human rights groups and the efficacy of the different steps. This is because the judgments expressed by the human rights groups have relevance not only to the government and the public, but also to the armed opposition groups in question. The legitimization function of human rights activity must not be undermined.

The majority of conventional NGOs in India have kept away from the controversy on state violence and violence by revolutionary groups. However, major civil liberties groups have condemned certain activities of armed opposition groups. For example, the APCLC stressed that 'all revolutionary parties had a right to chalk out their policies. This should not undermine the civil liberties of the people even in the name of revolutionary struggle'. Such activities reflect a growing concern for the violence committed by armed opposition groups. In a personal interview in 1998, Late K.G. Kannabiran logically explained this position as:

State violence and violation of laws by the State are greater threat to democracy and democratic values than private violence. I was never apologistic to this stand. This however does not mean that we are impervious or indifferent to large scale violence resulting in the loss of innocent lives by political groups and movements. We also criticise violence leading to loss of human lives and loss of property by Naxalite groups. Based on this conviction I have intervened in two kidnapping cases (involving senior bureaucrats of Andhra Pradesh in December 1987 and Bal Raju, MLA/Cong in

February 1993) and made all efforts for their release without any bloodshed. It is high time that revolutionary movements should try to foster humane relations along with revolutionary struggles'.[21]

The government response to human rights NGOs in the country was always negative. Kannabiran recalled that despite the crucial role played by APCLC in the release of hostages and other peace efforts, the attitude of the state and its agencies like police towards human rights NGO and civil rights groups was antagonistic. He quoted that in 1993 the DGP of Andhra Pradesh threatened 'to wipe out' rights activists as 'they were becoming a threat to society'. Moreover, half a dozen senior APCLC activists were allegedly killed by police or other security agencies, whereas a large number of cases were foisted against key functionaries linking them with LWE.

While analyzing the government response towards human rights NGOs certain clear trends emerge. In the immediate post-independent era and in 1950s, the nascent human rights NGOs could not make any noticeable presence, despite there being a plethora of human rights violations during Telangana uprisings and armed struggles in the North-east and J&K. Till the 1970s, the government simply ignored the allegations of right violations. The Naxalite uprisings of late 1960s and the National Emergency (1975–1977) gave an impetus for the formation and consolidation of human rights NGOs. This was largely due to the efforts by intellectuals, those sympathetic to Naxalite ideology and those opposed to the Emergency. Significantly, major civil liberties organizations were formed during this phase. However, the governments at the centre or in the states did not pay much heed to the feeble voice raised by these organizations in favour of the protection of civil and human rights of affected sections.

In the 1980s, the government policy was to deny all allegations of violation of human rights and tactfully refrain from replying any criticisms directly. More stringent measures were taken to silence the strong proponents of human rights. While international organizations like Amnesty were not given access to India, indigenous organizations began to be branded as 'anti-national' or 'front organizations of Naxalites.' There were organized efforts to harass the activists through investigation of their activities, preventing them from holding meetings/publishing materials or implicating them in false cases. The police and intelligence agencies were extensively used for such purposes. But this period also witnessed the genesis of PIL and the intervention of judiciary on civil/human rights issues such as extra-judicial killings, custodial deaths and so on at the instance of human/civil rights organizations like APCLC, PUCL and so on. Side by side, the international human rights organizations like Amnesty International came out with more authentic reports on the serious violations of human rights in India.

Thus, there was a clear shift in government strategy in 1990s. This was mainly due to judicial intervention on sensitive human rights issues and mounting criticism against India in various international forums for its poor records in human rights field. Firstly, instead of flatly denying allegations of rights violations, the government accepted that the abuse took place, but tried to dilute them as 'aberrations', and highlighted that it took prompt action whenever any incident was brought to its attention. Secondly, it began to focus on abuses by armed opposition groups in the Punjab, Kashmir, the Northeast, and left-wing extremist groups in Bihar and Andhra Pradesh, emphasizing that the police and paramilitary forces were operating in difficult circumstances. Thirdly, even while attacking rights organizations for distorting facts, and so on, the government permitted Amnesty to visit India for investigative purposes; and lastly, it enacted the Protection of Human Rights Act (1993) followed by the constitution of NHRC. Yet in real terms its attitude towards the human rights organizations has undergone very little change.

But things have again changed during the last two decades, especially in the light of the global threat of terrorism and the worldwide counter-terrorist operations. The easiest way to silence human rights NGOs or activists is to link them with a genuine or imaginary terrorist outfit in some remotest corner of the world. Draconian legislations have been enacted to ban any such organization in the name of fighting terrorism or extremism. Even the mere physical presence of literature construed to be of extremist ideology with an activist or philanthropist can be interpreted as a legal ground to put him or her behind the bars without bail or trial for months or years! Along with the intelligence agencies, sections of print and electronic media have been extensively used to discredit or tarnish the image of human rights NGOs through organized disinformation campaign. The Government Organized NGOs (GONGOs) play a crucial role to malign the NGO movement and their campaigns on civil and human rights. They were given the task of 'defending' the governmental violations in various international conferences. As a part of this task, they resort to very aggressive behavioural modes whenever there are some critical comments from the other Indian non-governmental representatives. Some of them operated as mere 'shouting brigades' without any intellectual acumen or calibre to defend the so-called 'sensitive tasks' assigned to them by their handlers. Ironically, they also wore the mantle of genuine NGOs in order to eat away the governmental money and largesse.

Meanwhile, the conventional NGOs dominated the NGO movement in India. In pre-independent India their activities were mainly confined to charity, relief and welfare. Raja Ram Mohan Roy's 'Bramho Samaj', Dayananda Saraswathi's 'Arya Samaj', Mahatma Gandhi's 'Khadi Village—Industries Commission', Acharya Vinoba Bhave's 'Bhoodan Movement' and so on were examples of such organizations. The revivalist organizations like Rashtriya Swayum Sevak Sangh (RSS) formed by Guruji M.S. Golvalker proclaimed such noble aims and objectives of reforming the society and people through selfless service. In fact, the NGOs were preoccupied with the reform of a society riddled with myriad of problems.

The mid-1970s witnessed a virtual 'NGO explosion' in the country with the formation of a large number of small and medium organizations, known under different names such as 'action groups', 'voluntary association', 'non-party affiliates' and so on, which strived hard for an alternative approach to development as well as emancipation of the exploited, marginalized and underprivileged sections. NGOs in India received a further fillip in their growth and consolidation when the government in 1982 formulated major policy guidelines for rural development with a direction to the states that they should enlist the support of NGOs for developmental activities. This had become institutionalized when the 7th Five Year Plan of Government of India highlighted the supplementary role of NGOs in the rural reconstruction programme. An amount of ₹250 crore was included in the Plan for channelizing through NGOs as part of such programmes. The formation of the Council for the Advancement of People's

Action and Rural Technology (CAPART) in September 1986 was intended to promote NGO movement in rural areas through rural development programmes with more focus on new technology. The above governmental policy decisions gave an impetus to many NGOs which took up a wide range of programmes in various fields such as education, health, poverty alleviation, sanitation, vocational training, rural development and so on, targeting vulnerable and marginalized sections, especially tribals, Dalits, slum dwellers, women and children. Many of them tried to bring the fruits of science and technology to the common masses, persuading them to shun the path of superstitions and obscurantist practices and leading them towards a new brave world.

Correspondingly, the NGOs have grown enormously in their numbers. One refers to more than one lakh prominent NGOs in the country, whereas another study reveals that there are more than 25,000 registered grassroots level NGOs in Tamil Nadu alone. However, what matters more is not the number of NGOs, but the quality of NGOs, the commitment of their functionaries, the nature of their activities and the credibility that they enjoy in the society and with the government. The committed NGOs were rightly described by NHRC as: 'the eyes and ears of the people of India'. Such NGOs can play a significant role in the protection and promotion of human rights, as their wide spectrum of activities are inextricably linked to human rights concepts and issues, especially in the case of marginalized and underprivileged sections which seldom get due justice from the government or its agencies.

8

Andhra Pradesh: A Role Model for Civil Liberties Groups and NGOs

Andhra Pradesh with its unique history of Telangana-armed uprising and decades-long violent struggles by left-wing extremist groups has been selected for the detailed analysis of the genesis and growth of civil liberties organizations and NGOs and the extent of their contributions towards human rights movement. The state that is the fifth largest in India with 23 districts has three distinct geographical regions—Coastal Andhra, Rayalaseema and Telangana. This geographical identity coupled with various socio-economic-political and developmental issues paved the way for the demand for separate Telangana state.

Andhra Pradesh has a distinct place in the history of social movements in India. The state was almost a laboratory for international institutions for experimenting with economic reforms. The political scientists attribute that one of the objectives of these experiments was also to capture the response to such reforms from varied social groups and those involved in social movements down the line, ranging from the extreme Left to autonomous groups. The state has witnessed many social movements involving marginalized and disadvantaged groups and regions. The Dalit and tribal movements in the state were the first in the entire country demanding reservation within STs. The frequent infringement of civil rights as a result of the presence and activities of radical Left parties and counter-extremist operations by state agencies led to the formation of strong civil rights movement.

The recent resurgence of the movement for land indicates the renewed demand for the distribution of land to the landless. The long survival of the movement for a separate Telangana is an indicator of the many regional identity movements in the country.

It is perhaps the only state with a vibrant women's self-help group movement. The presence of a strong women's movement, initially built up by the Left parties that later became autonomous, probably provided a base for this. Besides having these distinct features, the nature and impact of the social movements varied across the three regions of Andhra Pradesh. This was clearly reflected in the course of the study. Even these differences were noticeable in respect of the formation and spread of civil liberties organizations and NGO movement in the state.

The *genesis* and growth of civil liberties movements and NGOs in Andhra Pradesh can be mainly attributed to the dynamics of societal forces, socio-economic factors, demographic features and so on. The 'class–caste' orientation of the society, with 'elite section' dominating the socio-economic and political spectrum through neo-colonial strategy, that widened the gulf between the haves and have-nots, particularly in rural areas, the plight of sizeable chunk of Dalit-tribal and backward population immersed in poverty, illiteracy and so on led to a unique situation in which the formal developmental process could neither reach the lower strata of the society nor improve the socio-economic conditions of the overwhelming majority of population for many centuries. The insensitivity of the ruling elite classes to the genuine problems and aspirations of the large majority of tribals, Dalits and other backward sections coupled with their organized moves to exploit these sections with the direct or tacit support of various governmental agencies gave inspiration to many progressive intellectuals to prop up the cause of the exploited and oppressed. This has paved the way for the emergence of civil liberties groups and NGOs which stepped into political, developmental and social issues highlighting the plight of these sections. However, there were major differences in the ideology and strategy of civil liberties groups and NGOs. While the civil rights groups interpreted that social justice and egalitarian concepts cannot be attained so long as the state adopted its strategy of suppressing 'people's movements and struggles' by branding them as basic law-and-order problems, the conventional NGOs highlighted voluntary activities with mass participation as a panacea to all major ills in the society, which are the culmination of ill-conceived policies of development, administrative indifference, bureaucratic red-tapism and large-scale corruption.

The emergence of left-wing extremist groups greatly influenced the ideology and activities of civil liberties movements in Andhra Pradesh. As early as in 1970, a United Civil Liberties Organization was set up by all Maoist groups, comprising UCCRI/ML, Central Organizing Committee and Andhra Pradesh Revolutionary Communist Party (APRCP). However, ideological differences in the LWE had surfaced in the civil liberties movement as well. Thus, at the instance of UCCRI/ML, a new organization, viz. Organization for the Protection of Democratic Rights (OPDR) was formed in 1974. The main aim of OPDR was to mobilize mass opinion against the fascist acts, repressive laws and despotic rule by launching campaigns and struggles. For that purpose, the outfit also emphasized the proper collection and documentation of details pertaining to the repression and harassment of poor citizens by the state and its agencies. In line with the above aims and objectives, OPDR extended legal aid to undertrial left-wing extremists and organized a campaign demanding commutation of death sentence to some of the LWE detenues like Krista Gowda, Bhoomiah and so on. In the immediate post-Emergency period, OPDR played a major role in furnishing details/evidences before Bhargava Commission which was constituted in 1977 to probe into the encounter killing of activists during the period of 1968–1977. However, OPDR had lost much of its clout as the major civil liberties body in Andhra when another body, namely APCLC was formed in 1973. Since 1978, APCLC regrouped and strengthened its activities with the participation of urban intelligentsia mainly comprising lawyers, academicians, journalists and doctors. It soon emerged as the major civil liberties group in Andhra with wide-ranging activities such as Formation of Fact Finding Committees (FFC) mainly to probe into all 'encounter killings', documentation of all human rights issues, campaign against police excesses through protest rallies/meetings and so on. It also strived to create awareness among rural people on human rights violations and tried to mobilize mass opinion on issues like TADA, POTA and similar other legislations. APCLC also filed a number of cases in courts mainly espousing the cause of the victims of police atrocities/excesses, especially against LWE activists.

Peoples Union for Civil Liberties (PUCL), Andhra Pradesh

PUCL is an affiliate of the all-India body and is active in the civil liberties front of Andhra. PUCL, which came into existence at national level through its campaign/struggles against National Emergency (1975–1977), started its activities in Andhra since early 1980s. The objective of the organization is the 'defence and promotion of civil liberties through peaceful and democratic methods'. An equally important objective of the body is 'to combat social evils such as untouchability, casteism and communalism which encroach upon civil liberties'. The organization mainly took up issues such as torture and other custodial violence, repressive Acts like TADA and protection and promotion of human rights, especially of underprivileged sections. Their main activities included: (*a*) fact-finding missions on torture/custodial violence, (*b*) legal aid to the victims of civil rights violations and (*c*) seminar/workshop on police reforms, civil human rights issues and environmental hazards. Though PUCL stands for the unity of various civil/human rights groups and protection and promotion of these rights against the encroachment of the government/establishment, ideologically they are against any violent movement, campaign or struggles that they feel will weaken the democratic framework. In this regard, PUCL took a different line from APCLC and criticized the latter for not strongly denouncing the left-wing extremist violence, which according to them are blatant violation of human and civil rights and negation of the basic concept of democracy. The perception of PUCL leadership is that instead of blind criticism of police for their various omissions and commissions in the civil or human rights front, efforts should be made by civil rights activists to establish good rapport with progressive and humane police personnel and solicit their co-operation in the protection and promotion of civil and human rights during the day-to-day policing. It was in line with this approach that PUCL adopted a proactive role for radical amendments/changes in the Indian Police Act of 1861, so that the police became more sensitive and accountable to basic human/civil rights of common people.

All India People's Resistance Forum (AIPRF), which was formed in 1992 jointly by CPI(ML)-PWG of Andhra Pradesh, MCC and CPI(ML)-Party Unity of Bihar, occasionally took up civil/human rights issues mainly to safeguard the interests of Left-extremist groups. The main aim of the organization was to build up public opinion against the state violence by rallying the support/solidarity of Left intellectuals and human/civil rights activists. AIRF organized seminars and workshops in major cities and strongly deplored the wanton repression by the state on weaker sections, particularly in Bihar and Andhra in the name of counter-extremist operations. Simultaneously, they also tried to sensitize the masses on the adverse impact of globalization and liberalization in the domestic economy, the stranglehold of MNCs in the systematic plunder and depletion of natural resources depriving livelihood to indigenous people and the neo-imperialist role of international bodies like World Trade Organization (WTO), International Monetary Fund/World Bank and GATT in exploiting the developing countries and so on. Naturally, AIPRF was highly critical of Andhra Pradesh's overdependence on World Bank and other international financial bodies for mobilization of funds for investment in key infrastructural sectors, without considering the long-term interests of the state and the people.

Prominent Non-Governmental Organizations (NGO) in Andhra

The NGOs in Andhra Pradesh represent a mixture of various groups and functionaries with different ideologies, modus operandi, concerns, target groups and funding sources. The proliferation of NGOs all over the state, particularly during the last two decades was mainly due to the availability of resources facilitated by foreign funding agencies. A study of the voluntary organizations registered under Andhra Pradesh (Telangana area) Public Societies Registration Act (Act I of 1350F) and Societies Registration Act of 1860 indicated that a large number of organizations were registered in all the 23 districts mainly to avail such facilities. These societies were of varied in nature—educational, cultural, social, religious, rural-development oriented and so on. Vincent Ferror (Spanish) of Rayalaseema Development Trust (RDT), Anantapur district; Dr Parameswara Rao (Bhagavattula Charitable Trust, Ellamanchil, Visakhapattanam); Professor Windy (Belgium, Village Reconstruction, Hyderabad); Dr John David (AMG India International, Chilkauripet, Guntur District) and PKS Madhavan (AWARE [Action for Welfare and Awakening in Rural Development]) were the pioneers of NGO movement in Andhra. These NGOs generally known as 'Giant NGOs' of Andhra by virtue of their vast financial resources and wide spectrum of activities had given an inspiration to many others to float other NGOs. Side by side, some individuals associated with above NGOs acquired expertise in running NGOs, established linkages with foreign-funding agencies, formed their own organizations and extended their activities to new areas.

According to rough estimates, over 4,000 major NGOs are operating in the state. Based on the background of the promoters and nature of activities, they can be broadly categorized as 'independent NGOs', Christian Action Groups (CAGs), Social Action Groups (SAGs) and 'Muslim NGOs'. An analysis of the genesis and spread of NGOs in the state reveals certain clear trends. First, the concentration of NGOs is more in Coastal Andhra and Rayalaseema than Telangana, which is more backward in socioeconomic development. One main reason for this trend is the sizable presence of tribal and Dalit population in Rayalaseema and Coastal Andhra, which prompted the early 'activists' to float their organizations there. Moreover, these regions witnessed serious atrocities against Dalits and tribals from privileged castes/classes. On the contrary, the presence of left-wing extremists acted as a deterrent against such trends in Telangana region. Second, their intervention in the activities of conventional NGOs also hampered the spread of NGOs in Telangana belt. The Maoist groups, notably PWG in the past, had issued ultimatum to NGOs like Samata, Laya, AWARE, Spandana, Chaitanya Saravanti and so on operating in the agency districts of Visakhapatnam and East Godavari to stop their activities and leave the area. The reason for such ultimatum was the perception and ideological approach of Maoists that NGO activity hampered the growth of revolutionary movement in the area and influenced the backward and rural masses to depend upon the government machinery, courts and other agencies to solve their problems. PWG also accused NGOs of serving as agents of imperialists and working for the interests of bourgeoisie by depending heavily on foreign finances and their directives, instead of mitigating the genuine problems of the downtrodden and exploited sections. Some NGOs like Samata (East Godavari), Chaitanya Saravanti and Laya (both in Visakhapatnam district) shifted their area of operations, whereas others 'purchased peace' from the revolutionaries through negotiations and so on. Ironically, later PWG themselves admitted their lapses in properly assessing the ground-level situation vis-à-vis NGO activities and clarified that people themselves should shoulder the responsibility of supporting or opposing NGOs or other organizations on the basis of their activities and commitment to the downtrodden.

NGOs in the state are engaged in wide spectrum of activities targeting Dalits, tribals, rural poor, landless agriculturists/agricultural workers, women and children, victims of child/bonded labour, street children, slum dwellers and so on. These activities are in the form of:

1. Dalit-empowerment programme through training and financial support
2. Health-sanitation schemes in rural/Dalit-dominated areas
3. Rehabilitation of street children/victims of child labour
4. Financial incentives to women and rural poor for launching self-employment/ income-generating schemes
5. Creation of general awareness on the rights and privileges, especially of weaker sections
6. Human resources development programmes through training, seminars and workshop

A few organizations had done noteworthy work in the areas of rural development, health education and so on. On the rural development front, RDT, Anantapur, Young India Project (YIP) of Narendra Singh Bedi at Anantapur, Village Reconstruction Organization (VRO), Hyderabad and ASSIST of Guntur district had done moderately good contributions. Similarly, AWARE and SAKTHI could make some contributions in the Dalit-tribal fronts, whereas AMG India International of Gunter district had rendered notable service to the poor in the health sector.

The concept of 'networking' that did not exist among NGOs in the past has been gaining momentum mainly at the initiative of major foreign donor agencies/ voluntary bodies. This concept envisages the formation of a platform of NGOs working in the same field by pooling all their financial and manpower resources in order to attain significant results with the minimum misuse of funds. The networks are aimed at promoting common practices and standards in respect of policy and practices, identification of projects, their implementation and evaluation for which services of professional groups, if required, would be solicited. While a good number of NGOs have accepted the 'networking concept' and started implementing projects, many traditional NGOs like ASSIST, Village Reconstruction Organization and Creative Action for Rural Development CARD showed lukewarm attitude to the idea, fearing that they would lose their financial and organizational clout in any such arrangement. Some of the prominent 'networks' that had come up in the state are listed below.

Dalit Voluntary Associations Federation (DVAF): T.P.S Vardhan of Society for Integrated Development in Urban and Rural Areas (SIDUR), Hyderabad was the architect of this network. The DVAF has around 150 members (NGOs) in the state and work on the ultimate aim of unity among Dalits. The members of the forum are divided into three 'action groups', viz. big, medium and small. On an average, these groups receive ₹1 lakh per year with a monitoring budget to the tune of ₹10 lakhs. The entire budget is handled by SIDUR which receives the finances from EZE (Evangelische Zentralstelle Entwick-Lungshilfe), West Germany, and BILANCE (Netherland international development/donor agency; www. antenna.nl/bilance/en-index.ht), Netherlands, for their various projects. DVAF and its affiliates, despite its main slogan of Dalit unity, could not do much to bring various Dalit groups to a common platform. On the other hand, more dynamic outfits like National Dalit Human Rights Committee (NDHRC) could undertake more consistent programmes in the direction of protecting and promoting human rights of Dalits.

Guntur District Action Network: It was formed in 1996 at Pedakani, Guntur district at the initiative of T. Nageswara Rao, chief functionary of Creative Action for Rural Development,

Pedakani. This network has 33 member NGOs operating in Guntur district. It strives to bring about development through savings and political awareness among Dalits. Its bulk finances come from BILANCE.

Voluntary Action Network of Anantapur (VANA) came into existence in 1996 mainly at the instance of Gangi Reddy, chief functionary of Chaitanya Rural Education and Development Society (CREDS), Lekpashi, Anantapur district with the main aim of protecting the interests of NGOs from political harassment and mobilization of resources for common action programmes in the direction of uplift of Dalits and women. The long-term objective of VANA is to build up bigger movements on the pattern of CHIPKO[1] or National Fishermen Forum,[2] so that they can exert pressure over the governments in support of the demands of target groups. Around 20 NGOs working in Anatapur district have come under the umbrella of VANA which mobilizes its funds mainly from EZE, West Germany.

Cuddapah District Paryavarana Pariraksha Samiti (CPP) is a network of 14 NGOs formed in 1997 in Cuddapah at the initiative of P. Shiva Reddy, the chief functionary of Cuddapah-based NGO, Centre for Human Resources Development. Its objectives include forest conservation and afforestation under Joint Forest Management (JFM) programme.

West Godavari District Federation of Voluntary Organization (WEDFED) was formed in 1993 at the initiative of V. Prabhudas, the chief functionary of Centre for Reconstruction through Social Action (CRESA) which is operating in West Godavari. Seventeen NGOs are under its net.

Andhra Pradesh Rashtra Vyvasaya Cooleela Samakhya (AP State Agricultural Workers Federation) was formed at Chittor in 1989 mainly at the instance of YIP, an Anantapur-based NGO and Sakshi, another NGO of Chittor district. The primary objective of this Samakhya was to fight for legislation on the right to work and to unite the agricultural workers at national level. The Samakhya which has its units in 13 out of 23 districts in the state with around 60 NGOs as members also take keen interest on Dalit issues and extend active support for various campaigns and struggles by Dalit bodies such as Andhra Pradesh Dalit Mahasabha, Dalit Poratta Samiti and so on.

The Southern Collective: It is a network of various NGOs started by Narendra Singh Bedi of YIP in Anantapur district. There are around 70 NGOs from southern states and West Bengal in this network that work for the formation of a broad platform of NGOs at national level. It maintains links with National Network of Employment Guarantee Assurance (NNEGA) formed by Citizens for Democracy, Bandhu Mukthi Morcha and so on.

In late 1990s, Andhra had also witnessed other experiments in the NGO front. One such move was the 'Social Watch' for which inspiration came from the Copenhagen Social Summit of March 1995[3] and the follow-up action by the Voluntary Action Network of India (VANI).[4] The main slogan of the 'Social Watch' was 'development with social justice'. In Andhra its main endeavour is to work out better co-ordination and co-operation among NGOs and civil liberties movement in the state. Some of the major areas identified by the Watch include: State policies on poverty allevia-tion, health care, public distribution, primary education, public transport and so on and their impact over the masses, especially the poor; NGOs/people's movement/civil society and their inter-vention in policy formulation/development process; atrocities on women/gender justice vis-à-vis response of the state; democracy/ civil/human rights and state violence; social resurgence/Dalit/ tribal movements and religious fundamentalism/communal/caste conflicts.

One significant outcome of this move was the joint campaigns by NGOs and civil liberties movements, particularly Andhra Pradesh Civil Liberties Committee (APCLC) that in the past was keeping aloof from the activities and campaigns of conventional NGOs. The moves like 'Social Watch' by NGOs and independ-ent groups have become more relevant in the present millennium when concepts like religious fundamentalism, communalism, caste conflicts, social discrimination, mass displacement of indig-enous people due to new developmental projects by MNCs, new forms of people's struggles and so on have become order of the day, the state apparatus remaining a silent spectator of these developments. Only unbiased and independent NGOs can bring out real truth of such bizarre happenings, either neglected or cam-ouflaged by the state and its agencies.

The NGOs that mainly depend on foreign-donor agencies for their various projects and programmes are greatly influenced by these donors in the identification of tasks and selection of target groups. Thus, the issues like empowerment of marginalized sections like Dalits/tribals, women and rural poor, protection of human rights of weaker and oppressed sections, rural development, health and sanitation, housing for the shelterless, environmental protection and so on are the priority sectors of foreign donors like EZE, West Germany, BILANCE, Netherlands, Oxford Committee for Famine Relief (OXFAM), England, Bread for the World and so on. Thus, these sectors naturally find prominence in the action plan of majority of NGOs in the state. Some leading NGOs that have organized activities in these fields included: (a) CARD, Pedakani, Guntur Disrict; (b) Dalit Action and Research Centre (DARC), Chittor district; (c) Laya, Visakhapatnam; (d) Society for National Integration through Rural Development (SNIRD), Ongole, Prakasam district; (e) St Xavier's Society, Ongole, Prakasam district; (f) Rural Integrated Development Educational Society (RIDES), Gooty, Anantapur district; (g) Centre for World Solidarity (CWS), Taranaka, Hyderabad; (h) SIDUR, Hyderabad; (i) AWARE, Hyderabad and (j) SAKTHI, East Godavari district. These NGOs could build up considerable influence among Dalits, tribals, fishermen and agricultural workers by strongly espousing their various demands/issues. Through systematic activities and campaigns among the target groups, they could moderately contribute to the development and general awareness of these sections, as clearly manifested during the course of the study. These positive changes have also reflected in the human/civil rights scenario pertaining to these marginalized groups. Some overambitious NGOs like AWARE tried to capitalize the good will of these sections to fulfil political aspirations and floated their own parties (like Sama Samaj Party of AWARE) and contested the elections in the state. But, they could not meet with any major success in such endeavours. This was also indicative that NGO activities could not make any major impact in influencing the political perception of marginalized sections except in the case of tribals and rural poor, who had come under the radar and influence of Left radical groups as noticed in parts of Telangana area.

The annual inflow of foreign funds to NGOs in Andhra Pradesh, according to rough estimates is to the tune of ₹300–₹400 crores. The major foreign donors included: (a) Evangelische Zentralstelle Entwick-Lungshilfe (EZE), Germany; (b) Humanistic Institute for Development & Co-operation with Developing Countries (HIVOS), Holland; (c) BILANCE, Netherlands; (d) Inter-Church Organisation for Development Cooperation (ICCO), Holland, and so on which are directly funding the NGOs. Clubs formed in western countries are also a source of funding. A new concept of NGO funding has developed in the West, particularly in USA, Canada and so on where Indian expatriates raise consortium of funds to support particular NGOs. Besides, a number of voluntary organizations have been receiving indigenous funds from agencies such as Council for Advancement of People's Action and Rural Technology (CAPART) and other central and state welfare departments like District Rural Development Agency (DRDA) and so on for rural and women-oriented developmental schemes (details of major NGOs, their main target areas and funding agencies are given in the Appendix).

9

A Way Ahead

In the backdrop of the increasing instances of human rights violations, two crucial questions that were examined in detail were the effectiveness of the constitutional and legal mechanisms in safeguarding these rights and the role of state and its superstructures. The awareness' of the general public on their basic civil rights and understanding of NGOs were assessed along with the perception of police on NGOs and civil liberties organizations. Various research tools have been applied to collect empirical data from a wide spectrum of samples which included NGO—functionaries, academicians, bureaucrats, journalists, judicial-experts, police personnel and general public.[1] The views of prominent personalities closely connected with the theme of study, elicited during personal interview, were incorporated. The analysis of these data unfolded certain major conclusions.

On the question of the 'Role of state and its agencies in guaranteeing and protecting human rights', it was overwhelmingly felt that democracy is the best form of government for the protection and promotion of human rights as compared to other forms of governments like monarchy, oligarchy, aristocracy and so on. The Indian democracy that withstood many challenges since independence was not an exception to this truth. The Constitutional and legal provisions, a vibrant judiciary and vigilant fourth estate, are the major players in safeguarding human rights concept in Indian polity. But there are major lapses from the part of the state and its agencies in the enforcement of Constitutional and legal provisions safeguarding human rights.

Our Constitution is crystal clear on the issue of the protection and promotion of civil liberties and human rights of all sections of people. The preamble itself ensuring all citizens, 'JUSTICE social, economic and political; LIBERTY, of thought, expression and belief, faith and worship; EQUALITY, of status and of opportunity and to promote among them all FRATERNITY assuring the dignity of the individual and the unity and integrity of the Nation' unequivocally upholds the commitment of the nation in safeguarding these rights. The directive principles of the state policy also contain specific provisions to protect the human rights, especially of marginalized and underprivileged sections. But these rights could not be enjoyed by many sections of the society because the institutions created by the constitution have become the preserve of the dominant groups. So long as the constitutional provisions and safeguards are not implemented in their true letter and spirit, we cannot use constitution as protective shield for safeguarding human rights. Thus, many of the laudable ideals in the constitution remain as unfulfilled dream for the majority of the Indian masses, even after six decades of independence. The main reason for this distressing trend, according to constitutional experts like Dr M.V. Pylee (Kerala)[2] is the weakness of our institutions in the enforcement of various legislations and Acts.

The civil rights activists were bitter on these lacunae in our system. Late K.G. Kannabiran, the founder leader of APCLC was vociferous in his criticism of state and its agencies in this regard:

Indian State does not give much sacrosance to the concept of Human or Civil rights. For over 60 years in Jammu Kashmir and in the North East and around 30 years in Andhra Pradesh, such rights have been violated under one pretext or the other. The successive governments at the Centre adopted almost uniform policies in dealing with these issues. The emergence of regional political parties, in these States, failed to fulfill the aspirations of the masses, because of their over dependence on conventional politics. No serious attempt has been made by the Centre to sort out the socio-economic-political issues, projected by the people or the movements which spearheaded the struggles. Instead, political issues were handled as mere law & order problems with the induction of Army and paramilitary forces, which were instrumental for the large scale violation of human/civil rights and the alienation of people from the national mainstream.[3]

But, the limitations of the state in protecting the whole gamut of human and civil rights should not be ignored. As rightly pointed out by Ms Kiran Bedi, IPS, 'as the human rights now cover a wide spectrum of activities, which determine the 'dignity of human life', no state—whatever effective in the enforcement of these rights—can fully protect the human rights. In India, also, the situation is not different. Over the years, the concept of human rights has undergone radical transformation from the conventional, political and civil rights to 'collective rights', covering a myriad of issues such as environmental hazards, social security, health problems of aged and handicapped and so on. Such issues cannot be tackled by government alone.[4]

The reality that many of the institutional mechanisms by the state have virtually failed in the protection and promotion of human rights should not be undermined. The institutional constraints force the judiciary to keep human rights on low profile. The judiciary has their own limitations to enforce their decisions. A unique example is the guidelines issued by the apex court in all cases of arrest, while disposing a public interest petition, filed by Dr D.K. Basu, executive chairman of the Legal Aid Services, West Bengal.

> There is no decrease in the number of lock-up deaths or police torture in custody, even after the apex court judgment. The truth is that these guidelines have not been observed by police; nor there any effective mechanism to ensure the enforcement of judicial pronouncements whether in the case of police or other agencies in the country.[5]

But legal luminaries are of the view that of the various institutions, judiciary plays a pivotal role in the area of human rights. Justice (retired) V.R. Krishna Iyer of the supreme court has elaborated this aspect:

> The civil and political rights of citizens have been violated, whereas their socio-economic and cultural rights could not be safeguarded. Thus, on many occasions the courts intervene on such issues and give directions to the State, for the enforcement of these rights on the spirit of the Constitution. The genesis of Public Interest Litigation (PIL) gave further momentum to the concept of human rights. On issues like bonded labour, child- labour, denial of minimum wages

to contract workers, exploitation of women, jail conditions etc., the courts made far-reaching judgments, which helped to improve the human rights situation in these fields.[6]

But it is felt that the strengthening of human rights law at grassroots level has become imperative to deal effectively with the human rights violations. For that purpose, lower judiciary should be designated as human rights courts/judges for taking up the cases involving human rights violations. But the crucial aspect is that such courts or functionaries can effectively play their role of protecting human rights only when the provisions of international humanitarian law and the international covenants are incorporated in our municipal (local) laws.

On the other hand, the police organization has come under critical radar for their omissions and commissions in the field of human rights. The police who are duty bound to safeguard the life and properties of citizens has crucial role in protection and promotion of human rights. Unfortunately, the police could not effectively play this role. On many occasions, they negate their plenary commitment to the Constitutional/human values. This leads to police excesses and brutalities such as 'fake encounters', 'custodial deaths', 'third-degree methods', and so on which are the worst forms of human rights violations in a civilized society. A transformation in the political set-up with corresponding socio-economic changes alone can improve the functioning of police. So long as the police functions as an appendage to the existing political system, they would continue their excesses and violence in which the human rights would be the biggest casualty. There should be greater autonomy to police with stringent methods of accountability to the rule of law and people, where the slightest aberration should be initiated with major penalty as severe as they make it against terrorists. 'An erring policeman and a criminal should be treated one and the same'.[7]

Mere reforms in police organization would not help to develop a human rights friendly police. What is more important is an attitudinal change among the personnel coupled with their commitment to Constitutional/legal provisions and 'due process of law'. As rightly highlighted by the National Police Commission (1977–1981) in its final report, 'it is urgent and essential to devise new mechanisms of accountability to ensure certain amount of direct responsibility to the personnel at various levels of police administration'.[8] Thus, the need of the hour is the proper training and education, particularly to the constabulary, who is the cutting edge of the force. They should be familiarized with Constitutional provisions, every branch of law vis-à-vis human rights, legal parameters in the exercise of police powers, human rights and emergency situations, police and weaker sections and the major international covenants on human rights. 'Chief justice (retired) MN Venkitachellaih former Chairman of NHRC emphasized this aspect by holding that the incidence of human rights violations can be brought down only when there is radical change in the functioning and attitude of police'.[9] The NHRC has accorded top-most priority in creating human rights awareness among police personnel. The state police forces were sensitized on the need of organizing training to the personnel on human rights and interrelated aspects of police functioning. The commission prepared and circulated three-tier syllabus/training modules on human rights for constables, sub-inspectors/inspectors and SPOs.

In the backdrop of the ever-widening horizons of human rights and the limitations of the state/its agencies in fully protecting the mosaic of these rights the NGOs/civil liberties groups have a crucial role to play. Two trends were clear. While major civil liberties groups are vigorously pursuing human rights cause, majority of conventional NGOs are yet to accord priority to human rights agenda. Late K.G. Kannabiran, civil rights activist commented that 'majority of the NGOs are reluctant to step into the field of civil liberties movement, because of the inherent risk involved in this sector. They prefer to operate in risk-free sectors such as child labour, environment, welfare of weaker sections etc'.[10] This trend was more visible in LWE-affected states like Andhra Pradesh, Chhattisgarh and so on where human rights NGOs face dual threat from state agencies (branding them as pro-LWE) and from ultras for their alleged neo-colonial and imperialist nature of campaign and activities. Smt Nafisa D'Souza,[11] who is associated with leading NGOs like 'LAYA' (Visakhapatnam) actively among tribals has expressed such views that any 'action-oriented pro-grammes' by NGOs such as forceable occupation of tribal lands, now illegally occupied by non-tribals, would be misconstrued as 'Naxalite-inspired actions' followed by police repression.

T. Pratap Reddy,[12] a prominent PUCL leader closely associated with 'Vigil India Movement' highlighted that:

The conventional NGOs, which are more concerned on their foreign funds, chalk out their programs on the directions of the funding agencies. This strategy has caused much damage to the growth and consolidation of voluntary movements and in making significant contributions in the field of social resurgence or promotion of human rights.

Though NGOs in general could play a limited role in attracting the state/administration towards human rights issues, they were more successful in the creation of human rights awareness among masses. But there are certain sections of the society like police who have reservations to accept NGOs/CLM as protectors of human rights. This is indicative of the general trend that police which wields considerable power and authority do not pay much heed to community/volunteer organizations or their activities. In many respects, police–CLM relations remain strained, if not hostile. Despite such strained relations, NGOs could extend some assistance to police in preventing certain offences. This was at the instance of community policing and such other schemes in which NGOs have become an essential component.

Significantly, NGOs/CLM could create moderate awareness on human rights among masses, especially among weaker sections such as Dalits/tribals. Another interesting trend was that political activists were least influenced by the activities of NGOs, especially in human rights front. In a nutshell, one of the major hypothesis of the study that NGOs/CLM played a positive role in the protection and promotion of political, civil, economic and social rights of masses, especially of marginalized sections like Dalits and tribals stands proved, despite the known weaknesses of NGO movement such as propaganda-oriented and profit-oriented programmes and projects. The mushroom growth of NGOs and the genesis of government-sponsored NGOs (GONGOs) with motivated propaganda and campaign have adversely affected the credibility of the movement.

Basically, while maintaining identity, human rights NGOs and civil rights groups need to develop better synergy in their campaigns and activities as both are wedded to the task of protection and promotion of human rights. As rightly pointed out by R.V. Pillai, IAS, former secretary general of NHRC (1998):

> Unlike the conventional NGOs, the role of civil liberties groups is apparently different. No civil liberties movement can broaden their mass base through ideological propaganda alone, which will only influence a microscopic section. Instead they should take initiative for the proper rehabilitation of the victims of human rights violations. There should not be any discrimination in such endeavour.[13]

Many senior CLM leaders have similar views on the need of broadening the base of civil liberties organizations. Prof. Kodanda Rama Reddy,[14] Department of Political Science, Osmania University and a functionary of APCLC maintained (1998):

> CLM should change its scope and nature according to the development of various socio-political movements. Instead of strictly following the concept of rights enshrined in the Indian Constitution, the movement has to follow the concept of 'democratic rights'. APCLC, though originated in the context of Naxalite movement has expanded its scope to include the 'dalits and women-rights'. Another APCLC functionary Kannabiran was more specific when he commented 'for the protection of human rights, Civil Liberties movement should focus their attention in three major tasks viz. campaigns and activities in support of rights such as liberty, equality and right to life; attainment of credibility through autonomous and unbiased actions and more serious efforts for the proper rehabilitation of the victims of human rights violation'.

The reality that the issues and the campaigns raised by the civil society are getting more and more acceptance in the contemporary society should catch the imagination and policies and programmes of CLM. Thus, besides extending their activities to grassroots level, they should focus their attention on the new fields of civil/ human rights issues such as large-scale corruption and manipulations by political leaders/bureaucrats that adversely affect the common people or steady environmental degradation and wide use of banned pesticides/insecticides causing serious diseases/deformities to the people. Above all, rights and problems of marginalized sections such as Dalits/tribals, children and women should find priority in their agenda, apart from their continued tirade to uphold the civil and political rights of all sections of people.

NGOs, on the other hand present a different picture. As the state is unable to fulfil all the rights and privileges of different sections in a society, the participatory role of NGOs in strengthening the state's wide spectrum of activities and programmes has substantially increased in the present century. The NGO movement in the West, particularly in USA and UK proved this trend when NGOs undertook multifold activities, including the protection and promotion of human rights. For example, Ms Hillary Clinton was heading NGOs in the field of childcare and health when Bill Clinton was US president. Ms Clinton's[15] declaration in 1992 that healthcare is a 'non-negotiable human right' had evoked heated discussion in US governmental circles.

Basically, all well-intentioned NGOs can play a dual role in the society. On one hand, they can perform watchdog functions by highlighting human right violations and drawing the attention of the state for punitive and remedial measures, whereas on the other hand, they can equip and empower the people to enjoy their rights. Given the nature of rights, such a wide array of roles is inevitable. Strong expressions of outrage following illegal arrests, detention, fake encounters or custodial deaths capture the attention of the people at large and of the authorities in particular and create an atmosphere for prompt punitive and corrective action. Even though the role of voluntary organizations in such cases was earlier limited to articulating violation, there is a growing tendency, which is very welcome, to undertake enquiries and report the findings. Of late, the voluntary bodies have taken active interest in promoting the socio-economic and cultural rights of the people, particularly the marginalized sections. There are a number of NGOs, which work for the empowerment of women, elimination of child and bonded labour, literacy among the poor and rural sections, upliftment of Dalits and tribals and harnessing of resources and technology to ensure drinking water and pollution-free air. The crucial question of interest was how such diverse tasks would be effectively performed by NGOs.

A paradigm shift in NGO functioning is essential in order to improve their performance in the human rights front. Prioritization and professionalism are two key aspects in this regard. As many NGOs are overstretched with multiplicity of projects and programmes disproportionate to their resources and manpower, they are unable to make substantial impact among target groups, particularly in the human rights field. This lacuna, to a great extent, can be overcome through the 'networking of NGOs'. However, 'networking for networks' sake' or to comply with the directions of foreign-donor agencies will not serve any major purpose. The properly synthesized and synergized networks facilitate effective mobilization of resources and manpower and their rational utilization, leading to substantial impact among target groups. On the other hand, artificial ones that definitely lack integrated approach, commitment and sincerity open complex organizational issues.

Another equally important aspect is proper identification and prioritization of targets and tasks on the basis of the social milieu and dynamics. This is applicable to conventional NGOs, radical NGOs or action-oriented NGOs. When feudal issues or exploitation of weaker sections like Dalits, tribals, rural poor and landless peasants are rampant, the emphasis is on 'action-oriented campaigns' by mobilizing the affected sections. Then there is a phase of consolidation of NGOs through the establishment of institutions, training centres, income-generating projects and so on. No doubt, the foreign-funding agencies have greatly influenced this trend. Now, the stress is to transform the NGO movement as more indigenous and self-dependent, with their roots firmly grounded in the soil in which they work. Simultaneously, the concept and approach need transformation in line with the perception and aspirations of target groups. For example, for many 'tribal women' the non-tribals are alluring because the present new worldview is charming and attractive. Social evils like 'dowry system' slowly creep into tribal communities, which shatter the concepts of gender equality, integrity in interactions and community bonds. Such changes in the outlook of target groups should come in the purview of the policies, strategies and programmes of NGOs. Then only, they can do justice to their existence.

More co-ordinated efforts are needed to improve their performance. Too much dependence on foreign-funding agencies or their guidelines in the implementation of projects will prompt NGOs to deviate from their actual tasks/targets. Self-sufficiency, in resources, may argument their effectiveness as well as image. For that purpose, governmental support to NGOs is imperative. The strategies like channelizing a portion of the developmental

funds of government, through reputed and sincere NGOs, induction of NGO representatives in governmental committees, especially for social development/welfare may help to strengthen
NGO–government relations. They should enrol grassroots workers, motivate them, train them and field them with clear objectives
and goals. For example, in areas where percentage of literacy is
very low, door to door propaganda may be undertaken with wide
publicity and active involvement of the people. Cells or centres
in every locality may be opened to receive complaints/grievances
relating to human rights violations

Creation of awareness on human rights alone would not help
to check the violations. Awareness coupled with action would
improve the image or credibility of NGOs. These 'actions' should
be within the parameters of law and Constitution and should not
conflict with society. For example, NGOs or 'activists' can initiate PIL on grave violations of human rights. This is what has
exactly happened in Gujarat where the organized efforts of the
state to bury under the carpet the gruesome violations of human
rights were to a great extent defeated by NGOs and 'activists' like
Ms Teesta Setelvad through their relentless legal crusade. The
lawyer community and professionals can extend significant help
to NGOs in such campaigns and activities. These professionals while educating NGOs/volunteers on law and judicial process should strive to develop proper attitude to respect law and
human rights.

To improve the effectiveness of NGOs in the human rights
front, a number of practical and innovative mechanisms or strategies need to be developed. They include: (*a*) formation of human
rights watch group at village, taluk and district level with proper
training for effective intervention on human rights violations,
especially of marginalized sections. (*b*) Effective human rights
campaigns through multimedia network which includes telecast
of proper stories on human rights and publication of booklets,
leaflets and other literature on different aspects of these rights.
The electronic media should also be fully made use of. (*c*) Research
and documentation on major human rights violations/issues with
the publication of authentic fact-finding reports for facilitating the
intervention of the state/its agencies. (*d*) Taking up major human
rights violations in high courts/supreme court, particularly of
marginalized sections. (*e*) Promotion of human rights awareness

among students of schools and colleges through publication of literature, telecast of documentaries/films, talk by functionaries of NGOs, human rights experts and (d) establishment of data/documentation centres to collect, analyze, compile and disseminate information on human rights.

The perception of police and common public on NGOs assume considerable significance, especially from human rights angle. Conceptually, police are the protectors and promoters of human rights. But there is a wide gap on the concept and practice as clearly manifest during the study.[16] If the police develop cordial relations with civil society and voluntary bodies engaged in human relations issues, the greater would be their contributions on the protection of these rights. The human rights violations were not mainly due to lack of awareness on human rights among police personnel but due to other factors like the misuse of power, discretion and authority for vested interest or at the instance of extraneous forces. The weaker/marginalized sections were the worst victims of this 'police culture'. The political intervention on the functioning of police and the overzealous approach of a section of police leaders to appease the political masters were other causative factors for violation of human rights by police. Moreover, many police personnel had their own apprehensions on the actual intentions of major civil liberties and human rights NGOs that operate in LWE-affected states. Many middle-level police officers were blunt in their view that majority of these bodies functioned as 'front organizations of Naxalites'. Thus, police did not pay much heed to the campaigns of these groups focusing on human rights issues. On the other hand, police's approach towards conventional NGOs was different as they focused on socio-economic and cultural issues of marginalized sections like Dalits, tribals, women, children and landless farmers and seldom the conflict with police or other state agencies. A clear distinction is drawn between such NGOs and civil liberties groups as succinctly put by Ms Kiran Bedi (IPS):

> There are NGOs particularly from civil liberties side—which is totally biased and partisan in their approach and activities. For many of them, bashing police in the name of the violation of human rights has become a fashion of their campaign. Police is their whipping boy. For them, all other institutions are sacrosanct. The NGOs and Civil Rights Groups should be equally concerned over the

human rights of police personnel or the victims of militants. Their reluctance to denounce the violations by militant groups due to ideological or other reason is the major stumbling bloc in improving the relations between NGOs and police, at ground level.[16]

So long as police–NGO relations remain strained, the former do not expect much from the latter in policing tasks. Apparently, such trends are more focused and glaring in areas where police have stepped up operations, particularly against extremists/militants. In such a scenario, police do not find any major role from NGOs in assisting them in the law-enforcement tasks. The police personnel are also averse to the idea of giving rights to reputed NGOs to investigate into human rights violations by police. This clearly reflects that police personnel are not prepared to dilute their powers or authority. The fact of the matter is that police is generally against outside intervention in their affairs, including grave aberrations by the personnel. The general approach of police leadership is that the organization has effective internal mechanisms to deal with any major omissions or commissions by the personnel. This approach, on many occasions, evoke controversies and strain police–public relations, especially when police leaders try to exonerate personnel involved in grave offences.

The ground-level reality that the state and its agencies have limitations to fully comply with the constitutional and legal commitments to promote and protect human rights points to the need of NGOs and civil rights groups playing a major role in this field. A number of innovative mechanisms/strategies should be seriously thought of to better harmonize police–NGO relations to strengthen human rights concept in policing. These should include (*a*) better interaction between police and NGO functionaries by effectively utilizing community/proactive policing strategies. The NGOs can be well involved in preventive and proactive policing such as juvenile issues, drug menace, eve teasing, dowry and harassment and so on. Similarly, they can also assist police in reporting criminal activities and collecting facts and so on. Through such exercises, NGOs can harmonize and strengthen their relations with police, both at functional and leadership level. (*b*) Extending resources to reputed NGOs in order to launch propaganda against anti-social activities and to sensitize the general public on the constraints/difficulties of police in enforcing law and order. (*c*) Organizing of seminars/workshops/panel discussions on specific issues of policing/human rights for police personnel, especially the lower level functionaries, circulation/distribution of pamphlets relating to human rights among personnel with the participation of NGO functionaries and police leaders. (d) Annual planning strategy to protect human rights and check human rights violations need to be formulated jointly by state human rights commission, police personnel and NGOs. Similarly, joint endeavours by NGOs and police for imparting training/knowledge to lower functionaries of police on human rights and interrelated aspects during day to day policing should be initiated at district level. The meeting of district magistrates, SPs/SPOs, human rights activists/NGOs should be convened annually to review the overall law and order situation vis-a-vis human rights issues. (e) Formation of independent committees with the representatives of police, district administration and reputed NGOs at PS/district level to monitor the functioning of police as well as the campaigns/activities of civil rights groups/NGOs. The committee should interact with police and NGO representatives, at regular intervals, in order to create 'human rights friendly' atmosphere in that particular area and (f) Initiate effective steps to update the knowledge/understanding of subordinates/lower level functionaries on the legal and procedural changes, having relevance to human rights. Monthly meetings should be organized for such exercises. The representatives of civil rights groups/NGOs should be invited as guest speakers in order to share their views.

While the police are the important instrument of the state in the protection of human rights, the general public constitutes the major element of civil society in the protection and promotion of these rights. The more the awareness of the people on such issues, the more effective be the protection of these rights by the state and its establishments. Thus, the bodies like NHRC emphasized the need of creating awareness on human rights in the civil society through a number of campaigns and programmes in which NGOs can play a leading role. The public in general, particularly the urban and semi-urban sections have reasonably better awareness on their rights on situations arising out of day to day policing such as arrest, detention of women and ill people, detention after arrest, questioning of accused and so on. Another noticeable trend was that women, particularly of urban/semi-urban background had better awareness on such matters of policing. This also reflects the fact that any omission or commission by police such as illegal arrest/detention and use of third-degree methods against arrested persons in police custody get quick public attention and adversely affect police image. This speaks of the need of police strictly adhering to rule of law and due process of law in matters like arrest, which is imperative for maintaining their popular image.

The NGOs and civil rights groups play a crucial role in creating such awareness among the masses. Significantly, a number of NGOs are active among marginalized groups like women, children and Dalits. Another noticeable trend was that NGO movement has the potential to influence the psyche of these marginalized and underprivileged groups. The growth of NGO movement and the awareness created by them among marginalized sections have contributed in checking excesses by police and other agencies.

There are 'black sheep' among NGOs as well. They are nicknamed as 'briefcase NGOs' or 'pocket NGOs' primarily indicating that they are keen to mobilize finances and to fill the pockets of the functionaries, rather than doing anything constructive for the target groups. Ms Kiran Bedi, who runs her own NGO (Nav Jyothi in Delhi), has rightly commented: 'it is not correct to say that all NGOs have right objective or commitment or only spreading the Gospel truth.'[17] The people in general have goodwill towards sincere and committed NGOs. However, enlightened and elite sections have misgivings about NGOs on the ground that majority of them are dominated by vested interests and urge for foreign funds.

There was general consensus that more systematic and organized efforts should be initiated to inculcate 'human rights culture' in the society through education, for which human rights subjects should be introduced in schools and colleges. Interrelated with this is the adoption of effective steps for the improvement of literacy among women. For that purpose, NGOs working in the women front should chalk out special programmes in co-operation with state departments. The electronic and print media should be fully exploited to properly ventilate human rights issues during special occasions like Human Rights Day (10 December), Teachers Day (5 September) and so on. NGOs should resort to other strategies like dissemination of human rights themes through TV channels, cinema halls, wall postering at public places and so on.

Reorientation of the style and functioning of police organization is vital to make them human rights friendly. Recruitment of better educated persons to police forces, revamping of training curriculum by giving more emphasis on humane, moral/ethical subjects, intensive training of lower police functionaries on human rights and related legal aspects, end corruption and political interference in police functioning and improvement in the service and working conditions of police personnel and so on are imperative to make police organization more human rights friendly. There is a strong feeling that the improvement in police professionalism and their approach towards the general public would help to contain human rights violations of different nature.

The different shades of extremism, militancy and violence by various groups and counter-measures by the state and its agencies breed maximum number of human rights violations in the society. Thus, the NGOs and civil rights groups should make organized efforts to sensitize the people on such dangers in order to wean away the people from the influence of such forces. Side by side, the issues of development and social welfare, especially of weaker and marginalized sections, should be properly taken up to draw the attention of government and its agencies. An effective monitoring mechanism at grassroots level to be developed in order to monitor the implementation of welfare programmes for the marginalized sections.

All-round efforts should be made for the empowerment of women through better education, gender equality and guaranteeing jobs. Other measures such as model punishment to violations of human rights, compensation to victims and easy accessibility to public for approaching Human Rights Commissions and so on to mitigate their grievances should be enforced by the state which should demonstrate its sincerity and commitment in protecting and promoting human rights.

10

Conclusion

Findings

In the fast-changing world order, with the global trends towards powerful institutions and individualism and nation-states undergoing 'role transition' from 'provider' to 'policymaker', the NGOs which occupy a major space in 'civil society' represent a 'third way'[1] for collectivism and development. Their role is more important in fast-developing countries like India, where traditional strategies of socio-economic development, based on large-scale institutionalized methods and mechanisms, have not achieved the desired results or the upliftment of the target groups. Inevitably, malgovernance with corruption and indifferent bureaucracy has become the stumbling block in the challenging task of the nation emerging as an advanced affluent one in the present millennium. Thus, the fruits of development have not properly 'trickled down' to bring consistent and sustained improvement in the standards of living and quality of life of the poor and underprivileged sections.

The globalization and the new market economy controlled by powerful MNCs have widened the gulf between the rich and poor, relegating the marginalized sections particularly Dalits, Adivasis and rural poor to extreme poverty and deprivation due to new strategies of development, degrading nature and natural resources and displacing the sons of the soil. While planning experts and economists give mountain sermons on GDP or industrial growth or vibrant resilient economy surpassing the West, we hear the tragic stories of the suicide of farmers or the people dying in the streets due to starvation and poverty. Such internal contradictions in our developmental strategy acted as breeding grounds for organized struggles and movements, mainly by the deprived and exploited sections. These situations opened a floodgate of socio-economic and political issues in which the LWE has become the biggest challenge to the internal security of the nation coupled with human rights issues and violations in West Bengal, Orissa, Chhattisgarh, Jharkhand, Maharashtra, Bihar and Andhra Pradesh and perhaps in almost all states. The study, which was mainly intended to examine these issues and find out how far NGOs and civil liberties organizations were potential to protect and promote human rights in such a society, inflicted with major aberrations in socio-economic development and internal conflicts and struggles, brought out the following major findings.

Among the various forms of government, conceptually democracy is the best system for the protection and promotion of human rights. In such a system, the Constitutional and legal provisions are adequate to protect these rights. Though the state and its agencies are constitutionally and legally bound to protect and promote human rights, they are able to protect these rights 'to some extent' only. On many occasions, the Constitutional and legal guarantees in safeguarding human rights of various sections could not be enforced at ground level. In almost all forms of regimes, this dichotomy exists in respect of what nations profess and practice in the case of human rights. India, as per our findings, is not an exception. The increasing incidence of human rights issues and violations, as manifest in the annual reports of NHRC and the fact-finding reports of civil liberties groups and NGOs, demonstrated this trend. Meanwhile, bodies like NHRC have not got enough teeth to effectively carry out various tasks of protecting and promoting human rights. In many instances of gross violations of human rights, the recommendations of NHRC including compensation to the victims/families have not been conceded by the governments/authorities. Same is the case with other half a dozen custodians of interest of marginalized sections like Dalits/tribals, minorities, women and children. They include National Commission for the Welfare of SC/ST, National Commission for Minorities, National Commission for Women and National

Commission for the Rights of Children and so on. There is neither clear focus nor dynamic coordination among all these venerable institutions. Their studies, reports and recommendations languish without any interest whatsoever.

The various disturbing aspects of the socio-economic context that prevails in large parts of India have contributed to politics such as that of the Naxalite movement and other forms of sub-nationalist struggles. The movements such as LWE draw their main support base from the marginalized sections, especially tribals and rural poor who remain discontented and disillusioned for many decades because of the development paradigm insensitive to their needs and concerns. Development which is insensitive to the needs of these communities has invariably caused displacement and reduced them to a sub-human existence. In the case of tribals in particular, it has ended up in destroying their social organization, cultural identity, and resource base and generated multiple conflicts undermining their communal solidarity, which cumulatively makes them increasingly vulnerable to exploitation. The benefits of this paradigm of development have been disproportionately cornered by the dominant sections at the expense of the poor, who have borne most of the costs.

It should be recognized that calling and treating LWE or similar movements as unrest or a disruption of law and order is little more than a rationale for suppressing them by force. Ironically, our counter-extremist strategy focusing such movements as law and order issues is not conducive to work out permanent solution to serious internal security threats like LWE. It is necessary to contextualize the tensions in terms of social, economic and political background and bring back on the agenda the issues of the people—the right to livelihood, the right to life and a dignified and honourable existence. The state itself should feel committed to the democratic and human rights and humane objectives that are inscribed in the preamble, the fundamental rights and directive principles of the Constitution. The state has to adhere strictly to the rule of law. Indeed, the state has no other authority to rule in a democracy.

The NGOs and civil liberties organizations with a clear programme of action can play a pivotal role in such efforts. These bodies which have moderate space in the civil society have made contributions to improve the human rights scenario. The extent of their contributions varies from moderate to high, depending upon the areas/target groups, in which they are working for the promotion of human rights/related issues. Their impact was more in the tribal/Dalit front. When the civil liberties groups concentrated more on the protection and promotion of political and civil rights, the emphasis of NGOs was on the promotion of economic and social rights of marginalized sections. Their activities are significant considering the fact that human rights now encompass all different facets of human life.

The NGO movement in many states like Andhra Pradesh had accelerated the socio-economic development, particularly of Dalits, tribals and rural poor. These target groups have marginally succeeded in strengthening their economic base, including ownership of cultivable and irrigated land, better tenancy rights, and attainment of minimum wages, increased production and productivity, levels of capitalization and production of marketable surpluses. Socially, their status, had improved to some extent, as there was a noticeable change of attitude from the part of private and public actors like landlords and government officials towards these discriminated and exploited lot of the society. These socio-economic changes among the weaker sections led to a moderate improvement in their human rights awareness.

The awareness of the general public about human rights and their rights and privileges, especially the basic individual freedom and liberty vis-à-vis the role of major civil liberties groups/NGOs in espousing human/civil rights causes remained high among the urban and semi-urban sections as compared to rural people. The NGOs are engaged in accentuating the awareness of marginalized rural sections on these rights, through a process of 'social resurgence and 'social engineering' with the active involvement of these target groups and their representative organizations. However, the process of 'social engineering' is yet to gain momentum in many states where feudal neo-colonial forces are dominant.

The civil liberties groups, particularly in left-wing extremist states have occupied some space in the civil society through their campaigns and activities, focusing police excesses and fake encounter killings. Bodies like APCLC through their legal battles and intervention with NHRC could obtain certain significant orders against fake encounters and custodial violence. This has also opened a polemics on 'state violence' and violence by revolutionary/extremist movements. The approach of major civil liberties groups is that state-sponsored violence should not be equated with extremist violence and the fundamental duty of a civil/human rights NGO is to denounce state-sponsored violence without extrapolating wanton killings and violence by revolutionary/extremist groups. Taking cue of this line, prominent human rights NGOs vehemently oppose the counter-extremist strategy of the governments, especially state-sponsored private forces like *Salwa Judum* in Chhattisgarh. The above stand of civil liberties groups like APCLC has strained their relations with the government/police.

The police at cutting-edge level (sub-inspectors/circle inspectors), particularly in left-extremism affected states have high degree of awareness on the activities of major civil liberties groups/NGOs, as compared to lower-level functionaries notably constabulary. The relationship between NGOs/civil liberties groups and police remained strained, if not hostile. NGOs could make limited impact in making police human rights friendly; police could not find any significant role for NGOs in assisting them in the enforcement of law and order. In rural areas the general public suffers from 'police phobia' which the NGOs/civil liberties groups could not contain through their campaigns. This alienation of the public adversely affects community policing and such other programmes by police. Besides launching campaigns against police excesses, the other major activities of NGOs from human rights angle included: (*a*) Dalit/tribal development/empowerment projects, (*b*) health-sanitation schemes in rural areas dominated by marginalized sections, (*c*) rehabilitation of street children/victims of child and bonded labour, (*d*) empowerment of women, landless agricultural workers and rural poor, (*e*) self-employment and Income-generating schemes for weaker sections through financial incentives/loans and so on, (*f*) housing projects for the shelterless, urban slum dwellers, underprivileged and unorganized sections, (*g*) human resources development schemes/awareness campaigns of weaker sections, through workshop/seminars, training of volunteers and so on, (*h*) specific campaigns and propaganda on human rights issues such as untouchability, denial of minimum wages to agricultural workers, alienation of tribal lands, displacement of tribals, atrocities against women/Dalits and so on.

A shift in the strategy and operations of NGOs had come up in many states, largely at the instance of foreign-funding agencies. The major concept that was gaining ground in the NGO movement is the 'networking' and 'alliance building'. In this concept, NGOs identify common interest and concern; share information; provide support to each other and maximize the use of available resources to achieve optimum results in the target areas/groups. They are the manifestations of co-operative strategies to improve the impact of NGO operations. Such 'networking' of NGOs is active in the Dalit and landless agricultural workers fronts. The empowerment and the protection of the right and privileges of marginalized groups are the main tasks of these networks. Certain foreign-funding agencies, such as EZE (West Germany), BILANCE (Netherlands), OXFAM (England), ICCO and HIVOS (both in Holland), which have prioritized the socio-economic advancement of marginalized and underprivileged sections in backward areas of India, financially support the projects of these networks.

Though NGOs could make moderate contributions in the socio-economic development and the promotion of human rights among marginalized sections, unhealthy trends such as the emergence of fraudulent NGOs (nicknamed as 'briefcase NGOs), over dependence on foreign-funding agencies in policy formulations/ prioritization of projects, overstretching of resources by taking up multifold activities for mere propaganda and publicity without any tangible achievements, building up 'pressure groups' on political–ideological lines, advancing personal interests and, last but not the least, the improper accounting and utilization of foreign funds had also crept into the movement because of the omissions and commission of a few NGOs. Moreover, the emergence of GONGOs to toe the line of the governments on controversial issues had also eclipsed the image of NGOs among sections of people, notably the middle-class intelligentsia.

LWE and counter-measures to combat it constituted one of the major areas of human rights issues and violations. The extent and gravity of such violations could be well assessed from the staggering figures of killing of extremists, civilians and security personnel in LWE-affected states. The depredations by these groups in the form of wanton killings of innocent civilians branding them as police informers, abduction of citizens, bomb explosions/land-mine blasts resulting in the death of civilians/police personnel, fratricidal killings, destruction of public and private properties worth crores of rupees and the counter-extremist operations by law-enforcement agencies leading to the killing of extremists and civilians accounted for the largest number of human rights viola-tions in the country.

The untouchability in different shades and forms, which per-sists in the rural society, is the root cause of many socio-economic issues, particularly of Dalits, and tribals—two vulnerable sections which are subjected to exploitation and violation of human rights. There is an ongoing process of Dalit resurgence in the country, which has been accentuated by political parties, Dalit organiza-tions and NGOs in the Dalit front. But caste conflicts and discrimi-nation continue to dominate social scene of many states and cause human rights issues.

The human rights issues in the tribal front are closely inter-twined with the land issues and their apprehensions on the loss of cultural identity and livelihood. The alienation of tribal lands in scheduled (agency) areas by non-tribals, displacement of tribals due to developmental projects, depletion of their basic resources for livelihood and so on were the major issues, confronting the tribal community. The left-wing extremists could effectively exploit these issues to their advantage and build up their major support base in tribal dominated areas especially of central India.

Different shades of child labour constituted one of the worst forms of human rights violations in any society. Andhra Pradesh topped in the case of child labour with over 17 lakhs children. The intensity of the problem is more serious, as major percentage of the child labour in many states like Andhra Pradesh is girls, who are engaged in more strenuous works such as farm/agricultural labour in the most depressing conditions. Many of them are sub-jected to sexual exploitation. Poverty alone is not the sole causa-tive factor for this social tragedy. The subservice of the Dalit/backward sections to the landed gentry and their eagerness to get the patronage of the 'rural elite' in the form of tenancy rights, sup-ply of irrigation water and so on acts as motivating factors, for child labour. The existing state legislations or efforts of various agencies could not make much headway to eradicate the menace from the social spectrum.

The growing violence against women, gender inequality, lack of opportunities for the welfare/development of girl child, sexual exploitation of women camouflaged in traditional and obscurantist practices such as 'devadasis', 'yoginis' or 'basvinis' and so on in some states like Andhra Pradesh, Karnataka and so on are the major violations of human rights concerning women. A case study on violence/offences against women for a brief period of five years (1991–1996) in Andhra Pradesh revealed an increase of around 105 per cent in respect of registered cases relating to atrocities/offences against women. The situation is not much different in other states, including socially and educationally advanced ones like Kerala where the sexual and other offences against women showed a steep upward trend during the last one decade. This has clearly reflected the plight of women and the intensity of gender inequality and related issues in the states. The concepts like women empowerment through education and employment are yet to make any noticeable impact among rural women.

Recommendations

In any democratic society, the extent of protection and promotion of human rights depends on three major constituents, viz. the state/its institutions, the civil society and the nongovernmental or community organizations, which operate at the interface between the government and its superstructures. The major role, no doubt, vests with the state/its agencies, whereas the civil society is morally bound to create 'societal changes' or 'social transformation' in order to safeguard the human rights. Equally important is the role of NGOs, which are increasingly being recognized by governments as potent forces for social and economic development, important partners in nation building and national development and valuable forces in promoting the democracy. Needless to say that the better interrelationship and interface among these three components would not only accelerate socioeconomic development, but also promote concepts like community welfare and human rights.

1. The state/government, with its increasing role as a 'poli-cymaker' or 'facilitator' should involve more and more dependable NGOs in various socio-economic and developmental programmes meant for providing 'social goods' such as healthcare, drinking water, sanitation, poverty alleviation, literacy and so on for marginalized/weaker sections. Such a shift in developmental strategy has become imperative as the institutionalized strategies of social and economic development during the last six decades could not make significant qualitative and quantitative achievements in line with the expectations and aspirations of the people, especially marginalized sections.

2. The development paradigm pursued since independence has aggravated the prevailing discontent among marginalized sections of society. The development paradigm as conceived by the policymakers has always been imposed on these communities, and therefore it has remained insensitive to their needs and concerns, causing irreparable damage to these sections. Thus, developmental paradigm that suits better for the all-round development of target groups needs to be adopted with the active involvement of these groups.

3. A change in the strategy of NGOs is imperative to improve their operations, particularly their effectiveness in the field of human rights. Prioritization and professionalism on management lines are the two key aspects.

4. The operational strategies of human rights NGOs also need transformation in order to achieve better results in the protection and promotion of human rights. They should enrol grassroots workers, motivate them, train them and field them with clear objectives/goals. Cells or centres may be opened in their areas of operation to receive complaints/grievances relating to human rights violations. Human Rights Watch groups at village, *taluk* or district level may be constituted at the instance of NGOs. Extensive documentation on human rights violations through research/fact-finding missions, publication of authentic reports for the intervention of authorities/public consumption, creation of human rights awareness among public through special campaigns/media and so on should form the major tasks

of such watch groups. NGOs should also take up issues in high courts, apex court, NHRC and so on on major human rights violations, particularly of marginalized sections such as SC/ST, rural poor and so on, who have limitations to approach the corridors of justice. For that purpose, the lawyer community and professionals should be attracted to the NGO movement. PIL is the effective legal weapon, which the NGOs can use.

5. A shift in the strategy and the policies and programmes of civil liberties groups is essential in order to improve their credibility and image and thus to play a more important role in the protection and promotion of human rights. While continuing their campaigns and legal battle on police excesses and custodial violence, they should strive to extend their activities and campaigns focusing on the issues of marginalized sections particularly Dalits, tribals, women, rural poor, daily wage labourers and landless agricultural workers and so on.

6. Better interrelationships between NGOs and civil liberties groups may enable them to play an important role in civil/human rights issues, especially in areas infested by LWE or similar movements and people are sandwiched between extremists and security personnel.

7. The incidence of human rights violations can be brought down only when there is a radical change in the functioning of police. For that purpose police organization should be refined through proper training and education, particularly the constabulary, the cutting edge of the force. They should be familiarized with constitutional provisions, every branch of law and order vis-à-vis human rights, legal parameters in the exercise of police powers, human rights and emergency situations, police and weaker sections and the major international covenants on human rights. In enlightening the police through training and other campaigns, NGOs can also play a significant role.

8. Land and land-related issues are the major sources of human rights issues/violations in almost all states, especially those affected by LWE. The delay in the implementation of land reforms/Land Ceiling Act, absentee landlordism/tenancy issues, illegal occupation of governmental/forest

land, alienation of tribal land and so on are the major issues. Tribals, Dalits, landless agricultural workers and rural poor are the worst victims. These issues had given leverage to the left-wing extremist groups to build up their movement by exploiting the sentiments of the tenants, tribals and landless agricultural workers. Thus, effective steps such as (*a*) setting right the land records; (*b*) identification of governmental/tribal land in the 'enjoyment of non-tribals in agency areas; (*c*) rehabilitation/settlement scheme for non-tribals who are deprived of lands in agency areas; (*d*) distribution of surplus land among landless peasants, Tribals, Dalits and so on should be taken up by the government on priority basis.

9. Formulation of a comprehensive action plan to wean away the marginalized sections from the influence of left-wing extremist groups. A holistic approach should be adopted by acknowledging the reality that LWE is a socio-economic political issue. Thus, the action plan to tackle LWE should invariably include a combination of different tactics like development, dialogue and deterrence. While the theme of development should be specifically focused on the issues of marginalized sections of the affected areas, the dialogue or negotiations should include all stakeholders, instead of a couple of ex-bureaucrat/intelligence sleuths who wear the mantle of interlocutors and prolong the entire exercise for years to meet their vested interests. The irony is that such negotiations or dialogues to tackle LWE or insurgency and subsequent accords stage managed by handpicked interlocutors to suit temporary political gains fail to arrive at a permanent solution to the vexed issues. Thus, the history of insurgency in the Northeast or the Left radicalism in the country is full of such failed accords, smeared with blood, blood money or kick backs or foul-smelling stories of manipulations. Repetition of such a history will not lead us anywhere to permanently tackle major internal security threats like LWE. The following are some suggestions to deal with LWE tangle:

   i. Strengthening of law-enforcement machinery in the affected areas by opening more number of police stations/outposts with more manpower, sophisticated weapons and better intelligence set-up. As far as possible emergency deployment of central forces alien to the area may be dispensed with to avoid alienation of the forces from the local population. The operating forces should strictly uphold rule of law and due process of law and desist from encounter killings or fake encounters.

ii. Effective implementation of various protective legislations such as Protection of Civil Rights and SC/ST (Prevention of Atrocities) Act and laws meant for marginalized and weaker sections. Besides, the newly enacted legislations like Panchayats (Extension of Scheduled Areas) Act (PESA), 1996, National Rural Employment Guarantee Act, 2005, The Scheduled Tribes and other Traditional Forest Dwellers Act, 2006, and the National Rehabilitations and Resettlement Policy and so on should be effectively implemented in the affected areas so that many of the pending issues of discontent and frustration among tribals, Dalits and rural poor would be resolved.

iii. Revamping of administrative set-up and effective decentralization in which the three-tier Panchayat set-up would have decisive role in planning and execution of developmental projects and so on. The functioning of certain agencies/departments such as Tribal Welfare, Forest, Health, Rural Development, Irrigation and so on streamlined and improved with a monitoring mechanism at Mandal/district level to evaluate their performance in the development/sectors. Representatives of reputed NGOs and civil liberties groups may be included in the monitoring set-up in order to get objective assessment on such matters.

iv. The basic steps to tune up administration include establishment of credibility and confidence of government; keeping a continuous vigil for fulfilment of people's vision; effective protection, peace and good governance; rejuvenating tribal economy including social services; sustainable development with equity in tribal areas; holistic planning from below in scheduled areas; and negotiating crises by focusing on ending of confrontation.

v. Besides resolving land-related issues, amendments should be made in Land Acquistion Act and related legislations in order to check the liberal acquisition of traditional land of marginalized sections in the name of public purpose, leading to their displacement from homelands.

vi. Providing functional services to the people at affected areas at par with people of developed areas, especially in respect of elementary education, health/sanitation, public distribution, nutrition schemes, electrification, road connectivity and so on.

vii. Proper and speedy rehabilitation and resettlement of displaced persons with adequate infrastructure/facilities at the settlements and proper means of livelihood.

viii. Governmental incentives and encouragement to start small-scale/cottage industries in the affected areas in order to absorb the large number of unemployed sections. The state should arrange initial capital and the marketing strategies for the products manufactured in such units.

ix. All out effort to fight unemployment in the rural areas, for which the public and private industries operating in remote places with the subsidies/incentives from the governments, should be directed to absorb the maximum local unemployed and underemployed, especially of marginalized sections.

x. Formulation of a comprehensive surrendered and rehabilitation policy to surrendered extremists with certain amount of amnesty to them to encourage the surrender of ultras.

xi. The different forms and shades of untouchability and caste discrimination, which breed the issues of human rights, should be fought at social level by NGOs and in collaboration with other organizations/groups opposing such trends. An action plan to fight caste bias and social inequalities should be chalked out.

xii. In the tribal front, the NGOs, while striving to safeguard their cultural identity, should try to bring them more close to the national mainstream through their socio-economic advancement. Along with conscientization on their rights and privileges, areas of exploitation and so on, tribal empowerment through local initiatives and intervention should form the priority of NGOs working in this sector.

xiii. Proper empowerment of marginalized women of affected areas by involving them in local crafts/trades and governmental schemes for women. The NGOs should extend their co-operation and support to such programmes, notably in the fields of literacy, health, social-awareness, self-employment and so on.

Appendix

Major NGOs in Andhra Pradesh with Their Foreign Funding Agencies

S.No	Name of NGO	Target Area	Foreign Funding Agency
1.	Action for Welfare and Awakening in Rural Development (AWARE), Lake Hill Road, Hyderabad	Dalits/rural masses	NOVIB and ICCO (Holland), NCOS, (Belgium), DICONIA (Sweden)
2.	AMG India International, Chilakaluri-peta, Guntur district	Fishermen/ health/housing	Wort and Tat, Germany and other donor agencies from USA and Netherlands.
3.	Action for Food Production (AFP), Street No. 1 (Taranaka, Hyderabad) (Phone No. 7150413).	Fishing techno logy/fishermen	BILANCE (Netherlands)
4.	'ASMITA' East Maredpally, Secunderabad (Ph.7803745/7730632)	Gender justice/ girl child/ slums	Utilitarian Universal Assistance (UUA) (New York), Ford Foundation (USA), NCRAD HOLDIN and HIVOS (both Holland)

5.	'Anneshi', Osmania University Campus, Hyderabad	Women issues	Indigenous funds
6.	Andhra Pradesh Mahila Simatha, Society, Plot no. 134, Aravinda Nagar Colony, Domalaguda, Hyderabad	Women issues	Indigenous funds
7.	Adarsa Rural Integrated Development, Society, Bukkapattanam Manda, Anantpur district	Women issues	Centre for World Solidarity
8.	'ACTION', Womens Team, Janga- Reddy Gudem, 534447, W/Godavari	Women issues	Centre for World Solidarity
9.	'ASSIST', Chilakaluripeta, Guntur District	Rural development/ empowerment of Dalits	BILANCE, EZE and MISEREOR
10.	Action for Collective Tribal Improvement and Vocational Education, Khammam district	Dalit/adult	Action Aid (UK)
11.	ANKURAM, 1/8/702/32/35, Nallakunta, Hyderabad	Non-formal education/women issues	BILANCE
12.	'ARTIC', East Godavari District	Disaster preparedness/flood control	OXFAM, UK
13.	'BIRDS', House No. 9/102, Gandhi Street, Nagalapuram, Chittoor district	Women issues	Centre for world Solidarity
14.	Bhagavattula Charitable Trust, Ellamanchil, Visakhapatnam district	Village/rural development/Dalits	EZE and MISEREOR OXFAM, UK
15.	Centre for World Communication, Hyderabad	HRD/ communication/ networking	OXFAM, UK
16.	Centre for Human Resource Development, Cuddapah district	Training of vol/disaster management	OXFAM, UK MISEREOR
17.	'CRESA', Akiveedu, West Godavari	Water management	W/Germany
18.	Centre for Reconstruction Through Social Action, Akiveedu, W/Godavari	Rural development/ Dalit food security/ land development	OXFAM, UK EZE, Germany

19.	'CORK' Chittoor district	Dalit/women/ drought	BILANCE BILANCE,
20.	Chaitanya Rural Education & Development Society, Lepakshi, Anantapur district	Forest conservation/ afforestation	Holland Local Funds
21.	Cuddapah District Pariyavarana Samiti, Cuddapah district	Dalit issues/ networking	AIDE L'EN- France De'L
22.	Creative Action for Rural Development Pedakani, Guntur	Dalit/rural issues	INDE (AEE)
23.	Chaitanya Sravanti via Chintapally Gudem, Visakapatnam district	Dalit/network human rights	Luxumborg & ASW, Germany
24.	Centre for World Solidarity (CWS), Taranaka Secunderabad	Dalit/rural development/ environment	ICCO, Holland Bread for the
25.	Comprehensive Rural Operations Service Society (CROSS), Hyderabad	women/Dalit issues	World
26.	Comprehensive Social Service Society, Rompivalasa, Srikakulam district	Community development health programmes	BILANCE Action Aid, UK
27.	Community Development Centre, Ramabhadrapuram, Vizianagaram district		MISEREOR, Christian Aid
28.	Catholic Hospital Association of India (CHAI) Diamond Point, Secunderabad (Ph. 848293 & 848457)		
29.	Confederation of Voluntary Associations (COVA), Charminar, Hyderabad (Ph. 231 260, 23)	Women/street children/child labour/slums	Christian Aid, UK BILANCE, Netherlands
30.	Council for Advanced Rural Development, 234/31,S.K.Nagar, Yousafguda,Hyderabad	Rural development	Alternative & Asian expatriates in Canada
31.	Centre for Operational Research &Rural Development Adersh Vidyanagar Hyderabad	Child labour/ women/education	Indigenous funds
32.	Deccan Development Society (DDS), Hyderabad	Communal harmony/education Dalit/women issues	Local Funds/ CAPART EZE, W/
33.	Deenajana Abhivrudhi Seva Mandal, Medak District		Germany
34.	Dalit Voluntary Association Federation (DVAF), 2RT/144, Vijayanagar colony, Hyderabad Ph. 3342108/3348512	Dalit issues/slums/ child labour	OXFAM, UK MISEREOR, W/ Germany

35.	Guntur District Action Group Network (GDAGN), Pedakani, Guntur District	Dalit/rural development/child labour	DESWOS, Action Aid, Christian Aid, EZE
36.	Gandhi Peace Centre,2/2/ 1133,5/6/A New Nallakunta, Hyderabad		
37.	HEWSELF Society, Nandyal Hyderabad	Women/children rehabilitation homes	CEBEMBO/ BILANCE, Holland
38.	Council for Human Welfare, 4/6/365, Isamia Bazar, Hyderabad	Street children community	AVARD/ Gandhi Peace Foundation
39.	IRDS, 32, Railway Colony Picket, Secunderabad 500026	Development youth issues	Action Aid, UK
40.	Initiative Youth in Development (IYID) Vijaya Apartments, Central Excise Coloney, Bagh Amberpet, Hyderabad	Dalits/rural development/ community health	Indigenous Funds/Local Funds
41.	Jana Chetana, Goidi Village, Seethampet Mandal, Srikakulam district	Rehabilitation of ex-servicemen/ education	Indigenous Funds
42.	KRUSHI(Association Saikorian) Plot No.34, Methodist Colony, Begumpet Hyderabad	Women issues	Bread for the Word (BFW) Terres Des Hommes (TDH)
43.	Kanaka Durga Mahila Mandal, Mulagapudi, Natavaram Mandal, Visakapatnam district		Germany Local Funds Centre for World Solidarity
44	'LAYA', Lawsons Bay Colony, Visakhapatnam	Tribal/Dalit issues	OXFAM/UK EZE, Germany IGSSS, BILANCE, Community Aid Abroad, World Council of Churches 1)Manna Ministries International USA 2)Christian Church of North America 3) Door Fellowship Church 4) Joel Mitchel Foundation USA and so on Local Funds

45.	Manna Ful Gospel Ministries (MFGM) Amalapuram, East Godavari district	Missionary works/ education	Indigenous Funds
46.	Mahila Growth Centre, No. 1-2-56/76, Advocates Colony, Domalaguda, Hyderabad 500024	Women Community development	Centre for World Solidarity
47.	'Mahitha', 1/2/63, Domalaguda, Hyderabad 29	Women issues	Local Funds
48.	Mass Education and Organisation Society (MEOS), 1/337-26/A5-5A A.K. Nagar, Anantapur District	Women issues Child labour/ vocational training/ HRD	CAPART/ MISEREOR Action Aid, UK,
49.	Modern Architects for Rural India (MARI), 3/1/94, Kakatiya coloney, Hanumankonda, Warangal	Dalit/Women	MISEREOR/ West-Germany
50.	M.V. Foundation, West Marredpally Seconderabad	Community Development	EZE/W-Germany
51.	'MERISA', Kurnool district	Youth issues Dalit/rural issues	EZE/W-Germany
52.	Nalgonda Social Service Society, Nalgonda district	Street children	MISEREOR & BILANCE
53.	Navjyothi Youth Club, Medak district	Dalit/human rights issues	BILANCE,
54.	Nazarath Association for social Awareness, Tuni, E/Godavari district		MISEREOR
55	Navajeevan Balabhavan, Vijayawada		
56.	Prajwala Sanghom, Chittoor, Chittoor district		
57.	Praja Abhyadaya Sanstha (PAS) Gaddur Chittoor district	Nursery Promotion/ land management	OXFAM/UK
58.	Poor Peoples Service Society, Katragadda, Srikakulam district	Rural Development	EZE, West Germany
59.	Peoples Initiative Network (PIN), Moosa Nagar, Chaddarghut, Hyderabad	Child labour/ Community welfare	BILANCE & Christian Aid
60.	Pratyannaya, 12/2/709/C/8, Karolbagh Road, Mehdipatnam, Hyderabad 28	Rehabilitation of child labour/special school for children	Local Funds
61.	Phoenix Women & Child Organisation 1/8/703/9/B, Nallakunta, Hyderabad 114	Women and children issues	Supported by iCentre for World Solidarity
62.	'PARA'—Ravalapalam, Rajamundry, East Godavari District	Dalit/tribal issues	BILANCE
63	'PREMA Vihar', Benz Colony, Vijayawada City	Street children village upliftment	Supported by Canadian

64.	'PEACE' CROSS' Housing Compound, Bhongir, Nalgonda District	Women/Dalit issues Women/rural issues	Government & Agencies
65.	People Oriented Organisation for Reconstruction (POOR), Bairaganipalli Kuppam, Chittoor district	Tribals/Dalits Dalit/tribal issues Dalit/land/rural issues	BILANCE & CWS Centre for World Solidarity OXFAM, UK
66.			
67.	Rayalaseema Harijan-Girijan Backward & Minority Sangam, Rayachoti, Cuddapah district	Dalit/tribal issues Developmental issues	EZE & HKES Agencies from Spain, EZE, MISEREOR and so on BILANCE
68.	Rural Integrated Development Educational Society (RIDES), Gcoty, Anantapur district	Dalit issues Dalit issues	ICCO, Holland
69.	Rayalaseema Development Trust, Anantapur district	Village welfare Child welfare	Centre for World Solidarity OXFAM, UK Action Aid MISEREOR
70.	Rural Amelioration Service Society, Nalgonda district	Dalit/slums/ education	
71.	Rural Development Advisory Service (RDAS), Hyderabad		EZE, Action Aid, UK, DESWOS
72.	Rural Downtrodden Upliftment Society, Giddalur, Prakasum district		
73.	Sakthi, Rampachodavaram, E/ Godavari district		
74.	Social Service Centre, Eluru, W/ Godavari district		
	Society for Integrated Development in Urban & Rural Areas (SIDUR), Hyderabad		
75.	Society for Promotion of Health Education & Rural Economy (SPHERE) Gooty, Anantapur district	Dalit issues	EZE
76.	Social Action for Village Emancipation (SAVE), Vajrakarur, Anantapur district	Dalit/rural issues	Dutch Lenten Campaign

77.	SAMATA, Paderu, East Godavari	Tribal/Dalit issues	MISEREOR, EZE
	Society for National Integration through Rural Development (SNIRD) Ongole, Prakasam district	Dalit/fishermen/ tribals	BILANCE CAPART/Local funds
78.	Sramika Vidyapeet, 6/3/M9/19, Hindi Nagar, Banjara Hills, Panjagutta Hyderabad, R.R. District	Child labour/ training cent Women issue	Centre for World Solidarity
79.	Sarada Valley Development Society, Thunnapala-32, Anakapally Taluk, Visakapattnam	Tribal/women issues Land issues/tribal	OXFAM, UK and Local funds BILANCE
80.	'Samaskar Plan Internatkmal' Vani, Nizamabad district	Dalit/agricultural workers	EZE/ BILANCE
81.	'SALAHA', RTC Cross Road, Hyderabad	Dalits/women	EZE EZE, Action Aid
82.	'SAKSHI' Madanapally, Chittoor district	Rural development Agricultural	NOVIB, Holland EZE, Germany,
83.	Voluntary Action Network (VANA) Anantapur district	labourers/Dalits Peasants/	Action Aid, UK, ONEX, Switzerland
84.	Village Reconstruction Organisation (VRO), Hyderabad	agricultural workers	CAFART
85.	Young India Project, Pennkonda, Anantapur district		MISEREOR
86.	Young Farmers Rural Development		
87.	Society, Nagarkurnool, Mahaboob Nagar district		

Notes

Chapter 1

1. The word 'pharoah' is the rendering of the Hebrew word par'o which in turn renders the Egyptian word 'pr' (great house). From 15th century BCE, this title was used as synonym to denote the person of the king. They were the powerful ancient rulers of Egypt.
2. Cyrus the Great (580–529 BC) was the first Achaemenid emperor who founded Persia by uniting two original tribes—Medes and Persians; he showed unprecedented tolerance and magnanimous approach towards those defeated in war.
3. Hammurabi, the sixth Babylonian king enacted the code as early as 1772 BC. This code consisted of 282 law codes, covering various legal and moral canons in respect of various human transactions.
4. The *Rig Veda* (the book of mantra) is the oldest Veda as early as 12000–4000 BC covering social, political, religious, economic and moral codes.
5. The *Atharva Veda* (the book of spell) is the last of the four Vedas which deals with various aspects of Vedic society.
6. The concept of '*vasudhaiva kutumbakam*', also called '*hitopedesha*' upholds that the whole world is one family and hence all human beings are brothers and sisters. It is used as a theory presented by Marshal Mc Luhan on 'global village'.
7. Kautilya, also Chanakya or Vishnu Gupta, authored ancient India political treatise *Arthasastra* which covers all aspects of polity.
8. Thomas Aquinas, Italian priest, philosopher and theologian, is known for his modern philosophy on 'natural laws' and inalienable rights of human beings. Aquinas Thomas, 'The Summa Theologica', translated by the Fathers of the English Dominican Province, revised by Daniel J. Sulliven, Volume II (Chicago: Encyclopaedia Britannica, INC, 1952), p. 208.
9. Hugo Grotius is a legendary figure who is known as the 'father of modern international law'. His magnum opus, *Law on war and Peace*

specifically speaks about 'jus ad bellum' and 'jus in bellum'. Miller Jon, 'The Stanford Encylopaedia of Philosophy' url-http://plato stanford edu/archives/fall2011/entries/grotius.

10. Benedict Spinoza, the great rationalist of 17th century through his work, *The Ethics* laid the foundations of moral and natural rights. Edward W. Younkins, 'Spinoza-Freedom, Ethics & Politics', published in 'Le Quetoecois Lilove' Montreal, May 6, No. 178.

11. Lawrence C. Wanlass, *Gettell's History of Political Thought* (London: Surjeet Publications, in arrangement with George Allen & Unwin Ltd, 1981), pp. 247, 248–50, 252.

12. S.R. Maheshwari, *Comparative Government & Politics*, Fifth Edition (Agra: Lakshmi Narain Agarwal, 1997–98), pp. 211–12.

13. Wanlass, *Gettell's History of Political Thought*, pp. 294–95.

14. Ibid., pp. 318–19.

15. Samuel Pufendorf's famous work, 'On the Duty of Man & Citizen' (1673) is considered to be the succinct and condensed presentation of the natural law political theory developed by his monumental classic, *On the Law of Nature and Nations*. Wanlass, *Gettell's History of Political Thought*, p. 232.

16. Immanuel Kant, the German philosopher known for his metaphysical concept linking duties with ethics. Kant's famous statement of duty 'Act only according to that maxim by which you can at the same time will that it should become a universal law'. Wanlass, *Gettell's History of Political Thought*, p. 357.

17. Johann Fichte is another famous German philosopher who through his work, *Foundations of Natural Rights* laid down the concept of natural rights. Wanlass, *Gettell's History of Political Thought*, p. 358.

18. For Hegel's and Karl Marx's works see Wanlass, *Gettell's History of Political Thought*, pp. 392–94.

19. The English Revolution of 1640 was a great social movement like the French Revolution of 1789. The state power presenting the old order that was virtually feudal in nature was violently overthrown; power passed to the hands of a new class.

20. The Glorious Revolution of 1688 was the overthrow of King James II of England by a union of parliamentarians with Dutch stadtholder William II (William of Orange) and Queen Mary, also known as Bloodless Revolution.

21. Virginia Bills of Rights is a document drafted in 1776 to proclaim the rights of men, including the right to rebel against the 'inadequate' government. It influenced a number of later documents, including the United States Declaration of Independence (1776) the United States Bill of Rights (1789), and the French Revolution's Declaration of the Rights of Man and of the Citizen (1789).

22. 'Dictatorship of the proletariat' is the absolute control of economic and political power in a country by a government of the working class (proletariat), regarded in Communist theory as a means of establishing Communist regime.
23. Lt Col. David L. Roberts and Dr. S. Subramanian, IPS (Retd), *Hand Book of International Humanitarian Law& Human Rights Law* (New Delhi: Regional Delegation of the International committee of the Red Cross, 1998).
24. The Universal Declaration of Human Rights (UDHR) is a declaration adopted by the UN General Assembly (10 December 1948 at Palais de Chaillot) and contains various articles ensuring human rights such as right to life, individual freedom and so on.
25. Famous speech of former UN Secretary General Kofi Annan.
26. International Convention on the Elimination of all Forms of Racial Discrimination was adopted by UN in 1966; it came into effect in January 1969 and so far has been ratified by 175 nations.
27. The Convention against Torture and Other Cruel, Inhuman or Degrading Treatment or Punishment (United Nations Convention against Torture) was adopted by UN General Assembly in December 1975.
28. The United Nations Convention on the Rights of the Child (commonly abbreviated as the CRC, CROC or UNCRC) is a human rights treaty setting out the civil, political, economic, social, health and cultural rights of children. The Convention generally defines a child as any human being under the age of eighteen. It was adopted in 1989, came into effect from September 1990, and has been so far ratified by 140 nations.
29. As per Article 28 of International Covenant on Civil and Political Rights, Human Rights Committee will be constituted in order to examine issues if violations of human rights by contracting parties.
30. Protocol I is a 1977 amendment protocol to the Geneva conventions relating to the protection of victims of *international* armed conflicts. It reaffirms the international laws of the original Geneva conventions of 1949, but adds clarifications and new provisions to accommodate developments in modern international warfare that have taken place since the Second World War.
31. The Resolution 1503 of 27 May 1970 of UN Economic and Social Council (ECOSOC) pertains to the 'Procedure for dealing with communications relating to violations of human rights and fundamental freedoms'.
32. The United Nations Commission on Human Rights (UNCHR) was a functional commission within the overall framework of the UN from 1946 until it was replaced by the United Nations Human Rights Council in 2006. It was a subsidiary body of the ECOSOC,

and was also assisted in its work by the office of the United Nations High Commissioner for Human Rights (UNHCHR). It was the UN's principal mechanism and international forum concerned with the promotion and protection of human rights.

33. The 1235 Procedure is a procedure on the basis of which the commission holds an annual *public* debate on gross human rights violations committed by a given state. If the situation still does not improve, one possible outcome can be the adoption of an ECOSOC resolution condemning the authorities of a given state for the violations. Such a resolution severely affects the prestige of the ruling authorities.

34. Pursuant to United Nations General Assembly Resolution A/RES/ 48/141 of 2 December 1993, Dr. Ayala Lasso, was appointed first UN high commissioner for human rights and started his four-year mandate on 5 April 1994.

35. The Rome Statute of the International Criminal Court (often referred to as the International Criminal Court Statute or the Rome Statute) is the treaty that established the ICC. It was adopted at a diplomatic conference in Rome on 17 July 1998 and it entered into force on 1 July 2002. As of 1 February 2012, 120 states are party to the statute. Among other things, the statute establishes the court's functions, jurisdiction and structure.

36. Augusto José Ramón Pinochet Ugarte, more commonly known as Augusto Pinochet (25 November 1915 to 10 December 2006) was a Chilean army general and dictator who assumed power in a coup d'état on 11 September 1973.

37. The Supreme Court of India while disposing a writ petition filed by PUCL Rajasthan in April 2001 declared that food is a fundamental right and should be ensured to all citizens.

38. Omar Ahmed al Basir is the president of Sudan who came to power in a bloodless military coup that replaced the Prime Minister Sadiq Al Mahadi. He turned to be a brutal violator of civil/ human rights.

39. Richard Goldstone is a South African lawyer who chaired the Goldstone Commission, prosecuting war crimes in Yugoslavia and Rwanda, leading the United Nations Fact Finding Mission on the Gaza Conflict.

40. The Special Tribunal for Lebanon (STL) is an international tribunal for the prosecution under Lebanese law of those responsible for the assassination of Rafic Hariri on 14 February 2005. The Extraordinary Chambers in the Courts of Cambodia (commonly known as the Khmer Rouge Tribunal and the Cambodian Genocide Tribunal) is a forum established to try the most senior and most responsible members of the Khmer Rouge. Although it is a national court, it was established as part of an agreement between the Royal Government of Cambodia and the UN.

41. Kofi Annan's speech, 24 September 2004, at Dafur. V.S. Mani, 'The UN & Human Rights', The *Hindu* dated 6 September 2000.

42. UN Millennium Report/Freedom from fear/point216. *Millennium Report*, Chapter 3. 'Dayton International Peace Museu', Available at: www.daytonpeacemuseum.org/Contrib/Rfrncs/-MillenniumRepch3pdf.

43. Humanitarian militarism is the deployment of military personnel while undertaking relief or humanitarian activities in conflict areas. This is mainly interpreted as new US strategy to build up their presence in troubled areas.

44. Rudolph Joseph Rummel (born 21 October 1932), Cleveland, Ohio is professor emeritus of political science at the University of Hawaii. He has spent his career assembling data on collective violence and war with a view toward helping their resolution or elimination. Rummel coined the term 'democide' for murder by government and his research claims that six times as many people died of democide during the 20th century than in all that century's wars combined.

45. The case study of Jewish holocaust/1933 43 (www.gentricide.org). Daniel J. Goldhagen 'Hitler's Willing Executioners:' Ordinary Germans and the Holocaust (New York: Knopf, 1996) p. 418.

46. Raul Hilberg (2 June 1926 to 4 August 2007) was an Austrian-born American political scientist and historian. He was widely considered to be the world's pre-eminent scholar of the Holocaust, and his three-volume, 1,273-page magnum opus *The Destruction of the European Jews* is regarded as seminal study of the Nazi Final Solution.

47. Daniel J. Goldhagen's, *Hitler's Willing Executioners: Ordinary Germans and the Holocaust* (New York: Knopf, 1996).

48. Cathal J. Nolan, 'Longman Guide to International Affairs' (White Plains, NY: Longman, 1995).

49. Goldhagen, *Hitler's Willing Executioners, 1996*

50. Robert F Barsky, Noam Chosky-A life of Dissent (Cambridge: MIT Press, 1997).

51. Richard Pipes,'Russia under Bolshevik Regime' (US: Vintage Books, 1994).

52. Introduced by Mikhail Gorbachev in the second half of the 1980s, Glasnost is often paired with Perestroika (literally: restructuring), another reform instituted by Gorbachev.

53. Aleksandr Isayevich Solzhenitsyn (11 December 1918 to 3 August 2008) was a writer, who, through his often-suppressed writings, helped to raise global awareness of the gulag, the Soviet Union's forced labour camp system—particularly in *Gulag Archipelago* and *One Day in the Life of Ivan Denisovich*, two of his best-known works. Solzhenitsyn was awarded the Nobel Prize in literature in 1970.

He was expelled from the Soviet Union in 1974 but returned to Russia in 1994 after the Soviet system had collapsed.

54. Ibid., 45.
55. Sabrina P. Ramet, 'Balkan Babel—The Disintegration of Yugoslavia from the death of Tito to the fall of Milosevic' (Westview Press, 4th edition, 2002).
56. Robespierre (6 May 1758 to 28 July 1794) was a French lawyer, politician, and one of the best-known and most influential figures of the French Revolution.
57. Richard Roech is the editorial co-director of independent daily, *Terra Via*, who catalogued human rights violations/issues.
58. G-20 is a forum for the co-operation and consultation of international financial matters. Its members are: Argentina, Australia, Brazil, Canada, China, France, Germany, India, Indonesia, Italy, Japan, Mexico, Russia, Saudi Arabia, South Africa, South Korea, Turkey, United Kingdom, United States and European Union.
59. Taken from the title *Human Rights—A 21st century Agenda* authored by Sir Stephen Sedley. It was published by London Review of Books, London, Volume 17, No. 9, 11 May, 1995, pp. 13–15. A similar article by the same author titled *Human Rights in 21st century—Rights, Wrongs and Outcomes* was included in his book *Ashes &Sparks— essays on Law and Justice* published by Cambridge University Press in 2011 (pp. 348–64).
60. Patrick Naagbanton was co-ordinator of SDN partner organization the Centre for Environment, Human Rights and Development (CEHRD) in Port Harcourt, Rivers State. In the light of the threat to his life, Amnesty International launched a campaign for defending human rights workers working in difficult situations.
61. The Chhattisgarh Special Public Security Act, 2005, passed by the Chhattisgarh assembly in December 2005 and notified in March 2006 gave sweeping powers to police and security agencies in the name of combating LWE.
62. Barrack Obama's speech, 10 November 2008. Alex Spillius, Washington, 'Barack Obama proposes to move terrorist suspects from Guantanamo Bay', The *Telegraph* dated 10 November 2008.
63. This was used as a motto on the title page of *A Historical Review of the Constitution and Government of Pennsylvania* (1759); the book was published by Franklin, its author was Richard Jackson.
64. 'ISRO Espionage Case (1994)', in which senior scientists were implicated by Intelligence Bureau, was subsequently probed by CBI which found none of them guilty. The apex court also exonerated all the accused. Similarly, in Malegaon (2006) and Mecca Masjid (2007) blast cases, the initial charge sheet filed against accused (who were in jail for year) were subsequently cancelled during investigation.

65. Teesta Stelvad of Mumbai, Mrinalini Sarabhai and Mukul Sharma of Gujarat are prominent human rights activists who conducted relentless legal struggles and other campaigns to bring the culprits of Gujarat carnage before law.

66. In Gulbarg society, Ahmedabad, Ehsaan Jaffri, ex-MP Congress and many others were killed during Gujarat carnage (28 February 2002); in Naroda Patiya 97 people belonging to minority community were killed, whereas in Best Bakery Case (during March 2002, Baroda) 14 people were killed. There were conscious efforts by the political set-up to shield the perpetrators of these dastardly crimes.

67. Chief Justice of India K.G. Balakrishnan's presidential address at the inaugural session of the international conference of jurists on 'Terrorism, Rule of Law & Human Rights' in New Delhi on 13–14 December 2008. Balakrishnan retired from Supreme Court on 12 May 2010.

68. Substantive due process (SDP) is one of the theories of law through which courts enforce limits on legislative and executive powers.

69. Xiaorong Li, *A Question of Priorities: Human Rights, Development & Asian Values*, Report for the Institute of Philosophy and Public Policy (International Office of the Peoples Republic of China on Human Rights in China), *Beijing Review* 4–10, 1991.

70. Vienna Declaration of Human rights and Action Plan (made on 25 June 1993).

71. Ibid.

72. The Martens clause was introduced into the preamble to the 1899 Hague Convention II—Laws and Customs of War on Land. The clause took its name from a declaration read by Fyodor Fyodorovich Martens, the Russian delegate at the Hague Peace Conferences 1899 and was based upon his words: 'Until a more complete code of the laws of war is issued, the High Contracting Parties think it right to declare that in cases not included in the Regulations adopted by them, populations and belligerents remain under the protection and empire of the principles of international law, as they result from the usages established between civilized nations, from the laws of humanity and the requirements of the public conscience'. Theodor Meron, 'The Martens Clause: Principles of Humanity & Dictates of Public Conscience', *The American Journal of International Law*, Volume 94, No. 1, January 2000, pp. 78–89.

73. Roberts and Subramanian, *Hand Book of International Humanitarian Law & Human Rights Law*, pp. 114–15 (Section 1: Article 3, Common to the Four Conventions).

74. United Nations Security Council Resolution 1373, adopted unanimously on 28 September 2001, is a counterterrorism measure.

75. 'UN Security Council Resolution 1456,on combatting Terrorism' (clause-6) adopted by the Council on January 20, 2003; accessed from www.un.org/docs/sc/unsc _resolutions03html.

76. International Review of the Red Cross, September 1969. Jean Pictet, 'The need to restore Laws and customs relating to conflicts' published in *International Review of the Red Cross*, Vol. 9, no. 102, September 1969, pp. 459–83.

77. International Convention on the Elimination of all Forms of Racial Discrimination was adopted by UN in 1966; came into effect in January 1969 and so far ratified by 175 nations.

78. The Convention on the Elimination of all Forms of Discrimination against Women (CEDAW) is an international convention adopted in 1979 by the United Nations General Assembly. Described as an international bill of rights for women, it came into force on 3 September 1981.

79. V.R. Krishna Iyer, *Human Rights—A Judge's Miscellany* (New Delhi: BR Publishing Corporation, New Delhi, 1995).

80. Jolly George versus Bank of Cochin (international treaties do not automatically form part of international law. They must, where appropriate, be incorporated into the legal system by a legislation made by the parliament.

81. Preface of The Protection of Human Rights Act, 1993, Act No. 10 of 1994 (5 January 1994).

82. From the Third Annual Report of NHRC. The Annual Report of National Human Rights Commission (NHRC) 1995–96, 2.9, accessed from www.nhrc.nic.in/ar95-96-htm.

83. Based on the Annual Reports of National Human Rights Commission (NHRC) from 1993–94 to 2002–03 (under the sub-head 'Complaints before the Commission') accessed through the website: nhrc.nic.in/ documents-AR-ENG.pdf.

84. The Paris Principles were defined at the first International Workshop on National Institutions for the Promotion and Protection of Human Rights held in Paris on 7–9 October 1991. They were adopted by the United Nations Human Rights Commission by Resolution 1992/54 of 1992, and by the UN General Assembly in its Resolution 48/134 of 1993. The Paris Principles relate to the status and functioning of national institutions for the protection and promotion of human rights.

85. Justice J.S. Verma, who headed the NHRC during the Gujarat carnage, sent a personal letter to the then Prime Minster A.B. Vajpayee on Gujarat episode.

86. The Annual report of NHRC-2002-03, Chapter 3, pp. 28–41, accessed from www. nhrc.nic.in/documents/AR/AR02-03ENG.pdf (Justice

J.S. Verma's (Chairperson, NHRC) personal letter dated 3 January 2003 to the then Prime Minster A.B. Vajpayee on Gujarat episode).

87. Former Chief Justice J.S. Anand (Chairman/NHRC) to the Prime Minister of India on 7 April 2005 on Gujarat carnage. The Annual report of NHRC 2003–04, Chapter 3, pp. 13–22, accessed from www. nhrc.nic.in/documents/AR/AR03-04ENG.pdf.

88. Both the quotes were the observations of Chief Justice K.G. Balakrishnan of Supreme Court, who along with Justice P. Sadasivam and Justice J.M. Panchal heard a petition filed by Ms Nandini Sunder, Shri Ramachandra Guha and Shri EAS Sarma challenging the deployment of *Salwa Judum* in Chhattisgarh. The Court made these observations on September 19 2008, accessed from www.hindu.com/2008/09/20/stories/2008092055941300/html.

89. UN Accreditation Panel Report on NHRC—request for ISO status. Manoj Mitra, TNN 'India's clout ensures UN Status for NHRC', The *Times of India*, dated 21 July 2011.

90. From the paper 'Civil Liberties Movement: Response to Coercive Measures by the Indian State' presented in the seminar on Democratic Movement and Human Rights Perspective' in Hyderabad in June 1997.

91. Sumanta Banerjee, 'Civil Liberties Movement—Response to Coercive Measures by the Indian State' presented in the seminar on Democratic Movement and Human Rights Perspective held in Hyderabad during June 1997.

92. Seminar on 'Democratic Rights and Human Rights Perspective' in Hyderabad in June 1997.

93. The Annual Report of National Human Rights Commission (NHRC) 1995–96, accessed from www.nhrc.nic.in/ar95-96-htm.

94. Annual Report of National Human Rights Commission (NHRC) 1996–97, Annexure 1, 'Statement Showing Details of Custodial Deaths Reported by States/Union Territories', accessed through the website: nhrc.nic.in/documents-AR-ENG.pdf.

95. Ibid.

96. The speech of L.K. Advani, former deputy prime minister from the *Hindu*, 18 October 2002.

97. Leo Tolstoy 'War and Peace'. The original quote is from another non-fiction by Leo Tolstoy as Leo Tolstoy, 'What then must we do' (Cambridge, UK: Green Books, August 1991).

98. The Sohrabuddin Sheikh fake encounter is an ongoing criminal case in Gujarat where the police killed Sohrabuddin Sheikh on 26 November 2005, and then his wife also disappeared. A year later, his friend Tulsi Prajapati, the sole witness, died on 28 December 2006 in another Gujarat police encounter shooting.

99. Jessica Lal was a model in New Delhi, who was working as a celebrity barmaid at a crowded socialite party when she was shot dead on 30 April 1999. Dozens of witnesses pointed to Siddharth Vashisht, also known as Manu Sharma the son of Venod Sharma, a wealthy and influential Congress-nominated MP from Haryana as the murderer. There were major flaws in the police investigation. Due to mounting public opinion, the case, which was reopened, was tried by the High Court which convicted Manu Sharma.

100. Priyadarshini Mattoo was a 25-year-old law student who was found raped and murdered at her house in New Delhi on 23 January 1996. On 17 October 2006, the Delhi High Court found Santosh Kumar Singh guilty and sentenced him to death. On 6 October 2010, the Supreme Court of India commuted the death sentence to life imprisonment. Santosh Kumar Singh, the son of a police inspector-general, had earlier been acquitted by a trial court in 1999.

101. Nitish Katara was a 24-year-old Indian business executive in Delhi, who was murdered on 17 February 2002 by Vikas Yadav, the son of influential criminal-politician D.P. Yadav. Nitish had fallen in love with his classmate, Bharti Yadav, sister of Vikas. The trial court held that Nitish's murder was an honour killing because the family did not approve their relationship. Vikas and Vishal Yadav were later found guilty by the court and awarded life sentence on 30 May 2008.

102. The sensational '2006 Nithari Killing Case' related to the brutal killing of several young girls of Nithari Village of Noida area in the outskirts of Delhi. The killing took place in the house of one businessman, Mohinder Singh Pandher at Nithari during the period 2005–06. Though the affected families reported the missing of their children to the police, neither the police registered FIR nor conducted any proper investigation. They started to act only when some skeletons were found near the particular house. The entire episode demonstrated the deep-rooted insensitivity among police personnel at various levels of police organization.

Chapter 2

1. Theovon Boven was the director of what was then the UN Division of Human Rights (now known as the Office of the High Commissioner for Human Rights [OHCHR]) from1977–1982. He held other prestigious positions such as chairman of European Human Rights Forum

and the Special Rapporteur for Torture and so on. In 1985, he won the prestigious Right Livelihood Award.

2. Louis Henkin of Columbia University is one of the most influential contemporary scholars of international law and US foreign policy. He was attached to Columbia University Human Rights Forum.

3. Amartya Sen is the distinguished Indian economist who won the Nobel Prize for Economics in 1998 for his works on welfare economics and social choice theory. His works and concepts on the causes of famine attracted international attention. Dr. Amartya Sen, 'Social exclusion—concept, application and scrutiny', Office of the Economic and Social Development, Asian Development Bank, Manila, Phillippines, 2000.

4. P. Sainath who won Magsaysay Award in 2007 is a distinguished journalist. His well-researched articles on rural developmental issues, including farmers' suicide, published in the *Hindu* highlighted the plight of rural poor.

5. The 'decisional' approach that had been tried by Palsby, Dahl and some other researchers made use of empirical determination of actual decisions and persons who were involved in taking such decisions. The 'reputational' approach, the most popular in community-based studies was made use of by Floyd Hunter in his study of 'regional city'.

6. Intermediate Technology Development Group (ITDG), Bourton Hall, Bourton on Dunsmore, Rugby, Warwickshire, CV239QZ, UK, is an international development organization which works towards equitable and just work in which technology enriches and benefits the lives of poor people. Its major operations are in Africa, Asia and Latin America.

7. This definition is given in US Policy Document on Human Rights and is quoted from Lt Col David L. Roberts and Dr. S. Subramanian, *Hand Book of International Humanitarian Law and Human Rights Law,* (New Delhi: Regional Delegation of the International Committee of the Red Cross, 1998), p. 208.

8. The Protection of Human Rights Act, 1993 (Act no. 10 of 1994) came into effect on 28 September 1993.

9. (Retired) Justice P.N. Bhagwati of supreme court is known for his historic judgement upholding personal liberty and concept of human rights. In Francis Coralie Mullin versus Administrator UT of Delhi and others, he stated: 'We think that the right to life includes the right to live with dignity and all that goes along with it; namely basic necessaries like adequate nutrition, cloth and shelter, facilities for reading, writing and expressing views freely etc'. Francis Coralie Mullin versus Administrator UT of Delhi and others, AIR, 1981, SC 746.

10. 'Non-Governmental Organizations—Guidelines for Good policy and Practice' was prepared for Commonwealth Foundation by Colin Ball and Leith Dunn.

11. HRI is an awareness-raising and capacity-building organization based at Central European University. Formed in 1999, by the students of CEU Legal Studies Human Rights Program, it had grown into an internationally recognized human rights organization.

12. Inter-American Institute of Human Rights is a major academic and research centre in the field of human rights in Europe.

13. D.N. Banerjee, *Our Fundamental Rights: Their Nature and Extent* (Calcutta: World Press Private, 1960).

14. Professor Earnest Barker, English political scientist who served as principal of Kings College, London, was the author of *Social and Political Thought* (Camebridge, 1964).

15. J.H. Skolonick, 'Above the Law: Police and Excessive Use of force' (New York: Free press, 1994).

16. International Convention on Elimination of all Forms of Racial Discrimination was adopted by UN in 1965 and entered into force from 4 January 1969.

17. International Convention on Suppression and Punishment of the Crime of Apartheid was adopted by UN in November 1973. It is also known as 'Apartheid Convention' which treats Apartheid as crime against humanity.

18. The Convention on the Prevention and Punishment of the Crime of Genocide was adopted by UN in December 1948.

19. Vienna Convention on Consular Relations (1933) is an international treaty that decides the framework among independent nations in respect of diplomatic/consular relations. The convention with 79 articles was ratified by 173 nations.

20. David H. Bayley is a distinguished professor of the School of Criminal Justice at the State University of New York. He has authored a number of books on policing and law enforcement, *The Police for Future* (Oxford University Press, 1994) is one of his famous works.

21. Late K.G. Kannabiran and Late Dr. K. Balagopal, 'In the written arguments in the matter of case No. 234/1-6/ 93-94 NHRC', in respect of 'encounter-killings' in Andhra Pradesh.

22. Founded in 1983, the organization started with a group of Minnesota Lawyers who recognized the community's unique spirit of social justice as an opportunity to promote human rights worldwide. Its first project to attract international attention was the preparation and publication of the 'The Manuel on the Effective Prevention and Investigation of Extra-Legal and Arbitrary and Summary Execution' known as 'Minnesota Protocol' since 1992, the organization is named as Minnesota Advocates for Human Rights.

Chapter 3

1. The new democracy concept aims to overthrow feudalism and/or achieve a country's national independence from colonialism, but it bypasses the rule of the capitalist class that Marx and Lenin predicted would usually follow such a struggle, claiming instead to seek to enter directly into socialism through a coalition of classes fighting the old ruling order.
2. The great Naxalbari revolt led by comrade Charu Mazumdar in May 1967 proved to be the clarion call of 'Spring Thunder over India'.
3. Meerut-conspiracy case was a controversial court case, in which several trade unionists including three Englishmen were arrested for organizing Indian rail strike, this immediately caught attention back home in England, inspired the 1932 play titled *Meerut*, by Manchester-street theatre group, the Red Megaphones, highlighting the detrimental effects of colonization and industrialization.
4. The Chittagong-armory raid was an attempt on 18 April 1930 to raid the armory of police and auxiliary forces from the Chittagong armory in Bengal province of British India by armed revolutionaries led by Surya Sen.
5. The Tebhaga movement was a militant campaign initiated in Bengal by the Kisan Sabha (peasant's front of Communist Party of India) in 1946. At that time share-cropping peasants (essentially, tenants) had to give half of their harvest to the owners of the land. The demand of the Tebhaga (sharing by thirds) movement was to reduce the share given to landlords to one third.
6. People's war, also called protracted people's war, is a military–political strategy first developed by the Chinese Marxist–Leninist revolutionary and political leader Mao Zedong (1893–1976). The basic concept behind people's war is to maintain the support of the population and draw the enemy deep into the interior where the population will bleed them dry through a mix of mobile warfare and guerrilla warfare.
7. Buddhadev Bhattacharya's (former chief minister, West Bengal) letter to prime minister on the law and order scenario in the state (2010).
8. The Greyhounds are an elite commando force of Andhra Pradesh India. The force was raised in 1989 to control the Maoists who at one time had a strong presence in 23 of the state's 26 districts. Only the best policemen of Andhra Pradesh make it to the Greyhound squad, which is one of the highest paid in the country—even better than the elite National Security Guard.

9. The Telangana movement refers to a group of related political activities organized to support the creation of a new state of Telangana from the existing state of Andhra Pradesh.

10. Lalgrah movement, started during November 2008, was the struggle by Adivasis for their genuine rights. The Maoists who hijacked the movement launched a massive fight against police personnel and cadres of the ruling CPI(M). In June 2009, Indian security forces launched Operation Lalgarh against the Maoists in the village.

11. PPSS is a movement started by social activists/Left intellectuals against the large-scale exploitation of natural resources by MNCs to start their projects in Orissa.

12. Over 4,000 sq. km of land in Bastar (Chhattisgarh) that includes the thickly forested tribal heartland of Abujh Marh is considered to be the red bastion of CPI (Maoists).

13. The victory of the Chinese People's Revolution led by Chairman Mao changed the situation in the East and in the world, blazing a new trail for the revolutionary struggles. Mao, *Selected Works*, Vol. II, p. 318. Marxists Internet archive, accessed from www.marxists.org/reference/archives/mao/selectedworks.

14. The strategy and tactics document of Maoists adopted at the Ninth Congress of 2001 explains the importance of urban work as 'Work in the urban areas has a special importance in our revolutionary work in our revolution, which follows the line of protracted people's war, the liberation of urban areas, will be possible only in the last stage of the revolution'.

15. People's Committee against Police Atrocities was a pro-CPI(ML) movement that spearheaded the Lalgarh movement in West Bengal.

16. The Popular Front of India (PFI) is a confederation of Muslim organizations in India, including National Development Front (Kerala), Manitha Neethi Pasarai (Tamil Nadu) and Karnataka Forum for Dignity and so on. The PFI has about 800,000 members all over the country and claims to advocate for minority and underprivileged groups in India holding demonstrations and marches.

17. Arundhati Roy, the Booker Prize winner is noted for her crusade for the protection of civil and human rights of marginalized sections

18. The 'clear, hold and build' strategy was vigorously pursued by Bush Administration against Taliban in Afghanistan. The above strategy was also applied with limited success in India against LWE in their stronghold states like Chhattisgarh.

19. Kancha Illaiah is the noted writer and a protagonist of Dalit cause; who made a number of studies on Dalit paradigm in India. Interview with Kancha Illaiah by Anand, May 2000, www.ambedkar.org.

20. At least 54 upper-caste Rajput community members in Dalelchak–Baghaura in Bihar were killed in May 1987. The incident was the

worst massacre in the state until the Ranvir Sena killing of 61 Dalits in Laxmanpur–Bathe on 1 December 1997.

21. In 1968, T.N. Reddy broke with CPI(M) and formed the Andhra Pradesh Coordination Committee of Communist Revolutionaries (APCCCR). He succeeded in attracting a large part of the CPI(M) cadre to APCCCR. During a brief period APCCCR was part of AICCCR. Reddy was however very critical of the left adventurist line of Charu Majumdar, instead he wanted to promote a mass line. Thus, Reddy and APCCCR were expelled from AICCCR. Indian Vanguard, 'Relevance of T. Nagireddy line culminating from UCCRI (ML)', 8 November 2007.

22. The Maoist theory of people's war divides warfare into three phases. In phase one, the guerrillas earn population's support by distributing propaganda and attacking the organs of government. In phase two, escalating attacks are launched against the government's military forces and vital institutions. In phase three, conventional warfare and fighting are used to seize cities, overthrow the government, and assume control of the country.

23. India Report 2009 by Human Rights Watch. 'India/Human Rights Watch' (www.hrw.org/pt/worldreport/2009/india).

24. From the Report of the Institute of Peace and Conflict Studies. *The Naxal-Problem*, IPCS Conference Report, March 2012 (quoted from Naxalite-Maoist insurgency, Wikipedia).

25. Country Report on Human Rights Abuses by US State Department. US Department of State 'Country Report on Human Rights' (www.refworld.org/docid/3ae6aa980html).

26. V.S. Jafa serves in the Indian Administrative Service (IAS) and is a former chief secretary of Assam. He studied the Northern Ireland conflict as a visiting fellow at the University of Oxford (1986–1987), and as John D. and Catherine T. MacArthur fellow and a visiting fellow at the Massachusetts Institute of Technology (1988–89). He researched the revolutionary, ethnic and religious roots of violence, counter-insurgency and counter-terrorism in the context of the theory and practice of conflict resolution.

Chapter 4

1. Karl Gunnar Myrdal (1898–1987) was a Swedish Nobel Laureate economist, sociologist and politician. In 1974, he received the Nobel Prize in Economics with Friedrich Hayek for 'their pioneering work in the theory of money and economic fluctuations and for their penetrating

analysis of the interdependence of economic, social and institutional phenomena'. He is best known in the United States for his study of race relations, which culminated in his book, *An American Dilemma: The Negro Problem and Modern*. His another equally famous work is *Asian Drama*.

2. The Great March was a military retreat undertaken by the Red Army of the Chinese Communist Party to evade the pursuit of the Kuomintang (KMT or Chinese Nationalist Party) army.

3. Koratala Suryanarayana Rao was a senior CPI leader from Andhra Pradesh who strongly opposed LWE from the beginning of the movement. P.V. Ramana, 'Internal and international linkages of Naxalites', *Dialogue*, April–June, 2005, Vol. 6, No. 4.

4. The Coordination Committee of Maoist Parties and Organisations in South Asia (CCOMPOSA) is an umbrella organization of ten left-wing extremist organizations active in four countries of South Asia— Bangladesh, India, Nepal and Sri Lanka.

5. Praja court is the self-styled judicial set-up of Maoists in which the identified 'class enemies' of the movement are tried and punished for offences.

6. Justice M.N. Rao of Andhra Pradesh High Court in his directions on LWE violence. Shakumuri Appa rao and others versus Government of Andhra Pradesh reported in 1996(3)   ALD493 (Quote from the statement of Justice M.N. Rao).

Chapter 5

1. *Development Challenges in Extremist Affected Areas: An Expert Group Report to Planning Commission*, New Delhi: Government of India, 2008).

2. This study was undertaken by Action Aid (2001–2002). PACS: 'Untouchabilty still strong' 2007, New Delhi (news item regarding study undertaken by Action Aid during 2001–2002). A panel consisting of social activist Harsha Mander and Sukhdev Thorat (former Chairperson UGC) analysed the findings, based on which it was published in 2006. Ghanashyam Shah et al., (Ed). *Untouchability in Rural India* (SAGE Publications, New Delhi, 2006).

3. From Dr B.R. Ambedkar's speech in Constituent Assembly. Quotes by Dr B.R. Ambedkar on 26 January 1950, accessed from www. goodreads.com/ /7165680.

4. Formation of autonomous areas for STs and so on is enshrined in Article 244/A.

5. Grants from the Union to certain states/areas and special provisions are laid down in 275 Article.

6. The Scheduled Tribes Order,1950, promulgated on the strength of Article 342.

7. Formation of National Commission for SC/ST and so on are laid down under this Article.

8. Article 339, Control of the Union over the Administration of Scheduled Areas and the Welfare of Scheduled Tribes. H.M. Seervai, 'The Constitutional law of India' 4th edition, Universal Law Publishing Co, New Delhi, 2011 (Article 339, Control of the Union over the Administration of Scheduled Areas and the Welfare of Scheduled Tribes).

9. From the Report of SC-ST Commissioner, 1998. Government of India: Report, National Commission for Scheduled Castes & Scheduled Tribes (NCSCST), 1990, Atrocities against SC/ST.

10. *Development Challenges in Extremist Affected Areas*: An Expert Group Report to *Planning Commission* (2008).

11. Ibid.

12. Human Development Report 2006, Published for UNDP-Beyond Scarcity: Power, Poverty and the Global Water Crisis, accessed from hdr.undp.org/en/media/HDR06-completepdf.

13. Human Development Report 2008 of UNDP. Human Development Report 2008 :Human Development Reports, (UNDP)-accessed from hdr.undp.org/en/media/HDR08-completepdf

14. An honour killing is the homicide of a member of a family or social group by other members due to the belief of the perpetrators that the victim has brought dishonor upon the family or community. Honour killings are directed mostly against women and girls.

15. The creation of UN Women came about as part of the UN reform agenda, bringing together resources and mandates for greater impact in the empowerment and welfare of women.

16. Millennium Development Summit of UN 2000. 'The Millennium Development Summit & its Follow-up Global Policy Forum' accessed from www.globalpolicy.org/un-/un/millennium submit-and-its-followup, May 2009.

17. 'Children's Human Rights Training Programme for Civil Action Groups'—document prepared by Maheshwar Madan Lal (1994) for Malian Foundation.

18. The UN Convention on the Rights of the Child is a human rights treaty setting out the civil, political, economic, social, health and cultural rights of children. The Convention generally defines a child as any human being under the age of eighteen.

19. Office of the United Nations High Commissioner for Human Rights, Geneva, Switzerland: United Nations Convention on the Rights of

the Child,Adopted and opened for signature, ratification and accession by General Assembly resolution 44/25 of 20 November 1989, entry into force 2 September 1990, in accordance with article.

20. Nina M. Birkeland, 'Internal displacement: Global trends in conflict-induced displacement' *International Review of Red Cross*, Volume 91, No 815, September 2009.

21. UNCHR. 'Human Rights Watch, 'Small Change: Bonded Child Labor in India's Silk Industry' 23 January 2003.

22. *Development Challenges in Extremist Affected Areas: An Expert Group Report to Planning Commission* (2008).

23. From Ramachandra Rao Committee Report1993. G.O.Ms.No. 66, Social Welfare (J1) Dept. dated 2-6-1997 of AP Government (Ramachandra Raju Commission Report).

24. National Campaign on Dalit Human Rights is an Indian non-party based secular platform with offices in 14 states of the country. The objectives of NCDHR are the following: (*a*) to hold the state accountable for all human rights violations committed against Dalits; (*b*) to sensitize civil society by raising visibility of the Dalit problem; and (*c*) to render justice to Dalit victims of discrimination and violence.

25. UN Convention on the Elimination of All Forms of Racial Dicrimination held in Geneva in 2002. International Convention on the Elimination of All Forms of Racial Dicrimination, Committee on the Elimination of Racial Dicrimination, 55th session, Geneva, 2–27 August 1999.

26. James Baldwin, 'Letter to my Nephew on the One Hundredth Anniversary of Emancipation'; James Baldwin, 'The Fire Next Time' Vintage International, New York, 1963.

27. Bhopal Declaration adopted by All India Dalit congress held in Bhopal (January 2002). Venkitesh Ramakrishnan,'Dalit & Congress' Frontline, Volume 28, Issue 11, 21 May–3 June 2011.

28. Apart from Ahmedabad city, the worst fury was witnessed in the Adivasi *talukas* of Kawat, Panwad and Chhota Udaipur during 2002 riots. A research study by AP-based NGO 'AWARE'. AWARE | Action for Welfare and Awakening in Rural Environment, http://www.aware-group.com/.

29. Personal interview of the author with Ms Nafisa D'Souza, 1998.

30. The women's movement in Andhra Pradesh originated from the anti-arrack (anti-liquor) movement started by the state's rural women in the 1990s.

31. Based on the statistics of Women Welfare and Child development, Andhra Pradesh. Statistics on atrocities/offences against Women IN AP (1991–97): Department of Welfare and Child development, Andhra Pradesh, 1998.

32. Rameeza Bee was allegedly raped by sub-inspector Surender Singh and constables Mohammed Sultan and Mohammed Khaja at the Nallakunta police station in Hyderabad city on the night of 29–30 March 1978 and her husband was beaten to death for questioning their act. The public was greatly agitated and riots broke out in the city the following day.

33. One of the constables of the Tharoor police station (Andhra Pradesh) had beaten Parvathamma with *lathis* and leather belts and later raped her during April 2006. The case came up before NHRC.

Chapter 6

1. Union Government's Status paper on LWE (2005). Government of India: Development issues in Extremist affected areas-Expert Group report to Planning Commission of India, 2008.
2. Dwight D. Eisenhower from his speech before the American Society of Newspaper Editors, 16 April 1953. Classic quotes: Quotation No 9556 www.quotatHYPERLINK "http://www.quotationpage.com/quote/9556html"ionpage.com/quote/9556html.
3. Development Challenges in Extremist-Affected Areas: A Report of the Expert Panel to the Planning Commission. Government of India: Development issues in Extremist affected areas- Expert Group report to Planning Commission of India, 2008.
4. Government of India: Development issues in Extremist affected areas-Expert Group report to Planning Commission of India, 2008.
5. The National Rehabilitation & Resettlement Policy, 2007, was approved by the cabinet on 11 October 2007. It was published in the Official Gazette and came into force on 31 October, 2007. It covers rehabilitation and resettlement of displaced persons in all cases of land acquisition and in involuntary displacement due to other causes.
6. 'India's Forced Displacement Policy and Practice', Indian Social Institute, New Delhi. Fernandez Walter,'India's Forced Displacement Policy and Practice'-Is compensdation upto its functioning?' www.nesrc.org/NESRC/Walter/chap7pdf.
7. A Nyaya Panchayat is a system of dispute resolution at village level in India. Nyaya Panchayats can be endowed with functions based on broad principles of natural justice and can tend to remain procedurally as simple as possible. They can be given civil and minor criminal jurisdiction. But they should never follow civil and criminal procedure code in toto.

Chapter 7

1. Non-governmental Organizations—Guidelines for good policy and practice. Collin Ball & Leith L 'Dunn,Non-governmental Organizations—Guidelines for good policy and practice' Commonwealth Foundation, London, 1995.
2. The Second Vatican Council (also known as Vatican II) addressed relations between the Roman Catholic Church and the modern world. It was the 21st Ecumenical Council of the Catholic Church and the second to be held at St. Peter's Basilica in the Vatican. It opened under Pope John XXIII on 11 October 1962 and closed under Pope Paul VI on 8 December 1965.
3. The 1968 Medellin Conference, in Colombia, officially supported 'base ecclesiastic communities' and the liberation theology propounded by Gustavo Gutiérrez in his 1972 essay, 'A Theology of Liberation: History, Politics and Salvation'.
4. Liberation theology is a political movement in Christian theology which interprets the teachings of Jesus Christ in terms of liberation from unjust economic, political or social conditions.
5. Conference on Security and Co-operation in Europe is also known as Helsinki Final Act (1975). It discussed and adopted resolution.
6. Director, UN Centre for Human Rights (1977–1982). Theo Van Boven,' Human Rights & Rights of People' www.ejil.org/pdfs/6/1/1307pdf.
7. Felice D. Gaer, 'Reality Check: Human Rights NGOs Confront Governments at the UN' in eds. Thomas Weiss. Felice D. Gaer, 'Reality Check: Human Rights NGOs Confront Governments at the UN' in NGOs the UN and Global Governance', eds. Thomas G. Weiss&Leon Gordenker, Emerging Global issue Series (Boulder, Colo: Lynne Rienrer, 1996) USA.
8. Vienna Declaration and Programme of Action (1993).
9. The UN Working Group on Forced Disappearance deals with the numerous individual cases of human rights violations on a purely humanitarian basis, irrespective of whether the government concerned has ratified any of the existing legal instruments which provide for an individual complaints procedure. It acts essentially as a channel of communication between the families of disappeared persons and governments, and has successfully developed a dialogue with the majority of governments concerned with the aim of solving cases of disappearance.
10. Filártiga versus Peña-Irala (630 F.2d 876), 1980, was a landmark case in United States and international law. It set the precedent for United States federal courts to punish non-American citizens for tortious acts committed outside the United States that were in violation of

public international law (the law of nations) or any treaties to which the United States is a party. It thus extends the jurisdiction of United States courts to tortious acts committed around the world.

11. The Torture Victim Protection Act of 1991 is a statute that allows for the filing of civil suits in the United States against individuals who, acting in an official capacity for any foreign nation, committed torture and/or extrajudicial killing.

12. Amnesty International Report 1983 (London: Amnesty International Publications Ltd., 1983), pp. 113–5. Political killings by governments.

13. Amnesty International Report 1984 (London: Amnesty International Publications Ltd, 1984) Torture in 80s-campaigns.

14. Amnesty International. March 1992. India: Torture, Rape and Deaths in Custody. New York: Amnesty International USA.

15. Gita Saghal, who became the head of Amnesty's gender unit in 2003, resigned because of her differences with Amnesty on their campaign in respect of certain Islamic terrorists.

16. Moazzam Beggis, a British–Pakistani Muslim, was held in extrajudicial detention in the Bagram Theater Internment Facility and the Guantanamo Bay detainment camp in Cuba by the US government for nearly three years.

17. Munmum Jha, 'Nehru and Civil Liberties in India', in *International Journal of Human Rights*, Volume 7, issue number 3, 2003, pp. 103–115. Munmum Jha Human Rights NGO Strategies in India. In International Human Rights Perspective, Volume 1, Number 1, 2002, pp. 67–80.

18. Personal Interview of the author with T. Pratap Reddy (PUCL) of Hyderabad, 1998.

19. Article 3 of Geneva Convention (www.icrc.org/ihl/WebART/375-590006).Convention (III) relative to the Treatment of Prisoners of War.

20. Protocol II is a 1977 amendment protocol to the Geneva Conventions relating to the protection of victims of 'non-international' armed conflicts. It defines certain international laws that strive to provide better protection for victims of 'internal' armed conflicts that take place within the borders of a single country. The scope of these laws is more limited than those of the rest of the Geneva Conventions out of respect for sovereign rights and duties of national governments.

21. Personal interview of the author with K.G. Kannabiran, APCLC leader, 1998.

Chapter 8

1. In 1970s an organized movement known as 'Chipko' spread throughout India against the destruction of forest in various states, especially

Uttaranchal. Gaura Devi, Sunderlal Bhuguna and Chandi Prasad Bhatt were the founders of this movement.

2. National Fishermen's Forum floated mainly at the instance of Fr. Thomas Kocherry, alias Tom Kocherry, of Kerala is a typical example of the successful unionization of unorganized sections. The traditional fishermen of various states were organized under the banner of NFF which organized a series of agitations/struggles in the coastal areas in order to safeguard the livelihood of traditional fishermen.

3. The Copenhagen Social Summit of 1995 in its declaration reached a consensus by state heads on the need to put the people at the centre of development. It pledged to make the conquest of poverty, goal of total jobs and fostering social integration overriding development. After five years in June 2000, the heads of government again reassembled in Geneva to review the progress.

4. Voluntary Action Network of India (VANI) formed in 1988 is an apex body of NGOs having over 370 directly registered member organizations and around 4,000 indirectly represented member organizations. VANI could successfully launch advocacy at national and state level on a number of issues related to poverty, employment and development.

Chapter 9

1. Besides senior persons belonging to Judiciary, bureaucracy, Academic field, civil/Human rights, samples from police NGOs and common public were interviewed on the basis of structured questionnaire and inputs collected, collated and analyzed.

2. Dr M.V. Pylee is a former vice chancellor of Cochin University of Science & Technology. He is a known Constitutional and management expert. This was quoted a the personal interview by the author with Dr Pylee in1998.

3. Quoted from the personal interview by the author with Late K.G. Kannabiran, one of the founders of APCLC and a leading advocate of Andhra Pradesh High Court in 1998.

4. Quoted from the personal interview by the author with Ms Kiran Bedi, IPS.

5. The interview of Dr. MV Pylee, Constitutional expert by author (Cochin/1998).

6. Quoted from the personal interview by the author with (retired) Justice V.R. Krishna Iyer of Supreme Court, a legal luminary, Constitutional expert and human rights activist

7. The interview of Justice (retd) V R Krishna iyer,of Supreme Court by author (Cochin/1998).

8. From the National Police Commission (NPC) Report (1977–1981) (The Ministry of Home Affairs, GoI).

9. Quoted from the personal interview by the author with (retired) Chief Justice M.N. Venkitachellaiah of Supreme Court while holding the post of chairman in NHRC in 1998.

10. The interview of Late K G Kannabiran,(APCLC) by author (East Maradappally, Secundrabad/1998).

11. Quoted from a personal interview by the author with Smt. Nafisa D'Souza, director of Visakhapatnam-based NGO 'LAYA', active among the tribals of Andhra Pradesh.

12. Quoted from a personal interview by the author with T. Pratap Reddy, chairman, Vigil India Movement (1998) and PUCL leader from Andhra Pradesh.

13. Quoted from a personal interview by the author with R.V. Pillai, IAS and secretary general of NHRC (1998).

14. Quoted from a personal interview by the author with Professor Kodanda Rama Reddy, political science, of Osmania University and state executive member of APCLC (1998).

15. Ms Hillary Clinton's statement on health as a human right. Cliff Kincaid,'Hillary Clinton's Global agenda'-American survival inc, www.usasurvival.org/ck061903shtml (Human Rights day speech at Georgetown University on December 10, 1998).

16. The interview of Ms. Kiran Bedi, IPS by author (Hyderabad/1998).

17. The interview of Ms. Kiran Bedi, IPS by author (Hyderabad/1998).

Chapter 10

1. Anthony Giddens, former director of London School of Economics who authored around 40 books on political and sociological concepts through his remarkable work *Beyond Left and Right* propounded 'third-way politics', which is an alternative to capitalism and social-ism. He argued that the main aim of the third-way politics should be to help citizens to pilot their way through the main revolution of our time on globalization, transformation in personal life and our relations to nature. This concept has considerably contributed to the growth of social democracy and welfare state in many countries.

Bibliography

Books

Alderson, J. 1984. *Human Rights and the Police*. Strasbourg: Council of Europe Publications Ltd.

Aravind Rao, K. 1996. *Naxalite Terrorism: Social & Legal Issues*. Madras: East West Books Pvt. Ltd.

Ball, Colin and Dun, Leith. 1996. *Non-governmental Organisations: Guidelines for Good Policy and Practice*. London: The Commonwealth Foundation.

Bansal, V.K. 1987. *Right to Life and Personal Liberty in India*. New Delhi: Deep & Deep Publications.

Benner, Arthur. 1994. *Democracy in India: A hollow Shell*. Washington DC: American University Press.

Bowels, Stuart. 1984. *Police and Civil Liberties*. London: Camelot Press Ltd.

Baxi, Upendra. 1994. *Mambrino's Helmet? Human Rights for a Changing World*. New Delhi: SAGE Publications.

Chandra, Satish. 1990. *International Document on Human Rights*. New Delhi: Mittal Publications.

Choudhury, Paul. 1985. *Profile of Social Welfare & Development in India*. New Delhi: M.N. Publications.

Cox, Berry. 1975. *Civil Liberties in Britain*. Harmondsworth: Penguin Books.

Dev, Arjun. 1993. *Human Rights: A Source Book*. New Delhi: NCERT.

Diwan, Paras. 1996. *Human Rights and the Law*. New Delhi: Deep & Deep Publications.

Douglas, A. 1996. Stephen, *Economic Implications of the US-ASEAN Discourse on Human Rights*. Illinois: Centre for East Asian Pacific Studies.

Edword, Lawson. 1994. *Encyclopedia of Human Rights* (Vol. II). New York: Taylor & Francis Vermon Avenue.

Edgerton, W. Henry. 1960. *Freedom in the Balance*. New York: Cornell University Press.

Gadgill, D.R. 1987. *Human Rights in a Multinational Society*. Bombay: Asia Publishing House.

Gearty, Corner. 1966. *Understanding Human Rights*. New York: Mansell.

Gupta, Vijaya K. 1996. *Perspectives on Human Rights*. New Delhi: Vikas Publushing House.

Hargopal, G. 1988. *The Political Economy of Human Rights*. New Delhi: Himalayan Publishing Co.

Hingorani, R.C. 1987. *Humanitarian Law*. New Delhi: Oxford & IBH.

Jacobs, Francis A. and White Robin C.A. 1996. *European Convention on Human Rights*. Oxford: Clarendon Press.

Jaswal, Paramjit. 1996. *Human Rights and the Law*. Hyderabad: Asia Law House.

Jois, Rama (Justice). 1997. *Human Rights & Indian Values*. New Delhi: National Council of Teachers Education, IP Estate.

Kalaiah, A.B. 1986. *Human Rights in International Law*. New Delhi: Deep and Deep Publications.

Kapoor, B.K. and Singh Dharan Vir. 1997. *Rural Development through NGOs*. Delhi: Rawat Publications.

Kazmi, Fareed. 1987. *Human Rights*. New Delhi: Intellectual Publishing.

Krishna, Iyer V.R. (Justice). 1986. *Human Rights and the Law*. Indore: Vedpal Law House.

Madhava, Menon N.R. 1997. *A Training Manual for Police on Human Rights*. Bangalore: HR Centre, National Law School of India University.

Madhavan, P.K.S. 1998. *Farmers Suicide in Andhra Pradesh*. Hyderabad: AWARE.

Maheswari, S.R. 1998. *Comparative Govt & Politics*. Agra: Lakshmi Narain Aggarwal.

Mccabe, Sarah. 1988. *The Police, Public Order & Civil Liberty*. London: Routledge, Felter Lake.

Mukhoty, Govinda. 1984. *NTRs One Year—A Report on Democratic Rights in AP*. New Delhi: PUDR.

Narendranath, Gorrepati. 1984. *Communal Riots in Hyderabad*. Ahmedabad: Centre for Social Knowledge and Action.

Nickel, James W. 1987. *Making Sense of Human Rights*. Beckeley: University of California.

O'Neil, O'Neil. 1974. *Civil Liberties Today*. Boston: Houghton Mifflon Co.

Quirogy, C. 1988. *Battle of Human Rights*. London: Martins & Nighoff.

Rao Janardhan, B. 1984. *Administrative Response to Tribal Protest in India: A study of Tribal Movement in AP*. Andhra Pradesh: Kakatiya University.

Roberts, L. David and Subramanian S. 1998. *Handbook of International Humanitarian Laws & Human Rights Law*. New Delhi: The Regional Delegation of the International Committee of Red Cross.

Roech, Richard. 1994. *Human Rights: The New Consensus 1994*. London: Regency Press (Humanity) Ltd.

Robertson A.K. 1996. *Human Rights in the World* (IV Edition). UK: Manchester University Press.

Saxena, K.P. 1994. *Human Rights Perspective & Challenges*. New Delhi: Lancers Books.

Schgal Singh, B.P. 1993. Human Rights in India: Problems & Perspectives. New Delhi: Deep & Deep.

Sharma, Gokulesh. 1997. *Human & Social Justice*. New Delhi: Deep & Deep.

Sinha, Santha. 1989. *Maoits in Andhra Pradesh*. New Delhi: Gyan Publishing House.

Sinhadri, S. 1997. *Telengana: Dimensions of Underdevelopment*. Hyderabad: Centre for Telangana Studies.

Sohoni, Neera Kuckereja. 1988. *Anubhav Experiences in Community Health (AWARE)*. Lodhi Estate, New Delhi: Ford Foundation.

Subramanian, S. 1990. *Human Right and Police*. Hyderabad: Association for Advancement of Police Security Science.

Subramanian, S. 1997. *Human Rights: International Challenges* (Vol. I & II). New Delhi: Manas Publications.

Vadackumcherry, James. 1996. *Human Rights & Police in India*. New Delhi: SAGE Publications.

Articles in Journals/News Papers

Ansari, Iqbal. 1994. 'Human Rights Movement in India'. *PUCL Bulletin*, January.

Bajpai, G.S. 1995. 'Human Rights: Need to Realistic Approach'. Academy Journal Volume 47, July–December. 1995, *SVPNPA Hyderabad* .

Basu, V. 1991. 'Inter-Regional Variations in Health Services in A.P.' *Economic & Political Weekly*, 7 September.

Basu, Soma. 1997. 'Grants Withdrawn to Erring NGOs'. *Hindu*, Chennai, 1 October.

Bandopadhya, Parasun. 1991. 'On Human Rights'. *Ripples*, July.

Bhagawathi, P.N. 1998. 'Asian Concept of Human Rights', *Hindu*, 5 May.

Baxi, Upendra. 1999. 'Human Rights & Criminal Justice', *Hindu*, 14 September.

Chockalingam, K. 1996. 'Protecting Human Rights: Long Way to Go'. *Hindu*, 10 September.

Chatterjee S.K. 1997. 'Running for Rights'. *Statesman*, 1 January.

Das, Suranjan. 1996. 'Human Rights & Women Rights'. *Ripples*, July.

Deva, Rao and Srikrishna, P.E. 1995. 'Encounter Killings in AP'. *Economic & Political Weekly*, November, Vol XXX, No 44, 4 November 1995.

Dhillon, K.S. 1995. 'Indian Police and Human Rights'. *Indian Police Journal*, 42(2): 13–15..Gangrade, K.D. 1996. 'NGOs Underutilised in State Development'. *Hindu*, 6 September.

George Mathew, "U.N. World Summit on Social Development," Voices (Hong Kong: Christian Conference of Asia-Urban Rural Mission [CCA-URM], September-December 1995).

Hindwan, Sudhir. 1997. 'Human Rights Violations'. *Hindu*, 21 March.

Illaiah, K. 1992. 'AP's Anti Liquor Movement'. *Economic & Political Weekly*, 7 November.

———. 1991. 'Upper Caste Violence: Study of Chundur Carnage'. *Economic & Political Weekly*, 3 September.

———. 1998. 'Pushing Back Ignorance'. *Indian Express*, 5 November.

———. 1998. 'Genuine NGOs Facing Credibility Crisis'. *Indian Express*, 30 January.

Reddy, Jayachandra K. 1997. 'Human Rights Perspective Day to Day Policing'. *Police Professional*, January–March.

Jayanath, V. 1997. 'Two Standards over Human Rights Card Exposed'. *Hindu*, 14 April.

———. 1997. 'Aborigines & Human Rights'. *Hindu*, 5 July.

Jhunjanwala, Bharath. 1998. 'NGOs Can Do without Politics'. *Indian Express*, 31 January.

Kannabiran K.G. 1992. 'Disappearances in AP'. *PUCL Bulletin*, March.

———. 1993. 'Koyyaru—Reflections of a Killing'. *PUCL Bulletin*, March.

———. 1993. 'NHRC & Human Rights Act of 1993'. *PUCL Bulletin*, August.

———. 1996. 'Human Rights Education & NGO Movement'. *PUCL Bulletin*. March.

———. 1996. 'Emerging Consensus on Human Rights'. *PUCL Bulletin*, August.

———. 1997. 'A Lament for the Constitution'. *PUCL Bulletin*, July.

———. 1997. 'Appeal to all Human Rights Organisations'. *PUCL Bulletin*, July.

Khan, A.A. 1997. 'Human Rights & Police'. *Legal News & Views of ISI*, New Delhi, 2(12): 18–21 December.

Krishna, Iyyer V.R. (Justice). 1993. 'Dream or Reality'. Seminar 405, May.

———. 1989. 'Humans Go without Rights'. *PUCL Bulletin*, October.

Kunhikannan T.V. 1995. 'U.S. Double Standards on Human Rights'. *Indian Express*, 8 March.

Kumar, Praveen. 1997. 'Police & Human Rights'. *Hindu*, 18 March.

Liyakat, Ali. 1997. 'Women's' Dignity as Human Rights'. *Legal News & Views*, Volume 11, No 12, December 1997, Published by Social Action Trust, New Delhi, pp. 2–5.

Mathur, Krishna Mohan. 1995. 'Human Rights & Sovereignty: Some Random Thoughts'. *SVP, NPA Magazine*, 47(2), July–December.

Malhotra, Gyoti. 1997. 'India Bashing a Global Past Time'. *Indian Express*, 16 December.

Mathew, George. 1995. '*The Social Summit in Copenhagen*'. *PUCL Bulletin*, July.

Mitra, Nirmal. 1995. 'NGOs take Stock of UN Conventions'. *Statesman*. 24 September.

Nayar, Kuldip. 1997. 'Police & Human Rights'. *Hindustan Times*, 19 November.

———. 1997. 'Freedom of Expression'. *Hindu*, 22 May.

———. 1997. 'Due Process of Law Is Sacrosanct'. *Hindu*, 22 August.

———. 1997. 'Right to Information'. *Hindu*, 18 January.

Nages, Kumar S. 1998. 'Storm over Teacups in AP Villages'. *Hindu*, 7 May.

Pal, R.M. 1997. 'Police and Rule of Law'. *Legal Views and News*, Issue No 2, February 1997, pp. 14–17.

———. 1998. 'CRPF & Human Rights'. *Legal Views and News*, 2(1), January.

———. 1998. 'Dialogue on "Ancient Wrongs" NHRC's Role'. *Legal Views & News*, 2(1), January.

Pani, Kulangara (Vincent). 1998. 'Human Rights under Liberalised Economy'. *Legal Views. & News*, January, Volume 11, No 12, December. 1997, Published by Social Action Trust, New Delhi, pp. 6–7.

Pillai, R.V. 1997. 'Major Concern of India Today & NGOs'. *Legal Views & News*, 2(12), December.

Rao, K. Vijaya Rama. 1996. 'Human Right in the Criminal Justice System'. *UP Police Patrika*, 27(9), December.

Ramamurthy, M.V. 'Civil Liberties and Acts ol Violence'. *Hindu*, 22 July.

Sen, Shankar. 1997. 'Human Rights 1: Education Will Foster Growth'. *Statesman*, 16 April, Issue No 2, February 1997, pp. 7–9.

———. 1997. 'Human Rights II: Need for Proper Curriculum'. *Statesman*, 17 April.

———. 1996. 'Human Rights: Need for Developing Countries'. *Statesman*, 22 December.

———. 'Human Rights & Police'. *Legal Views & News*, Vol 2.

Singh, Prakash. 1997. 'Be Asian on Human Rights'. *Indian Express*. 6 October.

———. 'Human Rights in Inhuman Conditions'. *UP Police Patrika*, December.

Sorabjee, Soli J. 1994. 'UN & Human Rights: Scope for Improvement'. *Indian Express*, 4 October.

———. 'Educate Police on Human Rights'. *Times of India*, 13 January.

S. Subramanian. 1995. 'Human Rights & Law Intensity Conflicts'. *MP Police Patrika*, 38 (June–December), Volume 38, June–December 1995, Bhopal.

Subramanian, Chitra. 1997. 'Can Criminals in the Garb of Rights Activists be Granted Immunity?' *Indian Express*, 28 August.

———. 1997. 'Human Rights Inc'. *Indian Express*, 6 April.

Tarkundae, V.M. 1982. 'Immediate Programmes for PUCL'. *PUCL Bulletin*, December.

Tarkundae, V.M. 'Radicalisation of PUCL', *Radical Humanist* August, 1982

Warikoo, K. 'Report of a Symposium -Human Rights: View from Geneva'. *World Affairs*, December 1995, pp. 48–50 (Proceedings of Seminar on Human Rights: A View from Geneva, at India International Centre, New Delhi, 2 May 1995).

Umar, Mohammed. 1997. 'Human Rights & Judiciary'. *Legal News & Views*, 2(12), December.

Vanak, Achin. 1997. 'Human Rights Violations'. *Hindu*, 24 March.

Viswanathan, Prema. 1993. *Wrongs & Human Rights. Indian Express*, 12 August.

Warikoo, K. 1995. 'Human Rights View from Geneva'. *World Affairs*, December.

Documents/Seminar Papers

Amnesty International, Annual Report 1977 (London: Amnesty International Publications Ltd, 1977).

———. *Report 1994*

———. *Report 1997*

———. *Report 2007–09*

Andhra Pradesh Civil Liberties Committee (APCLC). 1983. 'Repression of the Rural Poor in Andhra Pradesh,' Hyderabad: APCLC.

———. 1985. 'Roll Call of the Dead-Killings by State'. Hyderabad: APCLC,

———. 1985. 'Right to Life in NTRs Andhra: Encounters as State Policy', Hyderabad: APCLC.

———. 1986. 'Encounter-Killings in Post-Emergency Period'. Hyderabad: APCLC.

———. 1991. 'Dowry Deaths in AP'. Visakapatnam: APCLC.

———. 1991. 'Political Militancy & Civil Liberties'. Hyderabad: APCLC.

———. 1991. 'From Karamchedu to Chundur'. Hyderabad: APCLC.

Andhra Pradesh Civil Liberties Committee (APCLC). 1996. 'Life, Liberty & Livelihood: Civil Liberties in Andhra Pradesh'. Vol. 1 (*Fact Finding Committee Reports* 1978–84), Hyderabad: APCLC.

———. 1997. 'Civil War & Uncivil Government', Hyderabad: APCLC.

———. 1997. 'Murders Most Foul: A Report on the Extrajudicial Killings by Police in North Telangana'. Hyderabad: APCLC.

———. 1998. 'Digest of Human Rights'. Hyderabad: APCLC.

Asian Human Rights Commission. 1998. Asian Human Rights Charter: A Peoples Charter. Asian Legal Resources Centre, Hong Kong.

National Human Rights Commission (NHRC). *Annual Report 1993–94* (published by NHRC, New Delhi).

———. *Annual Report 1994–95.*

———. *Annual Report 1995–96.*

———. *Annual Report 1996–97.*

———. *Annual Report 1997–98.*

———. *Annual Report 1998–99.*

———. *Annual Report 1999–2000.*

———. *Annual Report 2000–01.*

———. *Annual Report 2001–02.*

———. *Annual Report 2002–03.*

———. *Annual Report 2003–04.*

———. *Annual Report 2004–05.*

———. *Annual Report 2005–06.*

———. *Annual Report 2006–07.*

———. *Annual Report 2007–08.*

United Nations. 1991. *Human Rights: First Twenty Years.* New York: UN.

———. 1987. *Human Rights: Status of International Instruments.* New York: UN.

———. 1987. *Human Rights: Questions & Answers.* New York: UN.

———. 1991. *Manual of Human Rights Reporting.* New York: UN.

Index

About the Author

K.V. Thomas, a law graduate from Kerala University, has over 36 years of distinguished career in Intelligence Bureau, Ministry of Home Affairs, Government of India, in various capacities in different parts of India including the far-flung insurgency-affected areas of the North East.

For his outstanding contributions to the Bureau, he was decorated with President's Police Medal for distinguished service (2008) and Indian Police Medal for meritorious service (1996), besides special awards of the Bureau for his outstanding professional contributions in the field of Internal Security. The National Police Academy, Hyderabad awarded him Police Fellowship in 1997 for undertaking a research project on Policing which he successfully completed in 1998. He won Prime Minister's Silver Cup Essay Competition conducted by National Police Academy for the serving police personnel in the country on six times. As a delegate to All India Police Science Congress he presented research-oriented papers on various aspects of policing, including human rights issues, on half a dozen occasions.

K.V. Thomas (aka Toms Kara) superannuated from IB in 2010 as Assistant Director. He is now fully engaged in bringing out quality publications in various subjects especially Internal Security/law enforcement, Human Rights and Insurgency. He has authored two books: *Human Rights, Terrorism and Policing in India* (1999) and *Policing in 21st Century—Myth, Realities and Challenges* (2012).